James Franklin Love

The Southern Baptist Pulpit

James Franklin Love

The Southern Baptist Pulpit

ISBN/EAN: 9783743330870

Manufactured in Europe, USA, Canada, Australia, Japa

Cover: Foto ©ninafisch / pixelio.de

Manufactured and distributed by brebook publishing software (www.brebook.com)

James Franklin Love

The Southern Baptist Pulpit

THE

SOUTHERN BAPTIST PULPIT

EDITED BY
REV. J. F. LOVE

WITH AN INTRODUCTION BY
JONATHAN HARALSON, LL. D.

PHILADELPHIA
AMERICAN BAPTIST PUBLICATION SOCIETY
1895

Copyright 1895 by the
AMERICAN BAPTIST PUBLICATION SOCIETY

To
THE BAPTISTS OF AMERICA
A People who Love an
OPEN BIBLE and a PURE GOSPEL

THE EDITOR

PREFACE

As it is the province of the butler to serve the viands and not entertain the guests, we will not intrude on the reader a long dissertation on even so fine a dish as we are, by the graciousness of the brethren, able to provide. The intellectual and spiritual repast to which all are invited will proclaim its own excellence.

The Southern Baptist Convention constitutes the largest deliberative body in the world, and though a few excellent volumes of sermons by single individuals have been published, no book representing the pulpit of the Convention has yet appeared. It was thought that such a volume would be a fitting memorial to our fiftieth anniversary as a separate organization.

The book is truly representative though by no means exhaustive of the pulpit talent among us; and we believe its household value will be greatly increased by the portraits and biographical sketches of the contributors. All will welcome among the preachers, the face and sketch of the preachers' friend, Judge Haralson, the president of the Convention.

I wish here to record my profound thanks to my brethren, who, while averse to publicity, have, in the interests of the enterprise and through personal kindness, furnished the material for the book and made my cherished plan possible.

J. F. LOVE.

SUFFOLK, VA., October, 1895.

INTRODUCTION

The meeting of the Southern Baptist Convention at Washington City, on the 10th of May, 1895, was one, in some of its features, of unusual interest and importance. The Convention was organized in the city of Augusta, Ga., on May 8th, 1845. This meeting, therefore, was the semi-centennial of the Convention's existence, and we met for the first time in the capital of the country, to celebrate our jubilee. Nearly all who were present at the original organization, have passed from the scenes of earth. Only one of them, Rev. John Thomas Sankey Park, then of Alabama, now of Mexia, Texas, was present at the recent meeting. Besides him, only two or three others, so far as is remembered, linger on these mortal shores. During the organization of this session, when nominations were being made for vice-presidents, as a fitting tribute to this honored and venerable brother, and as a most appropriate and graceful thing to be done, by a unanimous vote of the delegates he was chosen as one of the vice-presidents.

This semi-centennial occasion was rendered the more enjoyable by the courtesy of the churches in Washington. To the average American no other city in the world compares with it. It bears the name of the most illustrious and honored man in the history of modern times, "First in peace, first in war, and first in the hearts of his countrymen." And it is a matter of ever-increasing pride and pleasure, to witness at the capital, and throughout America, and in every civilized country of the globe, the memorials of the greatness and goodness and virtue of the Father of our

Country. Let us never lose an opportunity to honor our greatest chieftain, to transmit from age to age the name and fame of a man so unselfish and incorruptible in his patriotism; so faithful, persistent, and successful in his advocacy and efforts for civil and religious freedom; so true to all public and private trusts committed to his hands; so reverent and devout in his Christian character; and so sublime in his life and death.

It was in this city, with all these objects of public and patriotic interests, and a thousand other attractions, that by the kind and hospitable invitation of the brethren and people of Washington, we were permitted to hold the recent session of our Convention. From every quarter of our extended territory, the representatives from the churches, with several thousand visitors, came. The total number of delegates present as shown by the rolls, was eight hundred and ninety, besides some hundreds of ministers and laymen whose names were not enrolled. The President of the Board of Commissioners of the District of Columbia (answering to the office of mayor of the ordinary city), the Hon. John W. Ross, visited the Convention at its opening, and greeting us with words of hospitable welcome, extended the freedom of the city to the delegates and visitors. The venerable and greatly beloved Dr. C. C. Meador, pastor of one of the Baptist churches of the city, gave us cordial welcome on the part of the Baptists and Christians of the community. The President of the United States tendered a reception, giving us the opportunity of meeting him and shaking his cordial and patriotic hand. The greeting we received, all around, was touchingly kind and cordial, and for it we cherish and express our profound and most grateful acknowledgments. God bless the brethren, people, and city of Washington!

There was not a visitor present who did not return

to his home with higher inspirations of religion and duty, and with a broader and deeper love of country. To their children and friends they will tell the story of what they saw and felt, and the influences for good thus set astir can scarcely be bounded as to place or time.

But it is not alone in the South that these benign influences are to be felt and ripen into fruit. The real dispositions of Southern Christians to the cause of Christ at home and abroad, and the love they bear our common country, were displayed on the border line between the sections. Northern friends and brethren, who honored us with their presence, had opportunity to observe the principles of religion and patriotism by which Southern Christians are animated, and to note that, no more in one section than in the other, is the sentiment dominant for "America for Christ," and for a united and happy country.

Had any one ever before entertained doubts as to the policy of the organization of the Southern Baptist Convention, of its very great and triumphant progress, and of the importance and necessity for its continued existence in the indefinite future, if for no other reasons than of convenience, and for the marshaling of greater armies of workers for the betterment of mankind and the redemption of the world,— he is a great disbeliever in facts if those doubts were not greatly shaken or dissolved at our recent session. Our struggles and triumphs, time and space will not here be taken to recount. Concerning these better information than can be given in this introduction may be found in the historical discourse of Dr. W. H. Whitsitt, delivered at the Convention and appearing in this volume.

The general enthusiasm in the interests of the Boards of the Convention and our Theological Seminary, and for an educated ministry, is attested in the fact that the Southern Baptist Convention is now the largest representative assembly of Christian men that anywhere assembles. And still it grows, until the question of its free entertainment, in our largest cities even, has become one of embarrassment. Its ambition and mission are to give the true gospel, as we understand it, to the perishing millions in our own country and other lands; to promote peace and good will among all men, and intelligence and enlightenment, by the spoken word and the printed page, to all ranks and conditions; to hasten, as far as may be, the millennial dawn.

Sunday was a memorable day at our recent meeting. The pulpits of most of the Protestant churches were tendered to the Convention, with solicitations for our preachers to occupy them. Accordingly, the usual committee having this matter in charge made assignments for preaching by members of the Convention at these several places of worship.

It was a happy suggestion to the mind of our brother, Rev. J. F. Love, pastor of the First Baptist Church at Suffolk, Va., to get together and publish in a volume some of these discourses, together with others, because contributed by leading ministers from all the States in the Convention. The volume will thus be of double interest, being in some measure memorial of the occasion and containing specimens of sermonic literature representative of the Southern pulpit.

In behalf of brethren and friends, North and South, the writer begs to express his gratification at the appearance of this volume, so unique and valuable, and to solicit for it the considerate attention of the brethren and Christians generally.

JONATHAN HARALSON

MONTGOMERY, ALA., July 17, 1895.

CONTENTS

I.	CIVIL GOVERNMENT AND RELIGION,	11
	BY GEORGE B. EAGER, D. D., MONTGOMERY, ALA.	
II.	A RETROSPECT,	30
	BY W. H. WHITSITT, D. D., LL.D., LOUISVILLE, KY.	
III.	THE CHRISTIAN HOPE,	46
	BY R. J. WILLINGHAM, D. D., RICHMOND, VA.	
IV.	GROUND OF JUDGMENT,	54
	BY B. H. CARROLL, D. D., WACO, TEX.	
V.	TRUTH A LIBERATOR,	67
	BY T. T. EATON, D. D., LL.D., LOUISVILLE, KY.	
VI.	ALL,	79
	BY W. W. LANDRUM, D. D., RICHMOND, VA.	
VII.	THE PRE-EMINENT NAME,	91
	BY J. B. HAWTHORNE, D. D., ATLANTA, GA.	
VIII.	SELF-HEROISM,	104
	BY H. A. TUPPER, JR., D. D., BALTIMORE, MD.	
IX.	THE DIVINITY OF JESUS CHRIST,	115
	BY G. A. NUNNALLY, D. D., MEMPHIS, TENN.	
X.	UNANSWERED PRAYERS,	127
	BY A. G. MCMANAWAY, D. D., ARKADELPHIA, ARK.	
XI.	CONSTRAINING LOVE,	133
	BY H. W. BATTLE, D. D., PETERSBURG, VA.	
XII.	GOD'S UNSPEAKABLE GIFT,	140
	BY REV. MALCOLM MACGREGOR, JACKSONVILLE, FLA.	
XIII.	THE HISTORY OF A SIN,	153
	BY REV. C. S. GARDNER, GREENVILLE, S. C.	
XIV.	THE DECEITFULNESS OF SIN,	163
	BY R. T. VANN, D. D., SCOTLAND NECK, N. C.	
XV.	CHRIST CRUCIFIED,	173
	BY J. C. HIDEN, D. D., RICHMOND, VA.	

CONTENTS

XVI. THREE STEPS UP, ... 180
   BY J. D. GAMBRELL, D. D., LL.D., MACON, GA.

XVII. UNBELIEVING BRETHREN, ... 191
   BY LANSING BURROWS, D. D., AUGUSTA, GA.

XVIII. THE TRIAL OF FAITH, ... 201
   BY Z. T. LEAVELL, D. D., CLINTON, MISSISSIPPI.

XIX. THE RESURRECTION OF CHRIST, ... 209
   BY M. B. WHARTON, D. D., NORFOLK, VA.

XX. THE FIRST RESURRECTION, ... 220
   BY REV. J. L. WHITE, MACON, GA.

XXI. THE EFFECTUAL CROSS, ... 231
   BY W. L. PICKARD, D. D., LOUISVILLE, KY.

XXII. A KINGDOM BUILT ON A CROSS, . . . 246
   BY REV. E. Y. MULLINS, RICHMOND, VA.

XXIII. HONOR FOR SERVICE, ... 255
   BY D. I. PURSER, D. D., NEW ORLEANS, LA.

XXIV. INFIDELITY AND CHRISTIANITY CONTRASTED, . 266
   BY T. H. PRITCHARD, D. D., CHARLOTTE, N. C.

XXV. A MAN IN HELL, ... 281
   BY REV. J. B. CRANFILL, WACO, TEX.

XXVI. GODHOOD IN CHRIST, ... 294
   BY J. J. TAYLOR, D. D., MOBILE, ALA.

XXVII. ABANDONED OF THE LORD, ... 305
   BY W. P. WALKER, D. D., HUNTINGTON, W. VA.

XXVIII. THE SUBLIMITY OF THE LIFE OF FAITH, . . 314
   BY REV. DAVID M. RAMSEY, CHARLESTON, S. C.

XXIX. THE FAITHFULNESS OF GOD, ... 324
   BY J. P. GREENE, D. D., LL.D., LIBERTY, MO.

XXX. THE CLEANSING BLOOD, ... 333
   BY R. R. ACREE, D. D., KNOXVILLE, TENN.

XXXI. THE MEAT AND MISSION OF THE MASTER, . 340
   BY H. F. SPROLES, D. D., JACKSON, MISS.

XXXII. THE CRUCIFIED CHRIST, ... 346
   BY C. A. STAKELY, D. D., WASHINGTON, D. C.

XXXIII. CONSECRATION AND ENTHUSIASM, . . . 356
   BY H. M. WHARTON, D. D., BALTIMORE, MD.

GEORGE BOARDMAN EAGER, now pastor of the First Baptist Church, Montgomery, Ala., was born near Rodney, Miss., February 22, 1847. He is the second son of Rev. E. C. Eager and brother of Rev. John H. Eager, our missionary to Italy. He did service as a soldier lad in the Army of Northern Virginia. Entering Mississippi College after the war, he graduated in 1871, with the first honors of his class, and from the Southern Baptist Theological Seminary in the Elective Course in 1876. His first pastorate was in the famous old university town of Lexington, Va., during which he took a post-graduate course at Washington and Lee University. He has since served with conspicuous success the First Church, Knoxville, Tenn.; St. Francis Street Church, Mobile, Ala.; First Church, Danville, Va.; Parker Memorial Church, Anniston, Ala.; and his present important charge in the capital city of Alabama. The degree of D. D. has twice been conferred upon him, first by the University of Mississippi and afterward by Howard College, Alabama. On the 20th of February, 1879, he was married to Miss Annie Coorpender, the gifted daughter of Dr. William F. Coorpender

Geo. R. Exxxx, D. D.

THE SOUTHERN BAPTIST PULPIT

I

CIVIL GOVERNMENT AND RELIGION[1]

BY GEO. B. EAGER, D. D.

"Render, therefore, unto Cæsar the things which are Cæsar's; and unto God the things that are God's." Matt. 22 : 21.

I NEED not dwell upon the unique circumstances that called forth these memorable words. Two hostile camps had united their forces against the new Prophet, whose claims so threatened the theocracy, and were now conspiring to compass his ruin. Pharisees and Herodians, zealots of Jewish orthodoxy and hated Jewish liberals, proud theocratic devotees and crafty Jewish royalists, had sunk their differences for the time in the ocean of a common hate. With dextrous cunning they will tempt Jesus to utterance on the burning question of the Roman poll tax. But they do not enter upon their work openly. They use "smooth dissimulation, taught to grace a devil's purpose with an angel's face." They feign the guileless spirit of inquirers. "Master," they say in softest accents of deference, "we know that thou art true, and teachest the way of God in truth, and neither carest thou for any man; for thou regardest not the person of men"—sublimest truths, but uttered in subtlest flattery. "Tell us, therefore, . . . is it lawful to give

---

[1] Convention Sermon at the Jubilee Session, Southern Baptist Convention, Washington, D. C., May, 1895.

tribute unto Cæsar or not?" Shall we, as God's people, owing allegiance to him as our King, pay taxes to Cæsar? Are these Herodians right who say that the tax is lawful and ought to be paid, or are we Pharisees right who claim that it is treason against Jehovah? Ought we, or ought we not, to pay tribute to Cæsar?

A PERILOUS ALTERNATIVE.

They must have waited in breathless silence and with gleaming eyes for the answer. He *must* say "yes" or "no," they thought. He cannot escape the artfully planned and perilous alternative. He will be thrown off his guard and fall into the trap. The Roman supremacy was certainly a usurpation. Jehovah alone was their King. And this Prophet of a new, divine kingdom, surely he will hold his followers free from fealty to this heathen power.

Danger lurked on either hand—death by the mob, or death at the hands of Rome—here the fierce fury of the fanatical crowds that thronged the temple courts, there the cruel craftiness of Herod's bailiffs waiting to arrest him for treason against Cæsar.

But "the forked tongue and envenomed fang of the serpent" were not hidden from Jesus. They had come fawning, "Master, thou art true and good and brave"; he flashes upon them the lightning of one scorching word, "Hypocrites!" "Why tempt ye me, ye hypocrites? Show me the tribute money!" And before the breathless crowd they hand him a Roman denarius. Holding it up—on one side the haughty face of the Emperor Tiberius, and on the other the hated title, "*Pontifex Maximus*"—he gives, as he was wont to do, an object lesson. "Whose is this image and superscription?" They say unto him, "Cæsar's." "Render, therefore, unto Cæsar the things which are Cæsar's." You have accepted this coin, and in so doing have answered your own question; for, as your rabbis have taught, to accept the coinage of a king is to acknowledge his sway. But he will not leave the matter there—he adds the weightier and more far-reaching words, "And unto God the things that are God's."

Is it a wonder that they stood before him amazed and silenced? that the evangelist simply adds, "They marveled, and left him, and went their way"?

A FAR-REACHING ANSWER.

The answer left nothing to be added. It met these treacherous questioners with a counter force of wisdom which crushed their conspiracy at once. It did more. The question which they asked that day was not simply a question of the hour, but a question of the ages—a great question that then, for the first time, had struggled to the surface and begun to clamor for solution. And more and more the world has come to see that the answer given so instantly and with such military brevity, affords the final solution of that question. It came, not only to give relief to Jewish minds, then perplexed with the problem of the relation of their civil government to heathen rule; but it came, as students of history and government everywhere are coming more and more to acknowledge, to settle forever the great problem of the relation of Church and State—the great generic question that lies back of so many of the grave, specific problems of our day—the question of the true relation of civil government to religion. To the consideration, or rather the reconsideration, of that question, according to the demands of our times, I venture to invite you to-day. If any apology be needed for so doing, I would have you recognize it in the fact that as Baptists we are committed by our principles and our history to be content with nothing less than a right solution of this great question; that we are reminded by this semi-centennial session of our Convention, of what our forefathers did and suffered for the principle involved, and that we hold this session in the nation's capital where so often the representatives of a free people have been called to face the problem in the halls of legislation.

A REVOLUTIONARY DOCTRINE.

Detaching this saying of Jesus, then, from its immediate historical connections, and viewing it as an aphorism of infinite wisdom given for the guidance of men in all ages, let us inquire afresh into its teaching.

Here is the clear recognition of man's twofold relation to government—human and divine. Here is an equally clear distinction between duties growing out of this twofold relation. Here is the implicit assertion of the separateness or independence of the two governments to which man stands related. And here, above all, is the unequivocal declaration of the duty and feasibility of absolute and uncompromising loyalty alike to Cæsar and to God, to human government and divine. In such teaching, the Master went beyond all precedent. He defied the wisdom of the ages. It was as radically at variance with the teaching of Moses as with that of the philosophers. Hebraism taught the doctrine of a perfect identification of the two governments and presented the sole instance known to history of a pure theocracy. Paganism demanded at least an alliance between the two; Egyptians, Greeks, and Romans considering the one as a sort of necessary adjunct to the other. In imperial Rome the emperor was also chief priest; and in republican Athens it was as the guardian of religion that the State decreed the death of Socrates. But here was one preaching a doctrine as far removed from Hebraism as Hebraism was from paganism in its highest form. As every form of this alliance in paganism had fallen into utter degeneracy, so now even the Jewish theocracy had grown corrupt, and was to be superseded. In the development of humanity the time had come when such union or identification of human and divine rule could no longer serve the highest interest of God's kingdom, or the true progress of the race. The old order was doomed, and the new order must rise out of its ruins. Henceforth human conduct was to be divided into two kinds: the conduct of the mind and the conduct of the body. Over the conduct of the body the State had rightful jurisdiction, but into the sacred domain of mind and conscience no State or legislature or officer of the law could ever rightfully penetrate, for in that realm God only could rule. These words of Jesus, then, cut into the very heart of things. Leopold von Ranke was not far wrong when he said it was the Master's most revolutionary utterance. It was right in the teeth of the most revered customs and institutions of the day, and utterly subversive of the great molding ideas and immemorial tendencies of antiquity. It was destined, as Richter says, to "Lift empires off their hinges and to turn the current of the ages out of its channel." It was the first streak of a new dawn; the sunrise gun of a great new day; the opening of the world's grandest era.

THE PRINCIPLE INVOLVED VIOLATED.

You need hardly to be reminded that not in the slightest degree, by either teaching or conduct, did our Lord or his apostles contravene or compromise the great principle he that day enunciated. For three centuries, indeed, or down to the time of Constantine, all of his followers, individuals and churches, Jewish and Gentile, were true to it. The Roman State, of course, ignored and violated it. You know the vicissitudes through which the truth it stood for then passed, and how frequently and variously it has been violated since. The periods that witnessed the most signal of these violations have been pithily summed up by one of our own honored leaders in four apt descriptive words: persecution, protection, power, and policy. The one word that designates the first period is persecution. Christianity, in the eyes of the Roman empire, was an illicit religion. But the pruning knife only gave vigor to its growth. Ten converts arose for every martyr. At last the heathen world stood awestricken before the spectacle of such constancy and yielded, at least outwardly, to the claims of Christ.

Then began the second period, from 325 to 1050, for which the word patronage is the fit designation. Constantine established a royal protectorate over the church. As his imperial predecessors had persecuted Christians, so now he will persecute the heathen. It became, therefore, of worldly advantage to profess Christianity; and the civil power combined with a lax morality and the unscriptural innovation of infant baptism to sweep whole populations into the church. The kingdom of God came to be identified with the church, and the church with a colossal hierarchy. Ecclesiastical arrogance knew no bounds, and the Church, nourished in the bosom of the State, stung to death its would-be protector.

A third period followed, from 1050 to 1250, in which the Church usurped the function of the State, and brought the world to her feet. The papacy arose to lord it over the bodies as well as the souls of men. Quietly appropriating to itself the prerogatives and traditions of pagan Rome, it wielded over the world an equally absolute and despotic power.

Then followed the period of power. In Hildebrand's claim to jurisdiction over all civil governments, in Henry the IV. purchasing his crown by penitential prayers as he waited barefoot in the snow at Canossa, and especially in the wresting from the emperor of the right of the election of the popes, and the giving of it to the cardinals as the princes of the church, we may trace, as the historian already quoted shows, the successive steps of hierarchy toward absolute dominion, temporal as well as spiritual.

Then followed a fourth period. As the first was the period of persecution, the second the period of patronage, the third the period of power, so the fourth has been as fitly called the period of policy. Papal assumption overleaped itself and provoked revolt. The sceptre departed from the church and she was forced to secure her ends by diplomacy. So from the year 1250 to 1517 she became the slave of the temporal powers, and by most unworthy concessions in spiritual things purchased their help in the extermination of her foes.

"Thus had the church run through its four stages of persecution, patronage, power, and policy. It had apostatized from Christ, sold itself for worldly gain, become a false church instead of a true church." Where then in that dark time, it may be asked, were the true people of God? And the answer comes, "Hiding in dens and caves of the earth, excommunicated, stretched upon the rack, burned at the stake. The Albigenses had been well-nigh exterminated; John Huss and Jerome of Prague had suffered martyrdom; and Savonarola's fiery appeals were preparing his doom."

A NEW ERA DAWNS.

But God fulfills himself in many ways. "The old order changeth, yielding place to the new." The year 1492 stands not only for the culmination of the old, but the rise of the new order of things. The practical demonstration had been complete that the alliance of Church and State was iniquitous and disastrous. "The turning point, the beginning of modern history," it has been well said, "is the discovery of America."

As the Renaissance was "the new birth of the human intellect," and the Reformation "the new birth of the human conscience," so what is known as the Revolution in England, France, and America was "the new birth of the human will"—the providential unfettering of human life for its highest activities. In spite of all the darkness, the morning hour had come of that glad day which we now enjoy, and which, however it may be overcast, can never, we may be sure, set in human bondage and gloom.

THE PRINCIPLE RECOGNIZED BY THE FOUNDERS OF OUR REPUBLIC.

In the providence of God it was reserved for the United States of America to abolish forever, as far as the general government could do it, this unnatural alliance of Church and State, and to secure the most sacred of all rights and liberties to all her citizens—the liberty of religion and the free exercise thereof. Thus there was given to the world the first example in history of a great civil government deliberately adopting this principle of separation, and depriving itself forever of all legislative control over religion.

The embodiment of that principle in the American Constitution and the actualizing of it in the administration of our government, forms, therefore, one of the great landmarks in human history.

THE AMERICAN IDEA.

The true American idea of the relation of civil government to religion, is not to be sought, of course, in old English legislation, or in colonial conceptions and institutions; or even in certain questionable Supreme Court decisions; but in that great instrument which is the organic law of the republic, the Magna Charta of our liberties, and the one authoritative exponent of the genius of our government. That instrument avowedly recognizes "the free exercise and enjoyment of religion as an inherent, inviolable, and inalienable right of man," and secures full liberty of religious thought, speech, and action, "within the limits of the public peace and order." It exacts that "no religious test shall ever be required as a qualification to any office or public trust under the United States." It makes as clear as human language can make it that the government does not adopt or establish Christianity, or constitute itself in any formal sense a "Christian nation." The fathers of the republic were God-fearing men. The foundations of the republic were laid in faith and prayer; but the Constitution is avowedly and skillfully framed so as not to give the Christian religion any more than any other the shadow of precedence or special privilege.

CIVIL GOVERNMENT HAS NO RELIGIOUS FUNCTION.

The American idea, then, as thus reflected in our organic law, is that civil government has no religious function. Not even Cavour's much-lauded doctrine of a free Church in a free State finds recognition or support in the American Constitution.

It does not undertake to define a "church," in its idea, essence, or marks. It gives no slightest sign of a recognition of the existence or non-existence of churches or of a church. As far as the government is concerned, the citizen may associate with his fellows in worship or worship individually and privately; yea, so far as the State knows or claims to have any right to know, he may be an atheist and absolutely hostile to religion; but if he is obedient to civil laws, he is *persona grata* before the law.

According to this idea, not only every Christian has rights, whether he be Roman Catholic or Protestant, Episcopalian or Baptist, Swedenborgian, Unitarian, or Seventh-Day Adventist; but the Jew also has rights, rights and immunities equal to and the same as those of the Christian. Yea, more, Jew and

Mohammedan; Buddhist, Theosophist, and Confucianist; Huxley, the agnostic; Frederic Harrison, the positivist; Felix Adler, the ethical culturist; Col. Ingersoll, the agitating skeptic; Emerson, the transcendentalist, if they are citizens, stand upon exactly the same plane of right and privilege. Only let them be law-abiding men, and they may be this or that religiously, or utterly nondescript otherwise; they are guaranteed freedom to enjoy their religion, or their non-religion, with "none to molest or to make them afraid." In other words, according to the American idea, the civil code is negative, not positive. The power of the State is power of police. Its function is justice, not love. Its demand of men is duty to man, not duty to God, and even this duty is limited so as to be not the positive doing of good, but simply the abstaining from doing wrong unto our fellows. As regards religion, it has nothing to do but to secure liberty to the individual and protection to the organized religious society or worshiping assembly.

SOME SIGNIFICANT SIDELIGHTS.

That this is the idea and spirit of the Constitution may be further shown in the history of the formation of that instrument; in the known opinions and public utterances of the founders and first president of the republic; and in the interpretation of the constitutional amendments and provisions touching religion by the most competent and incorruptible of American jurists and statesmen. It is a matter of record that in March, 1788, a meeting of Baptists was held in Virginia, at which were present representatives from New York, Rhode Island, Massachusetts, and other States, in which the question was taken up, whether the Constitution made sufficient provision for religious liberty. Upon consultation with Mr. Madison, they determined to address General Washington, and in August, 1789, they did so in these words:

"When the Constitution first made its appearance in Virginia, we had unusual strugglings of mind, fearing that the liberty of conscience (dearer to us than property and life) was not sufficiently secured. Perhaps our jealousies were heightened on account of the usage we received in Virginia under the British Government, when mobs, bonds, fines, and prisons were our frequent repast."

The great first president of the republic, though trained in an Established church, and at a time too, when men had not ceased to think that they who administered flogging, imprisonment, and even direr persecutions for religion's sake, were verily doing God's service, responded, setting forth the spirit of the Constitution in words which, like those of the Constitution itself, have been the wonder and the admiration of statesmen, historians, and lovers of liberty the world over:

"If I could have entertained the slightest apprehension that the Constitution framed in the convention where I had the honor to preside might possibly endanger the religious rights of any ecclesiastical society, certainly I would never have placed my signature to it; and if I could now conceive that the general government might ever be so administered as to render the liberty of conscience insecure, I beg you will be persuaded that no one would be more jealous than myself to establish effectual barriers against the horrors of spiritual tyranny and every species of religious persecution. As you doubtless remember, I have often expressed my sentiments, that every man, conducting himself as a good citizen and being accountable to God alone for his religious opinions, ought to be protected in worshiping the Deity according to the dictates of his own conscience."

Other dissenting bodies were also active in demanding explicit guarantees against any semblance or possibility of the establishment of a religion in the young republic; and it was in consequence of such demands that the first Congress, under the leadership of James Madison, proposed to the States the immortal First Amendment, which so explicitly and unmistakably provides that "Congress shall make no law respecting an establishment of religion, or prohibiting the free exercise thereof."

But let us note the idea, strictly speaking, is not American. It was no invention of our people or our times. Traced to its source it is found to be neither English nor French nor American nor even modern, but Christian. Its author is none other than He who spake these words, "Render unto Cæsar the things which are Cæsar's, and unto God the things that are God's," and who taught that great, new doctrine of the kingdom of God, "My kingdom is not of this world."

THE LEAVEN AT WORK IN OTHER LANDS.

The influence exerted by the United States in this respect upon other countries where the old order survives, has been incalculable. The forces and ideas that have been dominant here have been powerfully operative elswhere, especially in European lands. A new day has dawned in the British empire. The Protestant church of Ireland has been set free from the control of the legislature. Scotland is asking for the application of the same principle of religious equality. Thirty-one out of thirty-four representatives of the Welsh people are charged to seek the termination of the connection that binds the Episcopal Church in Wales to the British Parliament, and with this problem the House of Commons is now wrestling. Then the separation of Church and State is already accomplished in the habitual thought of the English people. Men are behaving on every hand "as though the formal deed of separation were already drawn and were only waiting for the signatures of the respective parties therto." "In theory," says Dean Stubbs, "Church and State were intended to grow together, but in practice the State has outgrown the Church, and left it, as it were, centuries behind." "Not by any law, expressed or implied, but by the assumption of the clerical party," says Canon Barnett, "the nation has become separate from the church." Episcopalians have come themselves to recognize the gradual detachment of the Anglican Church from the life of the people, and an elect few, among whom the new Bishop of Hereford takes primary rank, "are prepared, if not to welcome, yet unfearingly to allow, the total severance of the bond which has bound together for so many centuries the Anglican Church and the Crown." "Every year," says Dr. John Clifford, "adds to the number of Churchmen in England, as well as in Wales, who would rejoice in the Act of Separation, if only the resources of which the church is at present possessed were not in any way diminished."

As to English Nonconformists, they cling, not with less but with more tenacity than their fathers did, to the fundamental principle that any arrangement by which Parliament controls and administers the inward life and actions of societies of Christians, is contrary to the express teaching of the Lord Jesus, an invasion of his rights as the Sole Ruler and King of his people, and is historically proved to be fraught with great mischief to the disciples of Christ, to the progress of religion, and to the welfare of the people at large.

THE WHOLE QUESTION ENTERING UPON ITS FINAL PHASE.

These are but a few of many indications, says Dr. Clifford, that the whole question of the organization of the State for the promotion of religion has entered upon another, and probably its final, phase. It is no longer possible to ignore the new thought of men concerning the State and religion, the kingdom of God and the churches, now working with silent but surprising energy the world over. The divine right of any church to "establishment" and "endowment," has come to be recognized as but the survival of the "divine right" of kings to rule without the consent of the people, "a right introduced among English-speaking people only by a distinct violation of the historical principles of English development. "New factors indeed, of special significance, have found their way into the problem within the last fifty years. New conceptions of the State and of religion, of Christianity and of the churches and of their relation to one another, have come into play, and, as this great Englishman has said, are actually remaking our world.

There is growing up too, a fresh interpretation of religion, which is one of the formative forces of modern life. It is still recognized, if possible more clearly than ever, as the basis of morality, and as indispensable for the regulation of conduct and the building up of character; but men have come to see that ecclesiasticism is not of the essence of religion, nor is sacerdotalism, nor dogmatism, nor intellectual orthodoxy, nor even ritual observance. Religion is not a matter of rules and forms, but of spirit and truth; not a matter of doctrines and symbols merely, but of habits of mind toward men and toward God.

DISESTABLISHMENT CEASES TO BE DREADED.

Even English churchmen who a quarter of a century ago looked upon disestablishment as a dreaded calamity involving the fall of the "bulwark of Protestantism," are delivered from that fear now, for they see that the control of Parliament brings no advantage to Protestantism, while self-control, as in the

Colonies, in Ireland, and in the United States, would be attended with a quickened sense of responsibility on the part of the laity, a heightened appreciation of "Protestant principles," and a greater prosperity in all departments of the church's work. They have come to realize, as Lord Rosebery says, that "the essence of the church is spiritual; the inspiration, the traditions, the gracious message, the divine mission, the faith that guides us through the mystery of life to the mystery of death—all these were produced in poverty, in the cottage of a carpenter, and flourished under persecution; and that nothing can be so remote from their essence or their spirit as wealth, or power, or dignity in this world;" in short, that the supreme forces of Christianity are altogether beyond the touch of parliaments or senates. Moreover, they have come to feel profoundly that the church is no longer even approximately coextensive with the nation, and that, as Canon Moberly says, for the nation to continue to profess churchmanship nationally, involves "a necessary and considerable unreality in the profession." "The nation," he says, "is too much divided to be able longer to retain any single corporate religion"; therefore, "the maintenance of official profession involves us, from time to time, in scenes of painful religious unreality." Even Canon Liddon seemed to foresee the inevitable when in one of his great sermons he gave warning in these significant words: "Churches are disestablished and disendowed to the eye of sense through the action of political parties; to the eye of faith by His interference who ordereth all things both in heaven and in earth, and who rules at this moment on the same principles as those which of old led him to cleanse his Father's temple in Jerusalem."

REACTIONARY INFLUENCES IN AMERICA.

Coming back to our land, the integrity and full

extension of this great idea have been threatened at times all along the years by some persistent relics of the old order which survive in certain national customs, State constitutions, and popular ecclesiastical traditions. While the most marvelous progress has been making in the thought of other peoples in the direction of disestablishment, certain reactionary influences have been perceptible in the United States. The last few years, indeed, have witnessed a remarkable revival of the antique ideas and tendencies which it was the effort of our forefathers to throw off and leave behind; and as a result, the full embodiment and perpetuity of the great principles that constitute the most distinguishing characteristic of our national law and life seem to be threatened anew.

At a time when the British people are abandoning the idea that their religion consists in subscription to Articles of Faith, or in any formal definition of God or theories of the inspiration of the Bible, not a few over-zealous Americans are found making the most persistent and concerted efforts to secure new amendments to the Constitution by which the existence of God, the divinity of Christ, and the inspiration of the Scriptures shall be authoritatively recognized. When canons of the English church are pronouncing the maintenance of a national profession of religion in England "a necessary and considerable unreality," ministers of the gospel in free America are found laboring most strenuously with the avowed object of bringing our general government to a legal profession of religion—of Christianizing the Constitution! It becomes more and more apparent, of course, to intelligent and thoughtful people, that the proposition is utterly repugnant to our national history and principles, as well as to Christianity itself. The Constitution was not designed as "a Confession of Faith," but as "a compact between States, defining the powers and limitations of the general government, so as to establish and maintain a true and rightful union."

Akin to this is the effort that has been even more persistently made to secure a constitutional amendment making the religious use of the Bible and the teaching of the distinctive truths of Christianity obligatory in the public schools. "Let the devotional exercises be reduced to a minimum if necessary—to the reading of the Bible, the recital of the Lord's Prayer, and the singing of a hymn," men are found contending, "and let just the elementary truths of religion be taught—truths so simple and broad that none can reasonably object to them, and that is all that we ask." Good men, able ministers of the gospel, even Baptists of high standing, are found visiting committee rooms and halls of legislation, urged on by a zeal which is not according to knowledge, seemingly utterly oblivious of the truth that lies at the foundation of our government, that it is not the function of the State to conduct worship or to teach religion.

The principle is as really violated by a little worship as by the most elaborate—by the most elementary religious teaching as by the most developed theological instruction. Any such legislative enactment as is asked for would virtually give over the whole contention. It would be the beginning of a tendency; a first step backward toward the abandoned alliance of the past; the entrance of the camel's nose into the tent of our national life; and who then could secure us against the ultimate coming in of the whole dreaded body of religious legislation?

There is a sense, indeed, in which it is in vain to talk of drawing a line between the religious and the secular; for no such line really exists. Religion is the spirit in which all secular life should be carried on. Even the teaching and training of our public schools should be vitalized with the essential spirit of

Christianity. It is the right and duty of the State to prepare its citizens for citizenship, and this certainly involves moral training inspired by the spirit of reverence and love. Even a Huxley contends that our boys and girls are to be prepared not only for the discharge of domestic duties, but for duties as members of a social and political organization of great complexity; and to this end it is needful "that their affections should be trained, so as to love with all their hearts that conduct which tends to the attainment of the highest good for themselves and their fellow-men, and to hate with all their heart that opposite course of action which is fraught with evil." But this is far from granting the right of that worst form of paternalism, the paternalism of government that usurps the place of the home and the church in the religious training of the young. It does not require that we yield the point that the State as such, has no religious function.

The principle is evidently and palpably violated, again, by any and all appropriations of money from the treasury of the State or of the United States for religious purposes. It is this violation of the principle that has thrown us into such confusion over the school question. But we are coming to see, not only the inequalities, but the inherent unrighteousness, of the division of our public school funds to the support of any form of sectarian, or parochial schools, or charitable institutions. All government appointments or appropriations for religious purposes, or on religious grounds, are not only open to the charge of governmental favoritism for one church or denomination over another, but are in utter violation of the principle we are contending for, and of the spirit of our laws and institutions.

CONCLUDING APPEAL.

Bartholdi's statue, in the harbor of our great

metropolis, has more significance, as has been finely suggested, as applicable to soul liberty than to personal or civil freedom. That, in its glorious amplitude, is America's greatest contribution to the science of politics and to the art of government.

God forbid that her own citizens, Christian citizens, descendants of forefathers who counted not their lives dear unto themselves that they might secure the recognition and perpetuity of this great principle in our national law and life, in misguided zeal should do aught to dim the splendor of that light, or to neutralize its far-reaching influence!

II

A RETROSPECT[1]

BY W. H. WHITSITT, D. D., LL.D.

"Speak unto the children of Israel, that they go forward." Exod. 14 : 15.

THE earliest general organization among American Baptists was the "General Missionary Convention of the Baptist Denomination in the United States of America for Foreign Missions," organized by thirty-three delegates, representing eleven States, in the city of Philadelphia, on the eighteenth day of May, 1814. Baptist people throughout the entire country co-operated with this body for a period of thirty years.

In 1845 a division occurred between the Baptists of the North and those of the South. The Southern Baptist Convention was organized at Augusta, Georgia, on Thursday, the eighth day of May, of that year. Just fifty years have elapsed since that important event, and we have met in the capital of our country to celebrate our jubilee.

The separation that fifty years ago took place between Northern and Southern Baptists was happily circumscribed in extent. It related exclusively to the missionary operations which had hitherto been conducted in common. The fathers of that day were solicitous that this point should be clearly understood, and that the extent of the disunion should not be exaggerated. The official address sent forth by the Convention declared that "Northern and Southern

---

[1] Historical discourse on the Fiftieth Anniversary of the Southern Baptist Convention.

W. H. Whitsitt, D. D., LL. D.

WILLIAM HETH WHITSITT was born in Nashville, Tenn., November 25, 1841. When he was eleven years of age his father died, leaving him to the care and training of his mother, from whom he received the rudiments of an education. In 1857 he entered Union University and graduated with distinction. He then spent one year at the University of Virginia studying Latin, Greek, mathematics, and moral philosophy, and afterward took a two years' course at the Southern Baptist Theological Seminary. The two following years were spent in study at the universities of Leipzig and Berlin, Germany.

Returning to America in 1871 he entered the pastorate at Albany, Ga., from which he was called in 1872 to a professorship in the Southern Baptist Theological Seminary, which he held until his election in May, 1895, to succeed Dr. John A. Broadus in the presidency of that institution. That he should be chosen by men who knew them both to succeed such a man is a sufficient testimony to his character, his learning, and his piety to render unnecessary any comment here.

Baptists are still brethren. They differ in no article of the faith. They are guided by the same principles of gospel order. . . We do not regard the rupture as extending to foundation principles, nor can we think that the great body of our Northern brethren will so regard it."

Though the division related to nothing else than foreign and domestic missions, it was nevertheless unavoidable. One of our statesmen declared that the issues then pending between the North and the South constituted "an irrepressible conflict." History has justified the correctness of that conclusion. The best and wisest men in the North consented to a division because they regarded it as being, under the circumstances, a necessary evil; the wisest and best men in the South accepted the division as being imperatively required by the situation.

In many respects the separation has also been of signal advantage. It was of advantage to our Northern brethren, because it promoted their peace and union. They could never have been rightly at harmony among themselves so long as their Southern brethren remained in the same organization. It was of advantage to Southern Baptists in different directions, but especially because it developed their missionary enterprise and activity. To illustrate what is here affirmed, certain statistics may be cited with relation to the American Baptist Home Mission Society, which was the organ through which operations in domestic missions were prosecuted by the Baptists of the whole country from 1832 to 1845. During that period of thirteen years the entire sum of contributions from the Southern States was thirty-eight thousand six hundred and fifty-six dollars and forty cents. During a like period under the Southern Baptist Convention, the contributions for domestic and Indian missions amounted to two hundred and sixty-six thousand three hundred and fifty-six dollars and thirteen cents.

This gratifying advance was worth all the pain and sacrifice that we had to endure in breaking up the relations that had hitherto subsisted with our Northern brethren.

It is also a matter of sincere rejoicing that the separation here described was for the most part a peaceable one. Friction was unavoidable, and it is not denied that more or less of it was developed. But public negotiations on either side were marked by the dignity and moderation that become Christian brethren. That excellent result was due, in large measure, to the singularly elevated character and devout piety of the contending parties. Moreover, we cannot be too grateful that there were no questions regarding the division of a common property to excite the thoughts of men to undue asperity. It is likewise a special mercy of Providence that in all the fifty years of our history there have been no very important conflicts touching the boundaries that should exist between Northern and Southern Baptists. The evils of disunion would have been greatly enhanced if we had been forced to waste our resources and opportunities in building rival houses of worship for Northern and Southern Baptist churches in all the cities, and even towns and villages, adjacent to the border. Let us recognize our exceedingly fortunate situation and always do what lies in our power to keep the peace.

The half-century of our Convention's history may be divided into three separate periods, each of which has a well-defined character of its own.

1. The first of these is the period in which slavery still prevailed, extending from 1845 to 1865. It is not easy correctly to estimate the number of Baptist people within our bounds at the opening of this period. Dr. J. L. Burrows, in his excellent "American Baptist Register," estimates that we had four hundred and two thousand and sixty-eight members in our Southern churches in the year 1852. Possibly

there were not more than three hundred and fifty thousand in the year 1845. Of these at least one hundred thousand were slaves, who had few independent churches of their own, but almost uniformly belonged to the organizations of their masters. Subtracting these from the total, we shall have two hundred and fifty thousand as the approximate number of white Baptists in 1845.

The progress and development of our constituents during the greater portion of this period were rapid and steady. It is entertaining to consider how different was the tone that was observed in the year 1846 from that which prevailed in the year 1859. The excellent corresponding secretary of the Foreign Mission Board, Dr. James B. Taylor, gravely reminded the Convention that "the population of the South is comparatively small. Our churches are not of easy access, their members being often scattered over many miles of territory. . . Our country is not filled up with towns and villages, rendering it convenient to collect the masses together, but our brethren, being principally agriculturists, must be visited upon their farms or called together at their country places of worship." In the year 1859, on the contrary, we had begun to speak with a degree of exultation concerning the ample resources of our Southern Baptist churches, and to rejoice that God had blessed so many of our people with large financial means. A brief indication of the advance of the cause will appear in the fact that in 1847 the contributions to the Domestic Mission Board were nine thousand five hundred and ninety-four dollars and sixty cents, while in 1859 the same Board received from the churches almost three times as much, namely, twenty-eight thousand four hundred and eighty-seven dollars and ninety-six cents. In 1846 there was contributed throughout the Southern States eleven thousand seven hundred and thirty-five dollars and twenty-two cents to the Foreign Mission Board, while thirty-nine thousand eight hundred and twenty-four dollars and thirty-seven cents was received in 1859. It is not affirmed that the number of Southern Baptists had increased threefold, in keeping with their contributions, though it must be conceded that their progress in this respect also had been highly gratifying.

The constitution adopted by our Convention at its opening session in 1845 is, in some respects, a highly interesting document, and will repay attentive study. "The General Missionary Convention of the Baptist Denomination in the United States of America for Foreign Missions," with which we had co-operated since the year 1814, was in the beginning merely a society for the promotion of foreign missions. As such, it had only one Executive Board. At a later period the interests of home missions and of Columbian College were likewise imposed upon the same organization. Here was a single Board with three separate departments of labor. This arrangement worked very ill, and in 1826 the day of disaster appeared. In consequence of that disaster, the General Missionary Convention returned to its original function, and devoted itself to the prosecution of foreign missions exclusively. The work of home missions was temporarily interrupted, while Columbian College was left to its own exertions. The result of these changes was that in the Northern part of our country every separate and independent enterprise was henceforth to be prosecuted by a separate and independent society. The General Missionary Convention, now the Missionary Union, took charge of the work of foreign missions; the American Baptist Home Mission Society devoted itself to domestic missions, and the American Baptist Publication Society to the publication interests.

When the fathers of our Convention met together to consult about its constitution, they decided to go back beyond the convulsions of the year 1826, and as far as possible to adopt the principles and methods which had prevailed from the beginning in the General Missionary Convention. One change, however, was dictated by prudence and by an accurate knowledge of the facts. Instead of establishing a Southern Baptist Convention with a single Board, which should have charge of several different departments of denominational exertion, it was decided to establish two co-ordinate Boards, each of which should be dependent upon the body that had originated them. These co-ordinate Boards, one for foreign and the other for domestic missions, were but the forerunners of other interests. In 1851 the Bible Board was established at Nashville, Tennessee. In 1859 the Theological Seminary, with a certain relation of dependence upon the Convention, was set in operation at Greenville, South Carolina. In 1863 a Sunday-school Board was also established at Greenville. In 1888 the Woman's Missionary Union was recognized and assigned to a home in Baltimore. In 1891 another Sunday-school Board was created and sent to Nashville; and in 1893 the Southern Baptist Educational Conference began its existence in close touch with the Convention.

The relations of these different bodies to the central organization may not always be uniform; and yet they are each one in its own way dependent on the Convention. Historical development and the training that has been received by our people for fifty years require that every religious enterprise carried on among white Baptists within the limits of the Southern Baptist Convention shall be in one or other form auxiliary to the Convention. Whatever may be out of touch, and especially out of harmony, with this body, is liable to meet with more or less decided opposition, and to occasion more or less of conflict.

The earliest period of our history as a religious organization was closed amid the tremendous struggle and desolations of the war between the States. The Bible Board at Nashville passed away and was decently interred during this troublous season. The Board of Foreign Missions was greatly crippled in its operations, but disaster was averted by the devotion and sacrifices of some of the missionaries and of excellent brethren in Maryland and Kentucky, to whom we must always be under obligations. The Domestic Mission Board devoted its attention chiefly to the soldiers in the Southern armies, where it was useful and successful.

II. PERIOD OF POVERTY AND PERIL—1865-1879

It would be difficult to overestimate the extent of the poverty and distress that prevailed in the Southern country immediately after the war. Desolation reigned in every quarter. Almost everything was destroyed except the courage of the people. It goes without saying that our churches suffered along with other interests. The apprehensions of the people regarding the commonest necessities were so constant and so keen that there was often little time or thought for any other concern. Many houses of worship had been dismantled through military occupation or by the violence of conflict, and it was often a question whether it would ever again be possible to restore them to their original condition.

In the midst of these cares and sorrows our esteemed colored brethren retired from our churches almost to a man. The parting, though mutually painful, was accompanied by mutual good wishes. But it could not be prevented, and we were compelled to accept the inevitable.

Not long after the war came the trials and repression of the era of reconstruction. Ten years of confusion were entailed by this policy; a period in which our privations and anxieties were scarcely inferior to those we had endured during the four years of armed conflict.

To this aggregation of evils was added the remarkable financial panic that overtook the country in the autumn of 1873, whose results were keenly felt almost by every inhabitant of our section for six or seven years. The experience of those long days of torture and humiliation are still remembered and will haunt many people as an evil dream as long as they live in the world.

If the affairs of the Convention were in a sorry plight, this was nothing more than might justly be said of every other business enterprise. An attempt was made at Russellville, in 1866, to revive the Bible Board, and to establish its home at Louisville; but the Board was too dead for resurrection. If the resolution had not been faithfully embalmed in the minutes, it would not be known that any human being had been bold enough to recall the defunct institution.

The Sunday-school Board existed for ten short years, and in 1873 was dissolved at Mobile, its effects and its functions being committed to the care of the Domestic Mission Board. Unfortunately, however, the situation of the latter Board was by no means assured. As early as 1871, there were suggestions of merging it into the Board of Foreign Missions. The specious plea was urged that it would be more economical if we returned to the identical platform which proved so unfortunate for the General Missionary Convention and sustained only a single Board, which should prosecute the general work of home as well as foreign missions. These dangerous intimations were defeated, but the Board was not thereby restored to its former vigor. Centrifugal forces were everywhere at work. Several of the States had organized mission Boards to care for their own territory, and honorable State Conventions deliberately passed resolutions by which the Domestic Mission Board should be excluded from their boundaries. These proposed to take charge of the entire work of home missions, allowing the Convention to make no collections and to extend no assistance in any place where their authority was respected.

Still other States had entered upon terms of cooperation with rival organizations situated in other sections of the country. That was notably true of the district west of the Mississippi River, which, by one process or another, had all been lost to the Domestic Mission Board. It had no agent, and was rendering no assistance in any portion of that wide territory. This process of disintegration was not confined to the trans-Mississippi department. In some of the States on the eastern side of the river brethren had turned away from the Domestic Board and were working in connection with rival societies. The outlook was as gloomy as it well could be.

In addition to the above, the seminary was all the while in grave peril. It encountered three crises of cardinal importance: one in the year 1869, at Macon; another in 1874, at Jefferson, Texas; and a third in 1879, at Atlanta, Georgia. They must have been comparatively few who had courage enough in those evil days to conceive any firm faith in the future of the institution.

Under all these circumstances it was nothing more than one might expect, that questions concerning the life or death of the Convention should in due time be raised. That issue was brought forward and discussed at Atlanta, Georgia, during the session of the Convention in 1879. Here was indeed a "battle of the giants." No such momentous controversy has been brought before us in the entire course of our history. On the afternoon of the first day an impressive preamble and a couple of resolutions were proposed.

This document was expressed in diplomatic terms,

and yet it was generally understood that it related mainly to the question of "preserving our separate organization." As in the case of all issues of first-class importance, the business was referred to a committee composed of one from each State. When it came up for discussion on the morning of Saturday, May 10, 1879, after an address by the chairman, it was moved by John A. Broadus, of Kentucky, to strike out the two resolutions, and on that proposition a debate was held which lasted throughout the day. Shortly before adjournment in the afternoon, the motion of Dr. Broadus was carried, and an amended resolution was substituted in the following terms: "The committee to whom were referred the resolutions on co-operation with our Northern brethren, have had the same under consideration, and instruct me to report the following resolution:

"*Resolved*, That five brethren be appointed by this Convention to bear to our Baptist brethren of the Northern States, at their approaching anniversaries, expressions of our fraternal regard, and assurances that while firmly holding to the wisdom and policy of preserving our separate organizations, we are ready, as in the past, to co-operate cordially with them in promoting the cause of Christ in our own and foreign lands."

In this manner an issue was quietly closed which had threatened us with the most serious consequences, and there has never been a moment since the year 1879 when it was even remotely possible for such a question to be again discussed before the Convention.

The forces that conspired together to defend the life of the Convention in that dark and trying ordeal deserve respectful mention. The theological seminary, in its deep poverty and embarrassment, found in the Convention an indispensable support. It required an organization to which it could declare its sorrows year by year, and from which it could obtain much needed assistance. On these grounds, as well as many others, the seminary has always vigorously advocated the continued maintenance of the Convention.

But the sturdiest prop of an institution that was almost ready to fall was the Board of Foreign Missions. It had no rivals in prosecuting the foreign mission work of Southern Baptists. On either side of the Mississippi all States and Territories were open to it; its agents were kindly welcomed everywhere. By consequence it was in its power to exhibit a degree of prosperity that was unusual for that time, and to present reports that were always gratifying and often surprising. Friends of the Convention could urge with entire propriety that there was no serious call to surrender as long as this creditable work remained intact.

At the close of our first fifty years of success and trial it is becoming to bestow a deserved meed of acknowledgment and gratitude upon the sturdy Board of Foreign Missions, and upon its noble corresponding secretary, Dr. H. A. Tupper, for the splendid services it was given them to render us. They brought succor and strength and deliverance when other helpers all failed. Without their assistance we should not have been able to celebrate our jubilee to-day.

III. PERIOD OF PROSPERITY—1879–1895.

Almost every interest connected with the southern section of our country began to display marked energy after the year 1879. Our Convention took a new lease of existence, and after long years of weakness experienced afresh the joys of life.

The theological seminary, which it was apprehended might be suspended forever at the close of its sessions in May, 1880, found a deliverer in the person of Governor Joseph E. Brown, of Georgia. In March,

1880, he bestowed upon it a gift of fifty thousand dollars, coupled with the condition that within a specified period the amount should be raised to two hundred thousand dollars, and this kept forever sacred as an endowment fund. Here was the beginning of progress. The fund of two hundred thousand dollars was duly completed, and proved to be only the foundation upon which in the past sixteen years a large superstructure has been reared. Our seminary is one of the most important Baptist institutions of theological learning in the country, or in the world. A certain proportion of the means that constitute this large plant was bestowed by brethren from the Northern States, and it is a sincere pleasure to recognize their generosity and give them thanks. But we have not waited for other people. We have remembered the duty of helping ourselves. The great bulk of the property belonging to the theological seminary must be considered as a monument of the rising prosperity of the Southern States and of the increasing liberality of Southern Baptists.

The receipts of the Foreign Mission Board began to grow apace with the year 1880. In the thirty-four years between 1845 and 1879 this Board received from all sources, nine hundred and ninety-nine thousand three hundred and seventy-seven dollars and twenty-three cents. In the sixteen years that have elapsed since that period it has received one million four hundred and eleven thousand five hundred and twenty-nine dollars and fourteen cents. Here is no time to enter into minute details, but we cannot omit to congratulate ourselves upon the brilliant advances that have been recorded in foreign missions. The fields which up to 1879 had been cultivated in Africa, China, and Italy have been greatly reinforced and improved, while other fields have been opened and successfully cultivated in lands that were not then occupied by us. Our missions may not be all that we could desire, but we are heartily proud of them, and are willing for them to be compared with the work performed by other denominations.

The Home Mission Board, which had so long been in an enfeebled condition, began to receive new favor after 1879. In the year 1882 it was reconstructed at Greenville, South Carolina, and, under Dr. I. T. Tichenor, started upon a career of prosperity that has been the joy and the marvel of our recent history. Experience has amply demonstrated that this agency is necessary to the prosperity and efficiency of the Convention. Therefore we may well rejoice in every influence that contributes to strengthen the hands and to improve the resources of the Home Mission Board.

Something new under the sun began to display itself at Greenville. We had long been accustomed to comparatively small assemblies and slight attendance upon the sessions of the body. Some of us, hoping to correct this evil, were striving to induce our brethren to return to the former practice of holding biennial sessions. At Greenville the magnificent crowds began to appear that have recently become such a striking feature of our convocations. There were six hundred and sixteen members at Baltimore in 1884; Louisville entertained six hundred and fifty-six in 1887; and in other instances the figures have gone still higher. This remarkable change indicates the fact that our Baptist people have always felt a gratifying amount of interest in our affairs. I believe we have possessed the hearts of the people in a way that can be claimed by few of the religious organizations of our country. The people would have been present even in the darkest hours of our history, but poverty forbade them. As soon as it became financially possible for them to travel, they were delighted to put in their appearance. While we have a constituency of such numbers, character, and resources, there can be no further thought of surrender. A spirit of hopefulness and enterprise has been gaining ground for years. We feel that we can accomplish whatever it is sensible and prudent for us to undertake. The time has come when, without conceit, we may consider that we are well able to possess the land in which our lot is cast.

In the gloomiest period of our suffering and privation the wise and hopeful corresponding secretary of the Foreign Mission Board, Dr. H. A. Tupper, began to encourage and promote among our women an interest in the subject of missions. The earliest central committee was organized under his direction in the year 1876, and with persistent enthusiasm he pressed the enterprise wherever he could find an opportunity. There were many obstacles and many opponents, but in the year 1888, was finally established the Woman's Missionary Union. From the outset the women have been exceedingly helpful, but since the establishment of a central Board, they have become, in several important respects, the right arm of our power.

Members of the Convention were greatly mortified and discouraged by the failure of the Sunday-school Board, in 1873. For long years it was permitted to rest in peace. We were so often reminded that such an enterprise could not succeed in the South, that we were almost afraid to touch it a second time. But finally, some of our brethren screwed their courage to the sticking place and brought the matter to the attention of the Convention at two different sessions. After a thorough discussion of the subject in the press and on the platform, the Convention, in its session at Birmingham, in 1891, organized a new Sunday-school Board at Nashville. The result has transcended the most sanguine anticipations. The Sunday-school Board has done as much as any agency in recent years to excite a sense of pride in our Convention and of confidence in our capacities.

One of the best consequences of the new and firmer hold on life which we have gained in the prosperous period of our history has been the increased repose and dignity which have thereby been encouraged. Especially have our sentiments grown more kindly and more fraternal toward our Northern brethren. The fact that our footing has been more secure has likewise operated to increase our interest in our colored brethren, and it is possible that in coming years it may be given us to do more to "elicit, combine, and direct" their energies for their own advantage than we have ever accomplished in the past.

I have chosen as the motto of my historical discourse the word of the Lord unto Moses: "Speak unto the children of Israel, that they go forward." And I must needs return to it in my closing sentences. Last year the Baptists of the Southern States contributed only eight cents per member to promote the cause of foreign missions. It is presumed that a similar or even smaller amount was contributed for home missions and other objects; but as I have not the facts at hand, it will be desirable to speak only of foreign missions. We have made great progress since the opening year of the Convention. Our regular contributions have advanced something like tenfold while our membership has hardly increased above fivefold. But we are still much behind our privileges and our duty. The other great popular denomination of our section, the Southern Methodist, contributed last year the sum of eighteen cents a member for foreign missions. A comparison between them and ourselves is for several reasons more just than can be instituted between us and other religious denominations. We abide this test very ill. It seems to be the sacred duty of us all, as ministers of religion and friends of missions, to speak unto the Baptists of the South that they go forward. They are surely equal to the feat which has been accomplished by our Methodist brethren. Indeed, if they should give their mind to it, they might as easily lead as follow after the Methodists. Here is a reasonable and sober standard. Let us in coming years bestir ourselves and see that we measure up to it.

When the Convention was holding its opening session at Augusta, there was a lad just turned eighteen years, resting under the quiet shades of Culpeper, in far-distant Virgina. He was unknown to fame. Possibly no member of the body had ever heard his name. In due time he appeared upon the scene, and for a period of thirty years played the role of our "Great Commoner." For thirty years he was the leading force in our counsels and history, and yet throughout that entire period he did not occupy the smallest office directly in the gift of the Convention. This year of our jubilee, with all its light and gladness, has been sadly darkened by his departure. On the 17th of March devout men carried him to his burial and made great lamentation over him. The foremost leader of our history, great in the might of his gentleness, has passed away from us, but his fame and usefulness shall go and grow throughout the years and ages. When you who sit here shall be aged and feeble men and women, little children will gather about your knees with reverence and delight, to look upon one who has seen and heard and spoken with John A. Broadus.

III

THE CHRISTIAN HOPE[1]

BY R. J. WILLINGHAM, D. D.

"Which hope we have as an anchor of the soul, both sure and steadfast, and which entereth into that within the vail." Heb. 6 : 19.

WE are all creatures of hope. It enters into every relationship of human life. The day laborer goes forth in the early morning not having received his wages, but he labors in hope of the same at the end of the day, week, or month. The physician works in hope, the lawyer works in hope. The merchant lays in his stock of goods hoping to sell, hoping to collect. The tiller of the soil goes through heat and cold sowing, cultivating, waiting in hope. The parents in the home with the little child patiently do their duty in hope; you think the little one thoughtless, careless of the future; not so with them. Many fond hopes show them a bright future of usefulness for the loved one. What is true in all these spheres of life is true in the Christian life as the child of light looks to the days to come. We have not seen heaven, the great white throne, the angels of light, and yet we press on, day after day, year after year, because we have hope.

What is the basis of hope? Faith. Without faith there can be no hope. Strong faith gives strong hope. Weak faith begets weak hope. What is the basis of faith? Promises. What is the strength of

---

[1] Preached in the Central Presbyterian Church, Washington, D. C., during the Jubilee Session of the Southern Baptist Convention.

ROBERT JOSIAH WILLINGHAM was born May 15, 1854, in Beaufort District, S. C. His father, Deacon B. L. Willingham, now of Macon, Ga., has been for years a very prominent layman; quite successful in business, wise in counsel, and liberal in heart, he exerts a wide influence for good. His mother, Elizabeth Baynard, was a woman of rare gifts, of bright intellect, and very pious.

Robert joined the church at thirteen. He attended school at the University of Georgia and received the A. M. degree in 1873, graduating with high honors.

He went into business and at the same time studied law, but feeling called of God to preach, gave up all his plans and attended the seminary in Louisville one year.

His wife is a highly cultured and deeply pious woman. She was formerly Miss Corneille Bacon, of the noted Georgia family by that name. His pastorates were in Talbotton and Barnesville, Ga., and Chattanooga and Memphis, Tenn. He was very much blessed in all of these. The last six years of his pastorate he received over eight hundred into church-membership. He was called to the Corresponding Secretaryship of the Foreign Board in 1893, to a work which he loves and in which he has been prospered.

promises? The one who makes the promises. Here you have the whole connection. Hope depends on your faith in the one who makes the promises. This is true of the day laborer, the professional man, the merchant, of all. How is it with the Christian's hope? Do we have to take the word of any man? Do we have to build our hopes on the promises of any being of earth? By no means; we have the word of Almighty God. Day by day, and year by year, we press forward because we have faith in the promises of the King Eternal. When we consider, O mortal, our hope, let us realize that we build on the rock of eternal truth, the word of God. God has spoken and sealed it with an oath. At the old St. Giles' Church, in Edinburgh, Scotland, they tell you how the Covenanters would not sign the covenant in the church with ink, but went to the old gravestones near by and, opening their veins, signed the document on the tombstones with their blood. God has given us promises which he has signed in the blood of his Son on Calvary. Think of it; when the Lord God Almighty, the great eternal God, wished to make provision for you, poor lost man, weak, debased in sin, that he might deliver you, that he might help you, that he might hold you up, that he might finally give you an entrance into his home above—he wrote the promise in the blood of his only begotten Son. Hope, hope, blessed hope in God, through the promises which he has given us.

What of this hope? It is described as an anchor to the soul sure and steadfast. See the figure which is used. A ship in a storm driven on a lee-shore finds the anchor her safety. So hope is to the Christian an anchor, driven on the shoals of skepticism, in the whirlpools of disaster, in the dark nights of affliction, in the mists and fogs of intellectual doubts, yea, in every trial and difficulty which sweeps around the soul. Look up and trust. God's word says of this hope it is sure. What else of earth is sure? Mention only one thing. The longer we live the more we see how uncertain is all here. Man proposes, but he fails in his plans. You remember how the great Napoleon, in telling his plans, was reminded by an old lady of the mutability of human affairs in these words: "Remember, sire, man proposes, but God disposes." He replied with hauteur: "Napoleon proposes and Napoleon disposes." Even then he was going to defeat. One of our grandest, best men in a neighboring State not long since stood before an audience and told how he had accumulated property for his children, purposing to leave each one twenty thousand dollars. The means were in hand. The war swept it all away. He said, "If I cannot give it to them while I live, they shall have it when I die." He insured his life. The crash of 1873 came and the insurance companies failed. Then the children, one by one, continued to die until all had gone. He stood there alone, saying, "Property all gone, insurance all gone, children all gone, but Christ is mine still." The hope which had cheered his heart fifty years before, cheered him still.

This hope is also spoken of as steadfast. The idea is similar to the preceding. Nothing of earth is steadfast. The teachings of science are constantly changing. Not that the laws of nature change. No, never! God's laws in his works change not, but man's interpretations of them are constantly changing. Yet some people seem to think science and the Bible conflict. God's works never conflict with his words. It is only the puny interpretations which are put on one or the other that conflict. Teachings of science are constantly changing, and it is well. Copernicus was scoffed at for his theory. He revealed how planets, with their revolving satellites, revolve around the sun. When we find out all the truth, God's throne will be in the center and all revolving around that. God is the author and center of this universe. The teachings of science though are part of this earth, and that changes constantly. What is steadfast? Take the mightiest empires and dominions of earth and their very ruins tell of weakness and decay. Go to Egypt with her glory reaching back through thousands of years and the monuments of her splendor, whose very history is forgotten, tell of the weakness of man's power. Proud Babylon is the habitation of desolation. Go to Athens and stand on her Acropolis, look for her splendor, and you find only the broken columns of the grand temple of Minerva. The theatre of Bacchus is a waste; the prison of Socrates a hole in the rock. Desolate is the once thronged Pnyx where Demosthenes appealed to Grecian prowess, and Mars Hill, where Paul would awaken the still nobler instincts of manhood in calling on them for fidelity to God. Yet, all of these things cause a stillness to come over the soul, and an echo from the past intermingles with the sigh of the wind as it sweeps over the ruins with the ever-recurring refrain:

> Passing away, passing away;
> All of earth is weakness and decay,
> Passing away, passing away.

I might ask you to look at history and see how unstable it all is; history is but the biography and epitaph of men and nations—the account of how they rise and fall.

Take now your own experience. Go back twenty, thirty, or forty years; how all has changed. Go sit in the old church again. What has come to pass? The loved pastor gone. Dear man of God, he was faithful. But right there sat the young playmate, so bright and joyous. Where is he? Gone. He lies out yonder. Others nearer and dearer, where are they? Gone, also. But look no more without.

B

Look within, at your own self. You have changed, your affections, your desires, your longings. You say the world has changed. You have changed. But remember, one day sitting there in that church you felt a strange joy in your heart. You loved God, you loved all; you looked beyond earth; your trust, your hope was in Christ. Many changes have come, but this has not changed. No, no, the same old hope, the blessed hope is with you still—steadfast, fixed on God.

Again, we are told of this hope that it entereth into that within the vail. This probably refers to Christ going into the Holy of Holies, even heaven itself, to intercede for us. When on Calvary he was dying, the vail which hung in the temple between the holy and most holy places was by an unseen hand from above torn in twain from top to bottom. Christ has gone into the Holy of Holies for us. We can come to God through him. We need no priest, no pope. The simplest, plainest, poorest, can come boldly to the mercy-seat and find grace to help in time of need. Our hope takes hold on Christ himself, yea, Christ in heaven. It is said that in ancient times when the mariner wished to make a certain port, if tide or wind were against him and he could not proceed, he would send the anchor forward in a small boat and throw it out, and then with cable and capstan, draw up to that point, when he would again send it forward and thus proceed. The Christian has his anchor fixed in heaven, day by day he draws nearer. His progress may seem slow, but how sure when fixed, anchored to Christ. Do you feel tempest-tossed? Never mind, fear not, if anchored to Christ. I read some time since of a ship in a storm on the Mediteranean. The anchor was thrown out and held with remarkable firmness through the storm. Afterward in pulling in the anchor, it was found that one of the flukes had taken hold of the ring in an old anchor which had lain sunken in the sea. The security of the boat was thus made sure by the smaller anchor taking hold of the larger. So, O Christian, your bark on life's sea may be tossed, but is securely being anchored into the buried but ascended Lord and Master.

What does this hope do for us? It makes us rejoice in the Lord our God. God's people should be a rejoicing people. It is wrong to go around whining, complaining, and fussing as though we were fatherless and deserted. Think for a moment. God our Father; our sins forgiven, blotted out through Christ our Saviour; the Holy Spirit our guide and comforter; heaven our home. Shall we complain? We dishonor our Heavenly Father when we distrust him. If God has given his own Son to redeem us, how shall he not with him also freely give us all things? What good thing will he withhold from them that love him? Let us rejoice in God more, trust him, and hope in his word. Hope makes us strong; strong to endure. Trials and difficulties will come. Foes must be met. The fearful, timid heart cowers and flees. The hopeful heart takes courage, opposes, and overcomes. The man who hopes is the man who conquers.

Hope also makes us patient, and this is one element of genuine strength of character, and marks true Christian excellence. Paul stood on lofty heights when he could quietly say in the midst of difficulties and trials, "For our light affliction, which is but for a moment, worketh for us a far more exceeding and eternal weight of glory." He does not say, we think, or we suppose; but, "We know that all things work together for good to them that love God, to them who are the called according to his purpose."

Hope helps us to work. While Christ lets us stay here watching and waiting for his coming, how much is to be done, in heart, in home, in country, in the world. And how weak we are. Who, looking at self, so weak and unworthy, would not draw back in despair ; but looking at Christ, seeing, hearing him as he says, " My grace is sufficient for you," " Lo, I am with you alway," who cannot press hopefully forward, saying : " Master, lead, I will follow " ? Precious thought, we are co-workers with God. We sow the seed, he gives the harvest. He says in due season we shall reap if we faint not. He tells us to be faithful, not successful. He will give the crown of life.

And, lastly, hope takes the gloom from death and lights up the dying hour. What a desolation, a darkness to the man who looks at death and the grave without Christ there. The bottomless pit has been described as having written over the door, " He who enters here leaves hope behind." Oh, what a world of darkness and woe! No God, no heaven, no hope, forever, forever lost. The great Saladin, when dying is said to have told the attendants to carry a winding sheet on a spear before him to the grave to let all know that was all that the great chieftain took with him. Cæsar is said to have uttered in dying these words: " Is this all ? Is this all ? " How beautiful the picture as the aged Paul looks at death, and quietly says : " I have fought a good fight, I have finished my course, I have kept the faith : Henceforth there is laid up for me a crown of righteousness, which the Lord, the righteous judge, shall give me at that day ; and not to me only, but unto all them also that love his appearing."

Dear brethren, you have been, some of you, but a short time on the voyage ; may your hope grow stronger every day. Some have been many long years on the way. The anchor has held you through many a storm. You are almost home. The haven is at hand. Soon the billows will be passed, and you will rest in the presence of the King. I give an incident. Years ago a boy was returning home after having been away for months for the first time to a school in another State. He was on a boat going home. Somehow the boat seemed to move slowly and stop often. From time to time he would go on the upper deck and ask the captain: "Are we almost there?" And the answer would come, "Not yet." A drizzly, cold December rain set in, night came on, and the captain, seeing anxiety in the boy's face, said: "Your father told me to tell you he would meet you at the landing." By-and-by, as a turn was made in the river, the captain said: "You see that light away down yonder; well, your father is right there waiting for you." And sure enough he was there. Together through the darkness they went until they saw, at the head of the beautiful, broad avenue on the top of the hill, the loved old family mansion, with its lights and loving hearts, awaiting the son's coming home. Oh, how sweet the meeting, the greeting of the loved ones, the rest at home! The journey and the darkness were forgotten. At home again, at home again!

Years have passed. The old family circle is broken. The billows have beaten around us. Those who waited and watched for the boy that night have gone years ago, but somehow heaven has been nearer and sweeter ever since. They seem to be waiting and watching, still saying, "Brother, son, we are in the home and await you." The waves beat, the darkness lowers. Christ says, "I am the way, the truth, and the life." We trust, we hope, and through him we will meet again at home. "Which hope we have as an anchor of the soul both sure and steadfast, and which entereth into that within the vail."

IV

GROUND OF JUDGMENT

BY REV. B. H. CARROLL, D. D.

"Inasmuch as ye have done it unto one of the least of these my brethren ye have done it unto me. . . Inasmuch as ye did it not to one of the least of these, ye did it not to me. And these shall go away into everlasting punishment: but the righteous into life eternal." Matt. 25 : 40, 45, 46.

FOR four thousand years after the creation of the world one forecast of the future loomed up as the great coming event before the eyes of all intelligences. It was the highest mountain peak in the chain of coming events. I refer to the first advent of the Son of God. The prophets climbed up the highest mountains of inspiration, and from that lofty standpoint, having a wide sweep of vision, they strained their eyes and exercised their prophetic ken to discern the time and manner and purpose of that coming. And kings and princes longed to see that day. His coming was "the desire of all nations."

But when he came he so came as to disappoint the expectations of those who were looking for him. I mean that the guise in which he came was a terrible disappointment to carnal men who so long expected him. There was not enough pomp and pageant. He did not come as a king on a throne and surrounded by guards and attended by conquering armies. In coming he condescended; he who thought it not robbery to be called equal with God and who was God, stooped to take the form of a slave. That is what the word means, slave, not servant. He

B. H. Carroll, D.D.

B. H. CARROLL was born near Carrollton, Carroll county, Miss., December 27, 1843. When he was about six years old his father moved to Drew County, Ark., and in the winter of 1858 to Burleson County, Tex. He took the A. M. degree from Baylor University. Served four years in Confederate army, and was wounded at Mansfield, Ga. He was converted in 1865; ordained in 1866; married to Miss Ellen Bell, at Starkville, Miss.

Dr. Carroll has been pastor of the First Baptist Church, Waco, Tex., twenty-five years. Was made a D. D. by the State University, Nashville. The American Baptist Publication Society has brought out one volume of his sermons. The book supports his reputation for being a courageous and powerful preacher of a pure gospel.

left the throne of heaven to be born in a stable and cradled in a cow-trough. And he was poor. The foxes had holes, and the birds of the air had nests, but the Son of Man had not where to lay his head. He came in humiliation. He came as a sufferer. He came to endure the great passion appointed to him. And, coming in that guise and for such purpose, there was no beauty in him when men saw him that they should desire him. To them he was without form or comeliness, and in his great suffering they esteemed him afflicted and smitten of God. And he stooped unto death and into death and triumphed over death in his own realm and rose above the grave, and above Jerusalem, and above the mountains, and above the clouds, and above the stars, and ever up, challenging the heavenly portals as he rose: "Lift up your heads, O ye gates, and be ye lifted up, ye everlasting doors, and the King of Glory shall come in." And entering, he took his place upon the throne on high.

Daniel saw that. He says: "I saw in the night visions, and, behold, one like the Son of man came with the clouds of heaven, and came to the Ancient of days, and they brought him near before him. And there was given him dominion, and glory, and a kingdom, that all people, nations, and languages should serve him: his dominion is an everlasting dominion, which shall not pass away, and his kingdom that which shall not be destroyed." Concerning him thus received in heaven, the Apostle Peter now says: "Whom the heavens must receive until the times of restitution of all things." But before he ascended he said: "I will come again. I will come in like manner as I go up. I will come in the clouds of heaven." Now, from the death, burial, resurrection, and ascension of Jesus Christ, for nearly two thousand years the second advent of the Son of God has been the stupendous coming event of all the future. The eyes of the world and of the angels are fixed upon it. As the first advent caught and held with fascinating and attractive power the thought of all intelligences for four thousand years, so now the second advent fills the vision of the universe. "When the Son of man shall come in his glory"—mark the emphasis, in his *glory* —and the implied contrast. The first time he came in his humiliation. The first time he came as a slave. When he comes again he will come in his glory. He will come as a king indeed. He will come in all the splendid sheen of heavenly apparel. He will come environed by guards this time and with pomp and majesty and circumstance and pageantry enough to satisfy the greatest sensationalists that ever desired to see a startling thing.

But when he comes who will come with him? The context says: "When the Son of man shall come in his glory, and all the holy angels with him." They are said to be an innumerable company; seraphim and cherubim; holy angels, *all* the holy angels. For the first time since the creation of the world heaven will be emptied. When he starts to descend that next time the decree will go forth: "Let all the angels of God fall into line." "Wheel into column," and while the eye cannot look to the end of that line of fire, all of them, all of them will come down with him. Angels! You have heard of them. They were in paradise. They kept the way of the tree of life after expulsion from it. Abraham entertained them. When Jacob slept they came to him and he saw them descending and ascending the ladder to heaven, which symbolized the Lord Jesus Christ establishing communication between the upper and the lower world. When Jesus was born a special choir of them filled the welkin of heaven with hosannas when they sang: "Glory to God in the highest, and on earth peace, good will toward men." They released Peter from prison. They came to John. They smote Herod. And one of them breathed the cold chill of death into the hearts of one hundred and eighty thousand of the hosts of Sennacherib. Angels, holy angels! I will tell you directly why they will come with him.

Who else will come with him? We are informed in the twelfth chapter of Hebrews that now, with the innumerable company of angels in heaven and in the presence of God, are the spirits of the just made perfect, the souls of all good men and women and children, the spirits that had been by death released from the tabernacle which fell to pieces here upon this earth. Those disembodied, but perfected and justified spirits, now in heaven, they will come with him. What is the proof? In the letter to the Thessalonians Paul says: "For if we believe that Jesus died and rose again, even so them also which sleep in Jesus will God bring with him." And Jude says: "Behold, the Lord cometh with ten thousand of his saints."

And that will be a startling denouement. When the legions of the angels have been marshaled and the decree goes forth where the spirits are resting in the paradise of God in the presence of the blessed one: "Come out, ye spirits. Come out, spirits of Abraham and Isaac and Jacob. Come out, all ye disembodied souls and fall into line. I want to take you with me. I am going to visit the earth you once inhabited. I want to carry you there for a special purpose." And so they come with him. And they come down, descending with the sound of a trumpet, and the shout of the archangel and in the sheen of flashing wings, and in the glory and splendor of heaven they come, down, down, down. They pause in the air, poised above the earth.

Simultaneously with that descent from above, the descent of the King in his glory and of his holy angels and of the just made perfect with him, there is an ascent from below, and that is the calling up of the unholy angels. Satan, the great serpent, the dragon, the arch-fiend, Diabolus, the accuser of the brethren. From below, drawn by the imperious command of his Creator and Judge, he will come, and his demons with him. The demons that in the days of Christ took possession of men and made them blaspheme; the demons that defiled souls and obstructed the progress of the gospel by wiles and stratagems and delusions and every kind of fallacy and sophistry; the demons who seduced men, whose doctrines poisoned the souls of men; the demons who, under the guidance of Satan, fought every foot of the progress of Jesus Christ. They will come. I will tell you why directly.

And who else will come? The spirits of the lost will come with him. Dives and those like him in torment. Hell shall give up the dead which are in it. Men, spirits of men, who for sin on earth have been cast down in chains and darkness, are brought up from the prison-house of woe and despair, and they with the devil and his angels gather toward that central point. That will be a sublimely awful sight. Oh, it will be such a sight as no man has ever yet looked upon.

Now, as these two spiritual hosts approach to a common center, what happens? First, the dead arise. When it says the dead in Christ shall rise first, it does not mean that the dead in Christ shall arise before the wicked dead, but it means that the dead in Christ shall rise before the living Christians are changed. The first event in order is the resurrection of the dead, and living people will see it. They will witness the opening of the graves and they will see the body that has been buried or burned, or whose ashes have been scattered to the four winds of heaven, the dead from the sea, from the forest, from under mausoleums and from lowly and unmarked burial places, the dead will rise. The righteous dead will rise transfigured and glorified. Corruption puts on incorruption; mortality, immortality. That which was sown in weakness is raised in power. But they are as yet only bodies. Now, the king yonder, looking down at these still, lifeless bodies of his saints shall say to his angels: "Bring them here! Sever them from the unjust." And as they are brought, the spirits who once inhabited them recognize the houses in which they once lived, and with joy unspeakable, rush into the renovated and glorified habitation which they once animated; and the whole man, soul and body, is now united, perfected and glorified and sanctified.

Then what? The living Christians, the ones who have not died, and who will never die, these undergo a change. Paul says: "Behold I show you a mystery. We shall not all sleep, but we shall all be changed, in a moment, . . . at the last trump, for the dead shall be raised, and we shall be changed." And that marvelous change which took place when Enoch was translated and Elijah conveyed in a chariot of fire to heaven, that change takes place in every living Christian. Glorified without death, they are caught up with the resurrection bodies of the spirits already with Jesus—yes, together with the Lord in the air, and so shall they forever be with the Lord.

And the spirits of the lost find their bodies raised, raised immortal but not glorified, raised immortal but not conformed to the body of the Lord Jesus Christ, and these they re-enter, so that the whole man is together again. Then they stand with the unholy angels.

Now what? That leaves on earth only the living sinners. What awful things they have witnessed! How terribly suggestive their being left alone. Ah! what can it mean? "Then shall two be in the field; the one shall be taken and the other left. Two women shall be grinding at the mill; the one shall be taken and the other left." What does it forebode? You remember that when God took the one righteous man out of Sodom and left only the living wicked, what followed. If the salt is taken away, does not corruption ensue? If light is withdrawn, does not darkness follow? If those whose presence alone have hitherto restrained the wrath of God, if they are caught up to meet the Lord in the air, and only the living wicked are upon the earth, what follows? That passage read in Malachi is fulfilled. Fire leaps forth. It rushes out from the forest; fire from the plain; fire from river and lake and pool and sea and ocean, until Arctic and Antarctic and Southern and Indian and Atlantic and Pacific oceans, in one great conflagration meet the fire from the shore, and there is a deluge of fire as there had been a deluge of water. By the same word of God that brought the deluge of water, by that same word of God, the heavens and the earth which now are kept in store are reserved unto fire unto the day of judgment and the perdition of ungodly men; and the living wicked shall be burned up in that fire. I am not now talking about hell. I am talking about the literal fire, and they die in that fire. They do not escape death. They are not transfigured. They are not transferred across the river of death. They die; they die by fire, and they are ashes under the feet of the righteous literally and truly. And they are raised after that death, and their bodies are immortal but not glorified. The fire had come as the water came, but as the water did not annihilate, neither will the fire annihilate. There will be a new heaven and a new earth, as before there was a new heaven and a new earth. And now, that all the preparatory steps are taken, the King takes his place on the throne.

"I saw a great white throne, and him that sat on it, from whose face the earth and the heaven fled away... And I saw the dead, small and great, stand before God." And our context says: "He shall sit on the throne of his glory, and before him shall be gathered all nations."

Yes, all nations shall be gathered before him. There is the supreme court whose decision is infallible and irreversible. There is the tribunal which shall reverse ten thousand earthly decisions. The great white throne of eternal judgment! All men and all angels shall stand before it.

The question now arises: Who will be judged? And I say, angels, holy angels. And what will be the ground of the judgment of holy angels? Not that they kept their first estate—the result of that keeping hath already been with them—but because they worshiped the Son of God when they were called on to worship him; because they served him when they were called on to serve him; because they were the ministering spirits to them that are the heirs of salvation; because they furthered the gospel of the Son of God, therefore are the elect angels confirmed, and in that way is the Scripture fulfilled: "He shall reconcile things in heaven as well as things on earth." Then evil angels will be judged, not because they kept not their first estate—they are already cast out for that—but because they would not fall down and worship the Son of God when he was brought into the world. Because they opposed the gospel and fought it over every inch of ground. Because they beguiled men and kept them from believing in the gospel, hoodwinked and blinded them, took possession of them and degraded them. Because they persecuted the righteous. Because they worried and troubled God's people, therefore they will be judged. And there is no other ground of judgment for them. And that disposes of the angels, good and bad.

Now, the nations are gathered, all nations, all people in one congregation. There they are gathered together. What follows next? "He shall separate them one from another, as a shepherd divideth his sheep from the goats." Mark the word "separate," right and left! Right and left! Divide, open ranks. You stand there, and you there. Father here, mother over yonder. Daughter there, son here; brothers, one of you here, the other there. Right and left. Divide! Divide! Separate! That will take the light of hope out of the hearts of all evil men. Oh, there will be weeping at the judgment seat of Christ! There yawns the impassable chasm. No bridge can span it. No wing can fly across it. Separate! Separate! Separate! Good-bye forever!

And now comes to those on the right hand the final sentence. Oh, what a sentence! "Come." The invitation, the welcome in it. "Come ye blessed of my Father, come and inherit the kingdom prepared for you from the foundation of the world. Open wide the door, come in ye blessed, come in, come home, come healed, come cleansed, come washed, come whiter than snow. Come crowned. Come with harps. Come singing. Come with melody in your hearts. Come glorified. Come, ye blessed of my Father."

Why? Now, we will get into the very root of the matter. Why? For I was an hungered and ye gave me meat. I was thirsty and ye gave me drink. I was naked and ye clothed me: I was sick and in prison and ye visited me. That is why. That proves the proposition that only one thing is the ground of judgment, only one thing, and it is the sole ground of God's judgment of men and angels, viz., their treatment of his Son Jesus Christ. That is all. There is no other. It is not that these men fell in Adam. It is not that being fallen in Adam they cursed and swore and stole and murdered; not that. For that the sentence was already passed. They were condemned for that already. No trial about that up yonder, not a bit. But for what? That being fallen; being sinners; being condemned sinners, God brought the gospel to them. Jesus Christ came to them. An overture of salvation was made to them, and they rejected that. This is the ground of judgment. The condemnation is that light has come into the world and men love darkness rather than light. For no matter how great a sinner a man is, no matter how great a sinner he has been, if sinful as he is, fallen as he was and is, he will accept the overture of redemption in Jesus Christ, that sets him free from condemnation forever. That acquits him. Being justified by faith he is entitled to peace with God. As many condemned sinners as received him, to them gave he power to become the sons of God, even to them that believed on his name. If he received the Lord Jesus Christ, who came to rescue him from the condemnation that was already on him, well for him. If he rejected the Lord Jesus Christ, woe to him. No other ground of judgment, and no pleading will even be listened to based on your record in other things, for on that record sentence has already been pronounced, and that judgment has already been written, and it is righteous, and you are lost, and you stand lost. The sole question is, what did you do with Jesus who came to rescue you from that condemnation? And the word of God does not give a hint of anything else as the ground of final judgment.

But just here seems to be a difficulty. If everything depends upon our treatment of Jesus, how can we, who never personally knew, accord him treatment of any kind—either good or bad? If he says: "I was hungry and ye fed me; naked and ye clothed me; sick and ye visited me," making everything depend upon the treatment of him—what else can we say: "Lord, when did we see thee an hungered;

thee sick; thee in prison; thee naked? Why, you passed out of the world eighteen hundred years before I was born; or, I passed out of the world eighteen hundred years before you were born. When did I give food and drink to you, and clothing to you, and visit you?" Now, mark. This brings us to the text at the end of the service, and that is a good way to preach, lead up to the text. "Inasmuch as ye did it unto the least of these, my brethren, ye did it unto me." What does that prove? That the sole ground of the judgment is our treatment of Jesus Christ in his people and in his gospel, and he identifies himself with his people and his gospel. Now, I want to clear that up a little. I want to make it perfectly obvious to you by an illustration. He sent out some disciples, saying: "As you go, preach, and when you enter a city, preach in my name, by my authority, the message that I bid you, and if they receive you they receive me; and if they reject you they reject me. I make this treatment of you a personal matter." Here rises a wonderful scene. I cannot get some pictures out of my mind. See these preachers coming to a place and the people who receive them. What then? He tells the preachers to do a certain thing. I can see the picture of it in my mind. Two men standing in the street of a city where they have preached Jesus and Jesus has been rejected. Now, by the commandment of Jesus Christ, they stoop down and commence untying their shoes, loosening their sandals, and they take their shoes off and, clinging to their shoes, is the dust of the street of that city on which they stood and preached, and the word says: "Shake it off for a witness. Shake it off for a testimony." That dust on which men stood and preached Jesus Christ is brought up and put on the judgment bar and testifies: "O Son of God, we, the grains of sand upon which apostolic feet stood and preached Jesus to these men on the left hand, we were shaken off the feet of the apostles where Jesus was rejected. We testify in the court of heaven against them."

I have a little pebble about as big as the end of my finger, of no intrinsic value, though it is a beautiful pebble and it has a tinge of crimson running through it. As I was informed by the one who gave it to me, that pebble was picked out of the track of Maximilian after he was shot. He stood on that little stone and was shot to death. I had a gold fastening made for it and gave it to my little daughter, and told her that that pebble would be at the judgment bar of God as a witness of the righteousness or of the unrighteousness of the execution of Maximilian. And the rafters in the roof of the house and the beams in the wall shall speak out in that day and tell their stories of how men received or rejected the Lord Jesus Christ.

And when the Lord Jesus Christ shall come, saith Paul, in flaming fire taking vengeance upon them that have not obeyed the gospel, he will recompense tribulation to them that have troubled you, and he will recompense rest to you that were troubled. And what was the ground of that tribulation? That they troubled God's people. They troubled Israel. They brought a reproach upon Israel. They marred the purity of the white flag of Jesus. They obstructed the gospel. They put stumbling-blocks in the way of God's people. They caused strife and division. They, for selfish ends, and to satisfy their own greed, sacrificed the cause of the Lord Jesus Christ. And this I say, is the only ground of judgment. The sentence of Jesus Christ, when that comes, what will you do? How will you receive it? Let me speak for myself: I do not think that I am an undue enthusiast, nor do I think that intense thought and long study on this subject hath made me mad. I think I I speak but the words of truth and soberness when I say that I would rather my right hand should forget its cunning and my tongue cleave to the roof of my mouth in everlasting silence than to say "not at home" to Jesus Christ when he comes in his cause, whether he come by day or by night. When he comes and knocks and I hear it, and he says: "I am hungry, give me bread. I am thirsty, give me drink. I am naked, clothe me." When I hear his voice from the prison: "Come to me in bonds. Be not ashamed of my bonds." I hear him in his persecuted cause, crying: "Help, help, or I perish." Oh, God forbid that I should ever turn my back and close my eyes and ears and say, "Count me out, count me out."

THOMAS TREADWELL EATON was born November 16, 1845, in Murfreesboro, Tenn. His father was Joseph H. Eaton, LL. D., President of the University of Virginia. His mother was, before marriage, Miss Esther M. Treadwell, for some years editor of the "Aurora." He studied in Murfreesboro until after his father's death in 1859, and then entered Madison (now Colgate) University, where his uncle, George W. Eaton, D. D., LL. D., was president. In 1861 he returned to Tennessee on account of the war and soon enlisted in the Seventh Tennessee Cavalry, C. S. A., and served under Forrest. His education was resumed at Washington and Lee University after the war, where he graduated in 1867. Dr. Eaton has served the First Church, Chattanooga, Tenn.; First Church, Petersburg, Va.; and is now pastor of the Walnut Street Church, Louisville, Ky., and editor of the "Western Recorder." The Walnut Street Church is the largest white church of any denomination in the South. During Dr. Eaton's pastorate there have been over three thousand five hundred additions, and large colonies have been sent out. At one time seven hundred and eleven letters were granted. The present membership is one thousand five hundred and fifty. In 1880 he received the degree of D. D. from Washington and Lee University, and LL. D. from Southwestern Baptist University in 1886.

V

TRUTH A LIBERATOR

BY T. T. EATON, D. D., LL. D.

"And ye shall know the truth, and the truth shall make you **free**."
John 8:32.

THE extreme views on the subject of freedom which have followed the wild proclamation of liberty, have done great harm in the world. What we need, therefore, as the pendulum swings too far that way, is to insist with greater emphasis on the duty of obedience. Though a child be heir and lord of all, who is there that would be always talking to him of the delights of doing as he pleases and of the hardship of being under governors and tutors? Would you not rather urge upon him the obligation to obey his tutors, and emphasize rather the duty of submission than the delights of freedom? Would constant talking to the heir about liberty make him wiser and happier? His present duty is obedience, and this will remain his duty till the time appointed for him to be no longer under tutors and governors. We cannot make him free by all the eloquence we can use about the delights of liberty; all we can accomplish will be to make him restless and unhappy, disobedient and miserable. Then too we interfere with his progress. All his time and energies should be cheerfully given to mastering the tasks assigned him, and thus preparing himself for the responsibilities awaiting him, when he shall enter upon his inheritance.

Go into the schoolrooms and families of our land

and proclaim to the children, "You are free; these teachers and parents shall have no more authority over you; henceforth you are to be a law unto yourselves, and shall control your persons and estates." Would that be a kindness to the children? What would a child thus freed do with himself and with his estate? Is he free in the true sense of freedom? Nay, have you not rather placed upon him a burden greater than he can bear? And would a child be happy in possession of such liberty? Has he not a right to good guidance, and do you not wrong him by depriving him of it? If you really desired his welfare you would urge him to strict obedience to his parents and tutors, and would persuade him that they were working for his good. You would teach him to do gladly and with his might all his appointed tasks, although he could see no use in them, and they were dry and tedious; for his tutors and parents were wiser than he and knew those very duties were necessary for his right development. And the higher the rank of the child, the sterner is the necessity for strict obedience to the authority over him. It is related of that wise mother, the Duchess of Kent, that she allowed no one to tell her daughter, Victoria, how near she stood to the throne of England, and not till she was fourteen years old did she know that a higher destiny awaited her than awaited her cousins who were her fellow-pupils. Then it was deemed best to let her know, and the genealogical table of the House of Hanover was left in her text-book on history. She examined it carefully and found that she would succeed to the throne on the death of her uncle. Turning to her governess, who sat by watching eagerly what would be the effect of the disclosure, she said, "Now I know why you were so much stricter with me in Latin grammar than you were with my cousins. I never understood it before." A wise mother chose that governess, and she had trained the child wisely, showing the greatest strictness in training her upon whom the greatest responsibilites would rest. It might answer for the others to grow up with poorly trained minds, but not so with the future queen. And it speaks volumes for the character of Victoria that her first thought was not of the grandeur that awaited her, but of the wisdom of her governess.

Although we are heirs of God, yet are we children, and need to be reminded of the duty and dignity and glory of obedience, rather than of the sweets of liberty. Our highest honor is in a strict following of the appointed path, instead of insisting on making a path for ourselves; and the higher our destiny the more important that we be kept closely to the duties assigned us. Christians are heirs to higher thrones and grander kingdoms than was the young Victoria, and therefore they need to be more careful and thorough in their obedience. The chief care should be to be made exactly after the pattern shown them in the mount. They need to be urged to cheerfully bear the cross after their Lord, rather than to do as they please. There is little doing as one pleases in cross-bearing and crucifying the flesh. The more a man deserves freedom the more does he feel his need of guidance and the more cheerfully does he follow one wiser than he. It is always the man of least capacity and knowledge who is surest of his own infallibility. Humility and willingness to follow good guidance, are unfailing marks of wisdom.

But the time comes when the heir is of age and must pass from under the control of tutors and governors and enter upon the joys and perils of freedom. He is supposed, however, during his pupilage, to have learned to be a law unto himself. He must no longer cling to the guiding hands that have directed his youth; that would be to make his tutors lords of his inheritance, and would prove him unworthy of the destiny before him. Then is the time to speak to him of the responsibilities of freedom, and not when he is under age and needing to be trained in obedience. When Israel is at peace in Canaan, with every man under his own vine and fig tree, it will do to talk to them of freedom, but out yonder in the wilderness they need to obey Moses unhesitatingly and unquestioningly, and as they drive their foes before them they must submit heartily to the leadership of Joshua.

If, so soon as they crossed the Red Sea, every man had resolved to be "free" and to traverse the wilderness as he saw best, how many would have reached the Jordan alive? If after crossing the Jordan, they had been "independent" of Joshua, how long till the Canaanites would have destroyed them? Had the children of Israel remained in Canaan and walked in the footsteps of their father, Abraham, they would have needed no Moses and no Joshua. But they had gone down into Egypt and been slaves there, and coming out of the house of bondage, ignorant and untrained, freedom to them would have been destruction. Had our race remained in Eden, they would have been free and would ere long have been confirmed in holiness. But they sold themselves as slaves to sin, and rescued from that bondage, they need to be under tutelage. Though regenerated by the Holy Spirit, our evil propensities are not eradicated, the law of sin is still in our members; we need therefore to follow closely our Master, even though he lead us to the cross.

"Ye shall know the truth, and the truth shall make you free." What grand words are these—truth and freedom. What is freedom? We hear little else in these last days, "free thought," "free speech," "free country," "free press," "free men," "free trade," free! free! free!—the air is full of it, but what is freedom? It is well to stop occasionally and define these vague words that are going up and down the earth. There is nothing more dangerous than such vague words that all men speak, but do not define clearly to their minds. A truth to be effective must be incisive; you cannot pierce to the dividing asunder of joints and marrow with a column of mud or a sword of down. An error exactly defined can be met, while one that is vague eludes you. You cannot wrestle with a bank of fog. What is freedom? I would like to put that question to every one of you and see how many different answers I would receive.

One man thinks that freedom consists in choosing the rulers he wishes to be over him, instead of obeying an hereditary monarch. Go then and vote, but you do not get the rulers you wish unless a majority of your fellow-citizens choose as you do, so that in order for you to be free, a majority must think as you think. Unless you can compel them to think so, where is your freedom, and if you can, then what becomes of theirs? If the majority put in rulers you do not wish, are you practically any freer than if the rulers were born over you? To be free to choose your own rulers you must be careful to always side with the majority; though that is a freedom from principle not yet extolled in the pæans to liberty, though I cannot tell how long till it will be so. Then suppose you get the rulers you wish and they abuse their authority? Suppose they fail to protect your property and life from thieves and murderers, so that you have no feeling of security night or day, are you free while living thus, even though you had the high privilege of helping to elect such rulers? Think it out, and tell me whether political freedom does not consist in having good rulers, however they may come to be rulers, who shall so restrain evil-doers as to give well-doers security, who shall impose no tax upon you not absolutely necessary, and interfere as little as possible with all legitimate business? There can be no freedom for honest men without restraint for thieves.

Another man, and he voices the prevalent sentiment, defines freedom to be the right of every man to do as he pleases. But suppose he pleases to do wrong and injure others? Suppose he pleases to burn your house, and you please that he shall not do it, how can both be free? If the law restrain him from injuring others as he desires, is he free? But the man answers indignantly: "There is a wide difference between freedom and license." Exactly so; but what is that difference? Liberty to do as I please, whether good or bad, is not freedom but license, then. Very well, if I desire to do wrong and am restrained, I cannot be said to be free, in the popular sense, no matter what shape that restraint may take, whether bonds which prevent my using my hands, or fear of the punishment that will follow. So, tracing the matter up step by step we see that true freedom comes only with an absence of all desire to do wrong and a willingness to do right.

True freedom is opportunity to make the most and the best of all the capacities in us, and only when desire to do wrong is gone can we have such opportunity. This is what Paul meant by being "made free from the law." You are free from the law against murder, for you have not the slightest desire to commit that crime; so to you the law is dead. But if you should have such desire, then the dead law revives; and the penalty would restrain you—if only our laws were executed—alas! and your freedom would be gone. So long as your will is in conformity to the law, you are free, but let your will arise in opposition to the law, and you are in bondage. The law of God binds closer than the laws of the land, and Christians should be free from this law so that they need not be warned of the penalty of violation, but simply told of any given act, it is wrong. We are free from many of the laws of God in this sense. For example, the law against the worship of Moloch, though alive in the days of Solomon and Josiah, is utterly dead to us now, for we have no desire to worship that idol nor to pass our children through the fire. We would not do so even if that command were not in the Bible. Now the more of the laws of God and man we can thus make dead to us, the freer we are, and this is true freedom. Christ frees us from the law as his grace takes from us all disposition to violate the law; and the more we grow in grace, the more we grow in freedom. Christians are free in many things, and the angels are freer still.

What else can freedom mean than this, unless you make it mean lawlessness? If I must be allowed to do as I please in order to be free, every other man must have the same privilege or he is not free. Our freedoms clash, and we cannot both do as we wish. He pleases to take my purse and I please to keep him from taking it; we cannot both have our pleasure. And if freedom is lawlessness, we cannot both be free. Is it not the idea of many people, alas, that freedom means that I can do as I please but others cannot—there must be liberty for me, but restraint for them? Are we not drifting toward what was said to be the Frenchman's idea of liberty, "the right of every man to control every other man"? If all please to keep the law, then can all have their pleasure and all be free. There can be perfect freedom only where there is perfect obedience to rightful authority. The more sin the less freedom.

What then is freedom? It is the perfect harmony of our desires and actions with the law of God. If fond of modern lights, I might say freedom is being "in perfect harmony with our environment," but that is the solar system with the sun left out. We are slaves to whatever prevents our being free, and in preventing our hearts from being in accord with

God's law, we are the slaves of sin, no matter where that law is found. In the law governing our physical natures the definition holds good. No man is physically free who is suffering pain and weakness. But these follow in proportion to the disobedience to God's laws governing our physical natures; hence perfect freedom consists of perfect accord with those laws. A man is free from nerves when he is in such perfect accord with the laws of health that no pain reminds him that he has any nerves.

I have dwelt on this point till I fear you are wearied; but I do wish that we all had this definition of freedom firmly fixed in our minds. Satan has done untold harm in the world by giving men wrong ideas of freedom. There is nothing nobler than true freedom, no grander thing can man achieve than to bring himself into harmony with the laws of God; and nothing is more harmful than that lawlessness which seeks to get rid of obligation. No wonder all noble men yearn for freedom, and sad is it for them when Satan can blind their eyes to their bondage and make them think that liberty is license, and freedom lawlessness.

Mankind is a race of slaves to sin. "His slaves ye are," Paul declares, "whom ye obey, whether of sin unto death or of obedience unto righteousness." When our consciences are roused and we feel the chains of our bondage, Satan cunningly sets us seeking a spurious freedom, so that we may even boast, as did the Pharisees to Jesus, "we were never in bondage to any man," and the yoke of slavery was upon them while they spake. "Whosoever committeth sin is the bondservant of sin." Base bondage to a base master; while our heritage is the glorious freedom of the sons of God. How shall we win this freedom? Jesus answers, "The truth shall make you free." Then comes the great question from the lips of the ages, "What is truth?"

Grander words were never put together than "ye shall know the truth, and the truth shall make you free." Truth is a knowledge of God, and of the relations in which he has placed us to himself, to our fellows, and to creation. The highest and most important truth is the knowledge of God and of our relations to him. Nothing else deserves to be called "the truth." But I prefer the term *law*, to *relations*. Freedom being perfect accord with the law, we cannot be free unless we know the law. Even ignorant violation of law is followed by penalty. I may not know that fire will burn, but that ignorance will not free me from the penalty of pain if I put my hand in the blaze. But a knowledge of that law makes me practically free from it, for then I have no desire to put my hand in the flames. We cannot be free without the truth, and alas, that our hearts should be indifferent and even hostile to the truth, like the Pharisees who disputed with Christ, rejecting scornfully the truth which alone could make them free, and hugging the chains of their bondage.

How shall we gain the knowledge of God and of our relations to him? The sun says, "It is not in me;" the earth answers, "It is not in me;" and the soul declares, "It is not in me." Where can we find the truth we seek? In chemical action? in spectrum analysis? gravitation? insects and trilobites? Think it out for yourselves; think of all the sources whence man has sought truth in all the ages, and you will find but one answer to that great question of questions—what is truth? A voice comes to us from the Judean hills, "I am the truth," and lo, the great problem is solved. "God manifest in the flesh"—manifest—made evident that man may know him. Broken and fragmentary revelations of him are seen in the songs of the psalmist and the visions of prophets; still more broken and fragmentary in the world around us; but in Christ,

God is manifested, so that Jesus can say, "If ye had known me, ye should have known my Father also." "I am the way, the truth, and the life: no man cometh unto the Father but by me." Lofty words these, coming from the carpenter of Nazareth, but none too high, as thousands, who have found him all these, can testify. "The truth shall make you free," and because he is the truth, he goes on to say, "If the Son therefore shall make you free, you shall be free indeed."

"I am the truth." In Christ is God known in all his great attributes that concern us. How divine love and truth, holiness and long-suffering shine forth in every word and act of Jesus! Divine power and justice and sovereignty stand hand in hand with love and mercy round the cross of Calvary. God is manifest in the flesh to human eyes—no longer a God that hideth himself, but seen as clearly as he can be revealed to the eyes of fallen men. In Jesus stand revealed the relations binding God and man. Christ has broken down the dungeon walls that Satan had built around us and has let in the light of heaven. And he has done more. He comes, and laying his hands on our chains, says, "I will free you and open your eyes. No other can deliver you. If ye believe not that I am he, ye shall die in your sins." Shall we hug our chains when freedom is offered us? Shall we love darkness when that voice calls us to the light?

Freedom is perfect harmony between our souls and God's law. Jesus is the truth that shows us God and gives us hearts to love him; teaches us our relations to him and enables us to live in harmony with those relations. "If the Son therefore shall make you free, ye shall be free indeed." The choice is before you: the bondage of Satan or the liberty of the sons of God; slaves of sin or freemen in Christ Jesus; which will you choose? No other choice is open to you. You cannot say, "I will be free, but not in Christ." We cannot free ourselves, else the Son would never have come to free us. Adam was free as the angels till he sinned, but we can be made free only by the truth as it is in Jesus.

"If therefore the Son shall make you free, ye shall be free indeed." He frees us when we repent and believe in him. Then we stand before God justified, because we are washed in his blood and clothed in his righteousness. But we have not yet the whole of freedom, because although no longer the slaves of sin, we are not wholly free from sin. We are like babes in our weakness and ignorance, needing the care of tutors for our growth and training. We need the law to guide us in the pathway to perfect freedom. "If ye continue in my words, ye shall know the truth, and the truth shall make you free." "Continue in my words," this is the message to us, brethren. We are to meditate upon Christ's words, transmute them into action and make them part of our very being. So shall we grow into a manhood that needs no law, because the will of God shall have become part of our very existence.

"The truth shall make you free." From how many things does the truth free us! From all fear of harm—what can we fear when the everlasting arms are under us, and our Father's hand is leading us? From wearing care—he careth for us, even for the number of hairs on our heads. From the pollution of sin, so hard to bear despite our bravado, and from the remorse whose sting teaches us what we know of the undying worm. Pain and sorrow and sin, perfect freedom knows nothing of these, and the truth leads us into that freedom, which means all wisdom, all joy, all peace, and all holiness. We realize this more and more as we follow the truth. The way to love God with all our hearts is to act out what little love we have for him, by striving to please him in everything, and we will find our love growing deeper and truer every day. Our freedom will increase with our love, till we enter upon the perfect liberty of that inheritance we shall have with our Elder Brother, the noblest inheritance God himself could prepare, containing all that omniscience could devise and omnipotence provide of joy and glory. And over against that inheritance, for our choosing—what? "The wages of sin"—which "is death."

WILLIAM WARREN LANDRUM, eldest son of Rev. Dr. Sylvanus Landrum, was born at Macon, Ga., January 18, 1853; converted and baptized when thirteen years of age, and called to preach at eighteen years of age, and licensed by the First Church of Savannah, Ga.; educated at Mercer University, Macon, Ga., and Brown University, Providence, R. I., where he graduated as bachelor of arts in 1872, and at the Southern Baptist Theological Seminary. Ordained at Jefferson, Tex., May, 1874, and pastor at Shreveport, La., for nearly two years; at First Church, Augusta, Ga., for nearly six years; and has been pastor of the Second Church, Richmond, Va., for nearly thirteen years; was given the degree of D. D. by Washington and Lee University in 1885. His high character, affable manner, and pulpit gifts, have made him universally popular, both with the laity and clergy.

W. W. Landrum, D. D.

VI

ALL[1]

BY W. W. LANDRUM, D. D.

" All power is given unto me in heaven and in earth. Go ye therefore, and teach all nations, baptizing them in the name of the Father, and of the Son, and of the Holy Ghost: teaching them to observe all things whatsoever I have commanded you: and, lo, I am with you alway, even unto the end of the world." Matt. 28: 18, 19, 20.

PECULIAR interest belongs to what we know to be the last. On a mountain in Galilee our Lord gave his last command. Already he had discharged the duties of his redemptive mission. As prophet he had preached the scheme of God's universal love to sinners; as priest he had offered himself as a propitiation for the sins of the world by the sacrifice on the cross; as king he had triumphed over sin, death, and the grave. And now, surrounded by those who had caught his spirit and been saved by his power, Jesus Christ, before ascending to the right hand of God's throne, delivered to them his last great commission. That great commission is a compendium of the disciples' doctrine and duty. If we consider the apostles as soldiers, it was their "marching orders"; if we regard them as statesmen, starting to found a new and spiritual republic, it was their constitution; if they were philanthropists, it was their economy of universal beneficence; if physicians, the sovereign remedy for sick souls; if teachers, their text-book; if preachers, the subject-matter of all

---

[1] Preached in the First Baptist Church, Washington, D. C., during the Jubilee Session of the Southern Baptist Convention.

their discourses, directed to disclose God's character, the Saviour's love, and the soul's supreme good.

Accept this great commission as the Magna Charta of Christianity and you accept Christianity in its wholeness. Reject it, or any part of it, and you reject Christianity's fundamental principle. Modify it in any respect and you cannot claim to be a faithful disciple of him who issued the commission with unspeakable solemnity at the moment when he took his leave of the world.

Analyze the text and you will see four great "alls" loom up like mountain peaks. They furnish us with suitable observatories from which we may look out upon the world over which we are to go and to which the "glorious gospel of the blessed God" must be preached. Let us ascend these heights one by one.

1. "All power (authority)" is the first mountain. "All authority," says Christ, "is given unto me in heaven and in earth." This authority is the basis of the subsequent command. Without such authority the command would be presumptuous.

It is the highest human authority—that of Jesus Christ, "all authority on earth." No one questions that in the time of Tiberius there was a man called Jesus who was put to death by the Roman procurator, Pontius Pilate, and whose doctrines spread rapidly throughout the Roman world. The Gospels are not our only source of information; if they had never been written we should know that much from Tacitus, Suetonius, Juvenal, Adrian, Pliny, and others. Christ's historical reality is not only conceded by all, but his moral perfection by all without, as well as within, the circle of his followers. Christ's supremacy as a teacher of spiritual truth is gladly acknowledged by foe and by friend. Many who profess to be in doubt as to whether he is divine or human are willing to follow him as an ethical leader. Their cry is:

> If Jesus Christ is a man,
>   And only a man, I say
> That of all mankind I will cleave to him,
>   And to him will cleave alway.
>
> If Jesus Christ is a God,
>   And the only God, I swear
> I will follow him through heaven and hell,
>   The earth, the sea, and the air.

Beyond question the character of Jesus presented by the evangelists is a verity, a sublime reality. Amid the world's sin a perfect life has been lived; unto the world's doubt an authoritative voice has spoken; upon the world's darkness a heavenly light has shone. For these reasons Jesus Christ is the highest authority on earth.

He is also the highest authority in heaven. Repeatedly he made claims, be it said in all reverence, which, if he was not divine, seem to be nothing short of blasphemy. Christ, as we know, declared himself to be King of a heavenly kingdom; he exercised the divine right to forgive sins; he claimed a right to the supreme love of the race, demanding an affection stronger than the love of father or mother, wife or child; he asserted in the text that he possessed superhuman power, indeed that he sways the sceptre of universal empire; he predicted that, though he should die and be buried, he would rise again and ascend to heaven, but would return at the end of the age and finally judge all nations. Surely only a superhuman character could sustain such claims! And yet precisely such claims Christ vindicated. By a life of spotless purity and transcendent power he so completely vindicated such claims that the most enlightened peoples have for nineteen centuries pronounced him "God manifest in the flesh." Step by step the honest inquirer may ascend the mountain of authority, until, from its summit gazing up into heaven, he exclaims: "In the beginning was the Word, and the Word was with God, and the Word was God. . . All things were made by him; and without him was not anything made that was made." Like the author of the Hebrews, he will shout out to the Eternal Son: "Thy throne, O God, is forever and ever; a sceptre of righteousness is the sceptre of thy kingdom. . . Thou, Lord, in the beginning hast laid the foundation of the earth; and the heavens are the works of thine hands."

II. Naturally enough we pass from the authority of the Commander to the great command he gave. "All authority" issues an order which is to be delivered to "all nations." "Go ye, therefore, and teach all nations." "The field is the world."

1. Prophecy called Christ "the desire of all nations." The superscription on the cross was written in the three great languages of the world—Greek, Latin, and Hebrew—that all nations might know their regal Redeemer. Christ died in the fullness of time. The kingdom of heaven was inaugurated in the world only when "all nations," after long ages, had been made ready for it. That preparation required three conditions: First, a universal language in which the gospel could be preached and written; second, a universal government which would suffer missionaries to travel with reasonable protection; third, a universal people expecting a further revelation from God. The Greeks gave the universal language; the Romans furnished the universal government; the Jews, scattered by persecution into every land, were the expectant people waiting for the Messiah's coming. All nations were prepared by spiritual, intellectual, and physical conditions for the only religion that is adapted to save and civilize all nations.

2. Apostles were commissioned to go to "all na-

tions." True, they did not do so at once; they learned the lesson of world-wide evangelization slowly. Christian in heart they were Jews in spirit. They were naturally narrow and bigoted; they hated foreigners; in a word they were human, and the best of men are but men at best. The apostles did not leave Jerusalem till persecution thrust them forth; they did not go out among the Gentiles until years afterward the Holy Spirit moved upon the church at Antioch to dispatch Paul and Barnabas to the heathen. They found it difficult to be foreign missionaries. Before we condemn them too harshly let us remember ourselves. How long, alas, did it take to enlarge some of us into the foreign missionary spirit? When one is first converted he longs, in the gladness of his experience of pardon and peace, to lead some one else to the Saviour. Every one of us felt in that way. Naturally the young convert begins work among his friends. He believes in congregational missions, the duty of preaching the gospel to the lost of his congregation. As he grows in grace his heart enlarges. He hears of a city missionary society embracing members from several congregations and he comes to believe in city missions. As his renewed nature expands under the influence of the Holy Spirit he considers his State, with its multitudes of unrepentant and unsaved sinners, and comes to believe in State missions. Later he looks out upon his country, upon America, the nation of destiny, the asylum for the oppressed of all nations and gives in his allegiance to home missions. By an inevitable law he must go farther. He reads: "God hath made of one blood all the nations of the earth"; "Christ is the propitiation, not for our sins only but for the sins of the whole world"; Christ's command is, "Teach all nations." Thus, by a process of holy evolution, the growing believer comes, sometimes all too slowly, to champion the cause of foreign missions. It is not possible for any intelligent disciple to oppose foreign missions who will remember that God loves all nations, that Christ died for all nations, that the gospel is adapted to all nations, that Christ commanded it to be preached to all nations, and that many in all nations have believed the gospel and turned unto the Lord.

3. All nations are open to the preaching of the gospel to-day.

During this century the barriers which separated more than eight hundred million heathen from the rescuing power of the gospel have broken down. Before this century obstacles, almost insurmountable, interposed between the churches and the fulfillment of Christ's command. Obstacles to approach confronted the missionary. China was walled about; Japan's ports were sealed; India was held by an English company hostile to missions; Africa was impenetrable, even to the explorer; the isles of the sea were peopled with cannibals, more to be dreaded than the devouring waves of the angry ocean. Obstacles to intercourse with the heathen blocked the way. Languages, strange and hard to master, hindered all communication. At least sixty languages were without any literature, lexicon, grammar, or even written characters. Travel and transportation were slow and unsatisfactory. Women secluded within harems could not be reached; children and youth shunned the "foreign devil," as the missionary was called. Obstacles to impression were multitudinous and mountainous. Some races, like the Chinese and Japanese, claimed mental superiority to the missionaries and would not listen to them. Other races seemed to be on too low a plane of morality to be lifted up even by the lever of the gospel. In some quarters they were dumb beasts for shamelessness and wild beasts for brutality and ferocity, not only dehumanized, but actually demonized.

Once more, there were obstacles to action. Heathen peoples were prejudiced against all Christians because of the disgraceful practices and iniquities of certain so-called Christian countries. England forced opium on China at the cannon's mouth. Vessels carried missionaries to Africa from Christian lands, and then bore back to those lands stolen slaves. The Sandwich Islanders caught the consuming leprosy of lust from the merchant ships of Christian countries. North American Indians took the infection of drunkenness from contact with our "superior civilization." Missionaries were hated by the heathen as drunkards, licentious, mercenary, polluting, because the majority who came among them from Christian countries, sailors, soldiers, traders, and tourists, were such.

Now, thank God, these obstacles of approach, of intercourse, of impression, and of action, are removed as completely as if they were thrown into the sea. "India is now," in the words of another, "a starry firmament, sparkling with missionary stations." Turkey is planted with churches from the Golden Horn to the Tigris and Euphrates. Japan strides in her "seven league boots" toward Christian civilization. Polynesia's thousand church spires point like fingers to the sky. Africa is stretching forth her hands toward heaven. China, the very Gibraltar of heathenism, is crumbling down slowly but surely.

4. Souls, moreover, have been won to Christ among all nations. Converts abroad, in fact, exceed in number those of ministers in this country. These converts show as high a type of character, as self-sacrificing a spirit, as enlarged liberality, as obtains among brethren here at home. Compare, if you wish, the gifts and graces of the church at Canton, China, or at Ongole, India, with any church in Richmond or Baltimore or Washington. Tested in any way missions abroad are more successful than missions at home, and the nations of the heathen are producing

better and more numerous fruits than this elect nation, which we are pleased to call the pride and glory of the whole earth.

III. "All authority" issues to "all nations," "all commands," "Teaching them to observe all things whatsoever I have commanded you."

The gospel of our Lord Jesus Christ is intensive as well as extensive. The gospel reaches the whole man; it has a message for his body, his mind, his spirit, and it blesses him in all his relations, human and divine. The commands it lays upon men are for their highest well-being on earth and in heaven, for time and for eternity. These commands are moral commands, evangelical commands, positive commands. Moral commands embrace the decalogue; these, when obeyed, are the bases of the civilization which the gospel offers the world. Evangelical commands are those which concern our relations to Christ. They require us to repent of our sins before God and to put our trust in the Lord Jesus Christ for salvation. Positive commands relate to the ordinances of Christ, which exist only because of his appointment. Baptism is a positive command; the observance of the Lord's Supper is a positive command. Christ instructs us to teach all nations all commands.

Baptists dare not do less. Romanism may teach the heathen, more or less perfectly, Christ's moral ordinances; Protestantism may teach the heathen Christ's evangelical commands; Baptists, if true to their principles, must hold themselves responsible for teaching all Christ's commands, positive as well as moral and evangelical. For that reason, our mission as a people is to Protestant lands, to papal lands, to pagan lands. To pagans we must carry the moral, the evangelical, and positive commands; to Romanists we must carry the evangelical and positive commands; to Protestants we must carry the positive ordinances of our Lord Jesus Christ.

And we must teach all these commands to every single convert in the "all nations." If Baptists have one peculiarity more pronounced than any other, it is the stress they lay upon the worth of a single soul. Baptists are individualistic. The church exists for the individual, and not the individual for the church. Presbyterians are rather familistic; the family they are disposed to regard as a religious unit. Methodists are tribalistic; the Conference is the religious unit. Episcopalians are nationalistic; they have a State Church in England, and once had it here. Baptists are individualistic. They go forth to preach to every individual soul the broadest and deepest conceptions of personal responsibility. Starting with the doctrine of soul liberty, the right of private judgment, they commend personal repentance, personal faith, personal baptism, personal communion with the Saviour at the Lord's Supper, personal fidelity to all the moral, evangelical, and positive commands of the Lord Jesus Christ.

IV. It only remains to add the last of the four great "alls" of the great commission—"All days." "Lo, I am with you alway," or, as it is more correctly, "all days," "even unto the end of the world."

Do we really believe this? Where, let me ask, is our Lord Jesus to-day? That is a pertinent and pressing question. Does it not seem that in the minds of many professing disciples he is shut up in the pages of the New Testament, a mere doctrine to be believed? In the view of others he is dying on the cross still, a great historic fact to be treasured; as understood by others, Christ is up in heaven, an advocate, an intercessor; yet others intently look toward the east for his speedy second coming.

But where does Christ declare himself to be? On the earth. How on the earth? In the presence and power of the Holy Spirit. With whom is he on the earth? With all those who go forth to teach all nations the saving truth of his holy word. And why with his missionaries and ministers? That the excellency of the power of the gospel may be of God and not of men. Christ indeed, does not delegate power. "All power is given unto me," he said, "and lo, I am with you all days, even unto the end of the age."

Oh, my brethren, this is our only reliance as we go forth to the pacific conquest of the world, even the presence of the omnipotent, omniscient, omnipresent Spirit of Christ. It is that Spirit which convicts the guilty soul of sin, and it is that Spirit which leads the convicted soul to the Lamb of God which taketh away the sin of the world. An English preacher asked some British soldiers: "If Queen Victoria were to issue a proclamation, and placing it in the hands of her army and navy, were to say, 'Go ye into all the world and proclaim it to every creature,' how long do you think it would take to do it?" One of these brave fellows, accustomed to obey orders without hesitation or delay and at peril of life, replied: "Well, I think we could manage it in about eighteen months." Possibly they could. To deliver a message of salvation to all is not so difficult a matter. Suppose we ask this question: "How long would it take the army and navy of England, how long would it take the thousands of missionaries, all working together, to regenerate one single soul?" Army and navy combined, all the missionaries and the ministers of the world acting in concert, could not accomplish the task throughout all the cycles of eternity. Regenerating power is not in man. It is "not by might, nor by power, but by my Spirit, saith the Lord."

We may need more men, we do need more men to preach the gospel; we need more and better "machinery," churches, schools, hospitals, books, tracts; we need more money that we may equip more men and build more chapels; but the chief need is not men, machinery, or money. Our supreme want is more faith in him who said: "Lo, I am with you all the days, even unto the end of the age." Whenever we have failed, at home or abroad, the secret of every failure to save souls is due to our unbelief in the Holy Ghost. When Garibaldi had been defeated at Rome he issued his immortal appeal: "Soldiers, I have nothing to offer you but cold and hunger, rags and hardships. Let him who loves his country follow me." Instantly thousands of the youth of Italy sprang to arms and moved to victory. Garibaldi inspired his spirit into his men; Garibaldi was ever with his men as the communication of patriotism and courage. A greater than Garibaldi is with us. Oh, if we were all filled with the Spirit of Christ, if we felt his consuming passion for souls, if we were inspired by his high purpose of saving all men, the weakest among us would dare and do until the conquest of the world was won.

All power is in the hands of the Spirit of Christ. Dr. David Gregg illustrates Holy Ghost power in this way. An army is drawn up before a granite fort which it intends to batter down. We ask the general: "How are you going to level these great stones?" He points to a cannon ball and says: "By this." But there is no power in that. If all the men in the army should hurl it against the fort, it would make but slight impression, if any. The general replies: "True; but look at the cannon." Well, but there is no power in that. A child may ride upon that cannon; a bird may perch in its mouth; it is a machine and nothing more "But look," says the general, "at the powder." No power there. A sparrow may peck at it, an infant may spill it. Yet, given this powerless ball and powerless cannon and powerless powder and a spark of fire—what then? The spark of fire touches that powder. In the twinkling of an eye it is a flash of lightning; that ball becomes a thunderbolt which smites the fort as if it had been hurled from heaven, and its granite walls lie in ruins. China is that fort, or India or Africa. There is no power in the Bible as a mere book—it is an instrument simply; no power in the missionary—he is but a frail man. But put back of the book and the man the fire of the Holy Spirit and then God's omnipotence is brought to bear. The missionary's sermon is the cannon ball, the missionary's soul is the cannon, the missionary's zeal is the powder, but the Spirit of Christ is the all essential spark of fire which will cause the truth of the gospel to force its way through the citadel of pagan superstition and sin: "All power is given unto me in heaven and in earth, go ye therefore, and teach all nations, baptizing them in the name of the Father, and of the Son, and of the Holy Ghost: teaching them to observe all things whatsoever I have commanded you: and lo, I am with you alway, even unto the end of the world." Amen.

J. B. HAWTHORNE is a native of Alabama. He was converted at a very early age. After graduation from Howard College, Ala., he practised law in Mobile for a few years, but becoming convinced of a call to preach the gospel, he abandoned the profession in which he was already achieving success and distinction, re-entered Howard College and took a course in theology. Shortly after his ordination to the work of the ministry, he was invited to return to Mobile as pastor of the Second Baptist Church. Here he established a reputation as preacher and pastor which each subsequent pastorate has confirmed and increased. Selma, Ala., Franklin Square Baptist Church, Baltimore, First Baptist Church, Albany, N. Y., Broadway Baptist Church, Louisville, Ky., Tabernacle Baptist Church, New York City, First Baptist Church, Montgomery, Ala., First Baptist Church, Richmond, Va., have enjoyed his ministry. He is now pastor of the First Baptist Church, Atlanta, Ga., where large audiences wait upon his preaching, and his power and popularity are unabating.

J. B. Hawthorne, D. D.

VII

THE PRE-EMINENT NAME[1]

BY J. B. HAWTHORNE, D. D.

"Thou shalt call his name Jesus; for he shall save his people from their sins." Matt. 1 : 21.

VERILY there is something in a name. It may and often does represent a mighty factor in the life of the world. Back of all the world's history there were names that inspired human courage, purpose, and enterprise. The names of great men have become synonyms for the principles and institutions to which they devoted their lives. They have become slogans, watchwords, and battle-cries, to arouse the enthusiasm of men and to nerve them for heroic action in the midst of great crises. When the old Greek orators saw signs of dullness and inattention in their audiences, they could arouse every man before them and raise enthusiasm to the highest pitch by simply pausing for a moment, and then shouting, "Marathon! Marathon!" Since the day you first read the history of that struggle which culminated in the independence of the American Colonies and the establishment of the American Republic, the name of Washington has stood in your mind for patriotism, and the mention of it has stimulated your patriotic sentiment. That name has ever been a favorite countersign with American soldiers, and the use of it has helped many a weary, shivering picket to stand at his post and watch the stars.

---

[1] Preached at the First Baptist Church, Washington, D. C., during the Jubilee Session of the Southern Baptist Convention.

The day I was born my father named me for Boardman, that dauntless hero who preceded Judson in missionary work among the Karens. When I was old enough I read the history of the struggles, sufferings, and achievements of that brave young man. His name, which I so unworthily bear, has been to my soul an abiding and unfailing inspiration. Luther, Calvin, Knox, Bunyan, and Carey were long ago gathered to their fathers; but the power of their names is still invoked wherever Christian workmen need a higher courage, a steadier purpose, and a more fervent zeal.

But there is a name above every name—a name which is reconstructing our disordered planet, re-creating our fallen and ruined humanity, and which stands everywhere for the sweetest charities of earth, the synonym of the purest life, and the symbol of the highest civilization; a name which carries healing to the wounded, rest to the weary, pardon to the guilty, and salvation to the lost; a name which makes the dark gateway of the tomb the portal to a temple resplendent with the glory of celestial light, where the music of golden harps by angels' fingers touched is ineffable and eternal.

In the shock which followed the entrance of sin into the world man fell away from God, and heaven and earth went asunder. The sinful soul is diseased, polluted, fettered, imprisoned and hid away from God. Its deepest problem is how to be cured, cleansed, freed, and restored to the divine presence and favor. The solution of this problem is in the matchless and adorable name which we are to consider this morning: Jesus—Saviour.

"There is none other name under heaven given among men whereby we must be saved." Jesus himself stood up among men and boldly declared that he was the one and only way by which lost men could get back to God.

But in what sense is he the Saviour of men? A mistake here is radical and fatal. Is he simply the ideal man, showing by his own manner of living how other men ought to live? If he is no more than that, he is not the Saviour that we need. He is indeed the ideal man. His life was perfect. It was absolutely without spot or blemish. And he does require us to follow him in the sense of reproducing his virtues. But if he is only the ideal man, and does no more for us than show us how to live, he does not compass our necessities. Setting before us an example of right living, and inviting, entreating, and commanding us to follow it, will not save us from our sins and restore us to the favor of God.

Nor is he the Saviour of men in the sense that he shows them the way of salvation. If he is only a a law-giver, or a teacher of divine truth, or a fingerboard to direct us in the way of righteousness, he is insufficient for our needs. The man who shows me the way to New York is not himself the way. The person who merely teaches me the truth is not himself the truth. And if Jesus is only a teacher of the way of salvation he is not himself salvation. It is true that man is sadly and fearfully ignorant both of himself and of the infinite God to whom he must give account for the deeds done in the body; and it is also true that by coming to Christ he can be relieved of this ignorance. But if Jesus is only a pedagogue or schoolmaster, he does not touch the deepest necessities of man's condition. Such a view of him may improve a man's morals, and elevate him somewhat in other respects, but it can never save him from the power and consequences of sin. Jesus is himself the salvation which he taught, and which he commissioned his disciples to preach. He is the wisdom, the grace, the mercy, and the power that save men from their sins. The saved man is not he who attempts merely to copy the virtues of Jesus nor he who merely accepts his doctrines, but the man who trusts him, as the little child trusts its mother when it lies helpless and peaceful in her arms.

No man can have a true conception and appreciation of the mission of Jesus until he comprehends man's condition and necessities as a sinner. Why does that hired infidel go through the land outraging not only Christian feeling but common decency, by making sport of the question, "What must I do to be saved?" It is because the Satanic power to which he has sold his birthright has blinded him to the nature of sin and the condition of the sinner. If his worse than Judas Iscariot baseness and cowardice and his demoniacal blasphemy have not already placed him in the category of those who have committed what John calls "the sin unto death," and he could have just one glimpse into the fathomless abyss of his own iniquity, his cry of distress would surpass any wail of anguish that has ever vibrated the air of this globe, and his entreaties for divine mercy and salvation would exceed any prayer that convicted publican or harlot ever made.

Sin is no idle fancy or innocent hallucination with which circus clowns, street venders of patent medicines, low comedians, and such peripatetic infidel buffoons as I have just referred to, may with impunity amuse themselves and the frivolous people who listen to them. Sin is the most terrible fact in the universe of God. It is the intolerable burden of a soul that is destined to live forever. It is a black darkness which invests man's whole moral being, and conceals from his vision everything that belongs to the highest and grandest realms of realities. It is a disease that is converting him into a lump of rottenness and a feast for "the worm that dieth not." It is a fiend that has bound him hand and foot, and that is dragging him down and down to a region of infernal flames. From such a power man can be delivered only by the personal intervention and act of a personal God of infinite mercy and might.

The sense of sin is not something into which we, who live in a Christian country, have been educated. It is a universal experience, and inheres in the very nature of man. Wordsworth voiced the truth when he said, "The recognition of the fact of universal wrong-doing is perfectly independent of Christian teaching." Every man who has even a general acquaintance with the world's history, knows that every ancient religion and philosophy grappled with the problem of sin. All the records that we have of the races and tribes which have dwelt upon the earth show that men have ever been conscious of sin, and that sin is a stern fact of human nature which no people have ever been able to ignore or reason away. Men have never ceased to think and talk and write about it, because in every generation and in every region of the earth it has shadowed their pathway and burdened their hearts.

Ingersoll would have you believe that all of this talk about sin and its consequences originated with Christianity. How absurd! Buddhism antedates Christianity by nearly six centuries, and Buddhism is as full of the doctrine of sin as is the religion of Christ. Homer, the father of poetry, sang of sin and the wretchedness it had made. Sophocles, as he thought of the misery born of human depravity, declared that the best thing for man was death. Whether you read Greek poetry, Greek history, or Greek philosophy, you find not only lamentations over the woes of man, but a distinct recognition of the fact that all man's woes are traceable to human sin.

Sin figures in all the great poems and dramas that men have written. A semi-infidel critic has had the candor to confess that "a guileless hero would be no hero for a drama." Eliminate the part which sin plays in Homer's immortal "Iliad," and how much of it would be left? Take the thieves, hypocrites, liars, adulterers, conspirators, and murderers out of Shakespeare's tragedies, and who would go to a theatre to see one of them performed? Who was Macbeth? A murderer. And what was the inspiration of his challenge to the horrible shadow and unreal mockery that haunted him in his hours of seclusion? It was a conscience stained with blood and aching with remorse.

There is in every man's bosom a tribunal which pronounces judgment on his conduct and by which he is made to know that sin is a terrible reality. Or as Tennyson has expressed it:

> He ever bears about
> A silent court of justice in his breast,
> Himself the judge and jury,
> And himself the prisoner at the bar.

The Bible says, that "Fools make a mock of sin." Mr. Ingersoll calls a conviction of sin, "a nightmare —the result of too much appetite and too little digestion." It is not possible to conceive of a more unmitigated absurdity. Surely it was something more real than nightmare which David felt when he thought of his double crime of adultery and murder, and cried, "Against thee, thee only, have I sinned, and done this evil in thy sight." Surely it was something more serious than nightmare which made Judas throw down the price of his infamy in the temple and exclaim, "I have sinned in that I have betrayed the innocent blood." Surely it was more than a nightmare that inspired the prayer of the dying thief, "Lord, remember me when thou comest into thy kingdom." Surely it was something more serious than melancholy, born of indigestion, that afflicted a more honest infidel than Ingersoll, when he cried, "My principles have poisoned my friends, my extravagance has beggared my child, and my unkindness has murdered my wife! O God! is there yet another hell? But hell itself will be a refuge if it only hide me from thy face."

Among the many abominably false "isms" to which even some people who call themselves Christians have committed themselves, is one which declares that, "Evil is a blessing to mankind; a means selected from the infinite resources for our development; a ladder whereby we climb to moral heights yet unattained." Whether you call this pantheism, or Hegelianism, or Universalism, or monism, or Christian science, it is a plain and unmistakable denial of the word of God. That word forbids us in the most positive and intelligible terms to call evil good. It represents Satan as a distinct personality, as the father of lies, as the source of evil, and as the enemy of God and man. It teaches us not that sin elevates, but that it degrades; not that it leads to happiness, but to misery.

The doctrine of the Bible on this subject is supported by the everyday observations and experiences of men and by the common sense of the world. No philosophy in the universe can convince the average man that a participation in the vices, debaucheries, and deviltries of bar-rooms and gambling dens, is included in the divine plan by which men are to be disciplined into virtue and developed into the likeness of God. To the end of time the common sense of the world will support the Bible in saying that, "He that walketh with wise men shall be wise, but a companion of fools shall be destroyed," and that "evil communications corrupt good manners."

The application of this false philosophy would be the repeal of all laws forbidding vice and crime, the abolition of all agencies for the prevention of evil, and the glorification of all that is earthy, sensual, and devilish. I know of no reason why men and women who advocate such a system should not be sent to the lunatic asylum, except that they are too absurd to be seriously harmful.

Man is a complete and distinct entity. He is not a part of the Divine Being. What he does is not God's act, but his own. He is a distinct moral entity. He knows good from evil. He has the power to love the one and hate the other, and to choose the one and reject the other. In the exercise of this power he makes his glory or his shame, his happiness or his wretchedness, his meetness for heaven or his fitness for hell. Sin then is the will of the individual man asserting itself against the will of God. It is the deliberate and willful rebellion of the creature against the Creator. In its final analysis it is selfishness pure and simple. It is a man's defiant assertion of his purpose to be lord and monarch of himself. It is his absolute repudiation of any higher law than his own will. It is self-damnation—a man's own choice of "everlasting destruction from the presence of God, and from the glory of his power."

Here then the world is confronted with the most fearful of all realities—sin—God's enemy and man's destroyer. That reality makes the gravest problem with which human thought has ever grappled. Here is a disease that has laid its destroying hand upon every fibre of man's moral being. How can it be cured? Here are immortal spirits bound with infernal fetters. How can these shackles be removed? Here is loathsomeness worse than the rottenness of the grave. How can it be cleansed? Here are beings in communion with fiends. How can they be transformed and lifted into fellowship with the angels? Here is the great temple of humanity in ruins. Who can rebuild it, and make the glory of the latter house greater than the former? Here are two worlds—earth and heaven—separated by a great gulf of darkness and horror. Who will span it with an available highway, so that angels may come to us and that we may go to them?

All these questions are but different forms of the great question which the apostles answered on the day of Pentecost: "What must I do to be saved?" When Mr. Ingersoll gets upon the platform and sports with that problem he mocks the wail of a perishing world, dehumanizes himself, and speaks a language akin to the dialect of devils.

How can we get rid of sin? That is man's supreme question. The history of the world shows that there has never been a time when men did not believe that some remedy for sin had been provided. Abel expressed this belief when he kindled the first altar fire and made an offering to the Lord. Noah expressed it in the sacrifice which he made on leaving the ark. Abraham believed it and taught it to his children. Moses expressed it in the institution of the symbols and ceremonies of the tabernacle; and the prophets of Israel proclaimed it with almost seraphic zeal. The whole pagan world has ever cherished the belief that there has been provided some remedy for sin. It has always had its altars and sacrifices; and not knowing the true and living God, it has made its appeal to gods of its own creation. It has stretched out its hands into the darkness and laid hold on a thousand delusions.

Let us thank God there is a cure for sin. "There is a balm in Gilead, and a Physician there." There is an eye to pity and an arm to save. The angel of the Lord announced that remedy when he said to Joseph, concerning the child to which Mary should give birth, "And thou shalt call his name Jesus: for he shall save his people from their sins." A great multitude of the heavenly host proclaimed it when they hovered over the birth place of that Divine child and sang, "Glory to God in the highest, and on earth peace, good will toward men." John the Baptist saw it when on the banks of the Jordan he pointed the multitude to the form of a Galilean stranger, and said: "Behold the Lamb of God which taketh away the sin of the world." The people saw it who followed that man of Galilee from place to place and witnessed his mighty works. The poor distressed harlot saw it when Jesus said to her, "Thy sins are forgiven." The dying thief saw it and felt it when he heard those gracious words, "To-day shalt thou be with me in paradise." Three thousand people at Jerusalem saw it and felt it when they gladly received the message of salvation from the lips of the apostles. It was seen by Lydia when she attended unto the things spoken by Paul. It thrilled the soul of the Philippian jailer when he "rejoiced in God with all his house." It was known in Macedonia, Greece, and Rome, and wherever the apostles and their co-laborers told the story of the life, death, and resurrection of Jesus. It is known and felt to-day by the millions of happy men and women who bear aloft the banner of the Cross and sing the coronation hymn. The sun in his course shines upon no land where there is not a sacramental host rending the air, and making the welkin ring with the rapturous shout, "Messiah is come, and his people are free."

"He shall save his people." The point to which I would give special emphasis in closing is, that the Saviour of men is not a doctrine, not an ordinance, not a church, but a person—a divine-human person. The Word that was in the beginning with God and was God, was made flesh and dwelt among us in the person of the man Christ Jesus. Salvation is in him, and not in anything he ever said, nor in anything that he commanded others to say. The doctrines of the Bible are only finger-boards that point us to Christ. You may accept every one of them, and contend for them with a martyr's zeal, and then die in your sins.

A man may know the saving power of Christ without being able to define any of the great fundamental doctrines of the gospel. Doubtless the woman who bathed the Master's feet with her tears and wiped them with the hairs of her head, knew scarcely anything of his doctrine. But she knew him. She believed on him, and in believing felt his saving power. That demoniac of Gadara, when he went down to his home to tell the story of his rescue, knew nothing about the system of truth which Jesus taught, but he knew him; he knew that he was a Divine Redeemer, and that much he could declare to others with the utmost clearness and zeal.

The woman of Samaria to whom he gave to drink of the water of life, ran into the city and told the story. What was the story? Something about the doctrine that he taught? No, for of that she was utterly ignorant. It was something about him, and about the redemption which he had bestowed upon her. Many a child has known Jesus and his salvation before it had read one-third of the New Testament.

Oh, my brethren, I do know that there is a vital difference between believing on the Divine Christ and believing in a creed. I do know that the former brings salvation to the soul and the latter does not. I do know also that the faith of many in this day reaches no higher than a creed and never touches the person of the Living Redeemer.

The power of redemption is not lodged in theories of the atonement, nor in definitions of regeneration, nor in Confessions of Faith, nor even in the Bible as such. This may seem to you extravagance of speech, but I cannot believe that it is. There is a condition of things about us to-day which warrants me in saying all this and even more. There are no words of reprobation too strong and severe for that conception of Christianity so common in our time which reduces it to a mere pedagogic arrangement, and puts it on a level with every human system of philosophy and ethics.

If every church creed, and even every copy of the Bible, were burned to ashes, Christ and his salvation would remain the same. He would still sit on his mediatorial throne, and save his people from their sins. The doctrines of the Bible are divine, and yet as I have already said, they are only finger-boards to point us to Christ. You can believe them and be lost; but if you lay the hand of faith on that living divine personality whose name is Jesus, you shall be instantly and eternally saved from your sins; your transgressions of divine law shall be forgiven; your whole moral being shall be unfettered, cleansed, and reconstructed; every barrier which separates you from God shall be removed; the Lord will make you his tabernacle, and will be the comfort and joy of your life; in the power of his might you shall have the mastery of every spiritual foe; and on the stepping-stones of conquered difficulties you shall rise day by day into a diviner life and a more glorious freedom. Coming to the margin of death's cold and sullen stream, its dark waters shall divide and make you a passage to the shining shore. As you approach "the city that hath foundations whose builder and maker is God," the gates of pearl shall be lifted high, and as you step upon the golden pavement within those jasper walls, the same benignant Jesus who saved you from your sins will greet you with every token of welcome, robe you with resplendent beauty, crown you with imperishable honor, and conduct you to a seat at his own right hand, high above all principalities and powers, where you will sit and reign as long as immortality endures.

When we think of the sublime significance of this name which is above every name, and of the unspeakable grace and ineffable beauty of the adorable being who bears it, we are lifted into sympathy with him who wrote:

> Oh, could I speak the matchless worth,
> Oh, could I sound the glories forth
>   Which in my Saviour shine,
> I'd soar and touch the heavenly strings,
> And vie with Gabriel while he sings,
>   In notes almost divine.

If present contemplations of that best and most glorious of all beings are so fruitful of bliss, who can conceive of the blessedness of an abiding place in his immediate and visible presence?

> The delightful day will come
> When our dear Lord will call us home,
> And we shall see his face.

VIII

SELF-HEROISM [1]

BY H. ALLEN TUPPER, JR., D. D.

"Be strong, and quit yourselves like men." 1 Sam. 4 : 9.

IT is what is in a thing that determines its value. The rough rock of the mountain, the wild wave of the sea, the vaporous veil of the sky shut from the eye, mines, oceans, worlds of wealth. The invisible is more potent and more permanent than the visible; the intangible is richer and more real than the tangible. Fame is more fashionable than foundation, in an age when life finds its sufficiency on the surface of things. To the question: "What is he worth?" the answer is invariably given from a materialistic point of view. The value of a man is estimated by the dollars or dirt that he owns or that own him. He may be poverty-stricken in the lack of those possessions that honor true manhood; but if he has built and owns a golden calf, the people are ready to fall down and worship. Money is monarch over the multitude of men, for they have been educated, by the spirit of the times, to think that under its royal rule they enter the Golden Age of life. Does it not change a cot into a castle? Does it not put a crest on the carriage? Does it not cover, with a golden cloth, the humble origin of grandpa, or even grandpa's grandson? Does it not bring us into the courts of kings? Does it not change the hazy horizon of life

---

[1] Preached in the Seventh Baptist Church, Baltimore, Md., before the "Commercial Tourist Association."

H. A. Tupper, Jr., D. D.

H. ALLEN TUPPER, JR., is the son of Rev. H. A. Tupper, D. D., late Secretary of the Foreign Mission Board of the Southern Baptist Convention. His mother was sister to Rev. J. P. Boyce, D. D., LL.D., for years president of the Southern Baptist Theological Seminary and the Southern Baptist Convention. Dr. Tupper, Jr., was born in Washington, Ga., June 22, 1856. At the age of thirteen he entered Charleston College, S. C., and after a course in this institution he became an alumnus of Richmond College and the University of Virginia. In May, 1879, he took the full diploma from the Southern Baptist Theological Seminary. He has been successively pastor of the Harrodsburg, Ky., Baptist Church, Broadway Baptist Church, Louisville, Ky., and of the Seventh Baptist Church, Baltimore, Md. These have all been important pastorates, and in each of them his labors have been signally blessed. At this writing Dr. Tupper is preparing for a tour around the world. Dr. Tupper received his degree of D. D. from Georgetown College, Ky. He married Miss Marie L. Pender, a niece of Mrs. Dr. J. B. Jeter.

into a ring of rubies? But the outward is delusive rather than conclusive. The world of sense and sound holds not within its lap the best or brightest prizes of life. Within himself each one has a world to discover, to explore, and to conquer; and in this hidden realm, as the metal lies beneath the mass of the mountain, wealth below the waves, the stars behind the shifting sheen of the sky, may be found the true treasury of man's life. Root, and not fruit, is the source and secret of life; the one is inner life, the other outer life; the one may be the fountain of life, while the other may be in the embrace of death. Strength and stability are secured by seeking below the surface. He who is not, while he moves through the years, engaged in character-building, by diving beneath the driftwood of to-day's current, and grasping the granite of immutable principles, is one whose fall is inevitable. He may be supported by stocks and bloated by bonds; his position may lend him crutches, and his frail frame may be lifted by tender, loving hands upon a pinnacle of power; but, by so doing, these only hasten a downfall as certain as the law of gravitation. Greatness, as well as growth, moves from within, without; never from without, within. It is from the core to the bark, and not from the bark to the core, that yonder tree finds its expansion and power. A man's real self is within, not without; and any permanent progress must move from the center toward the circumference of his life. "His value must not be estimated by what is on him or around him or in his possession. Above position, above wealth, above culture, above genius even, is nobility of character. The fundamental question in human life is not one of possession or of attainment or of standing, but of being." The aristocracy of character includes the members of the real nobility of earth. They give value and significance to their possessions and surroundings; but these are powerless to give value to them. Such are they who fight the bravest battles and win the most valiant victories.

> Real glory
> Springs from the silent conquest of ourselves,
> And without that, the conqueror is naught
> But the first slave.

My sermon this evening is dedicated to these victors; and my subject is their namesake. "Self-Heroism": The heroism of self-examination; the heroism of self-preparation; the heroism of self-concentration; the heroism of self-perpetuation.

I. THE HEROISM OF SELF-EXAMINATION.

Nothing is insignificant. There is a divine meaning in the existence of everything. To doubt this is to doubt the intelligence of the One by whom all things exist and consist. There are no alternates nor duplicates in creation; and the Creator knows no surplus in his works. As the greenness of no two blades of grass is the same, as the light from no two planets is alike, as the weight of no two pebbles on the beach is equal, so each life is the working out of individual principles and possibilities. No life can infringe upon another's right of way in living; for the legitimate property of no two lives lies along exactly the same track. Each life is a monopoly in itself; for to each has been given the sole permission to exercise certain exclusive powers.

What is the meaning of my life? This is the supreme question for each to ask. Why have I been given an existence, with endowments peculiarly its own? Where is my position and what is my mission in this complex life about me? The Author of my being has made a mistake, or my life is of tremendous significance. His intention in giving me life is of momentous importance to me, and the knowledge of this problem should be my ceaseless pursuit. Introspection partakes of the heroic. It is much less difficult and much more delightful for us to look upon and live by the visible than the invisible; and it demands higher heroism to master the science of self than to explore and to know the wealth of the world about us. "Distance lends enchantment to the view" in spiritual as well as in physical vision. To view and review another's life, to analyze it, to weigh it, to point out the weakness of it, to know how it ought and ought not to be spent, to examine into the cause of its fall and failure, is a very easy job for most of us to work out to our perfect satisfaction. But to reverse the eye of the microscope, and carefully scrutinize self is quite another matter. "Know thyself" is one of the most useful and comprehensive precepts in the whole moral system. Thales, the prince of philosophers, is said to have been the author of it; and he declares, "For a man to know himself is the hardest task he can master." Ignorance of this knowledge has proved to be the reef upon which many of the conquerors of the world have been wrecked. They knew others; but did not know themselves. They mastered others; but could not master themselves. They guided others; but failed to guide themselves. The fields upon which they were victors lay beyond themselves; the fields upon which they were victims lay within themselves; and they were losers in the real battle of life. If self-examination were an applied science, I venture the opinion that some who are now in the pulpit would be behind the plow; some who are at the bar would be in the blacksmith shop; some who are in Congress would be in the cornfield; some who sit in faculties would lie in fossil-beds; and others, with heretofore undiscovered El Dorados within, would awake to their native right and riches and put honor upon lives divinely gifted. Whoever you are, wherever you are, be brave enough, be honest enough, to get intimately and accurately acquainted with yourself; and with Jean Paul Richter be enabled, at last, to say: "I have made as much out of myself as could be made of the stuff, and no one can require more."

II. THE HEROISM OF SELF-PREPARATION.

"Every one has two educations," Gibbon tells us, "one which he receives from others, and one, more important, which he gives to himself." We are debtors, it is true, to all the past; and in beginning life we enter upon the labor of ages. "There is not a philosopher who has not thought for us; not a martyr for truth nor a defender of human rights who has not bled for us." The past has indeed bequeathed us a rich inheritance; and what we are and what we know depend largely upon this wealth. But the highest education and the noblest preparation for life's duties and responsibilities come not from the process of reception or absorption. The popular idea of education seems to be, the art of allowing others to do as much for us as we have the capacity of receiving. "He is not capable of receiving an education," is a suggestive expression. True education is self-preparation. It is not a question of pouring in, but of drawing out. Not so much the effect of something on you, as your effect on something. It does not create; but it takes creation for granted. It must find something within you, or it brings nothing out of you. It would lead you to recognize and honor your inner self rather than your outer succor. It converts your possibilities into practical powers. "I accept without qualification," says James Anthony Froude, "the first principle of our forefathers, that every boy born in the world should be put in the way of maintaining himself in honest independence. No education which does not make this its first aim is worth anything at all. There are three ways of living: by working, by begging, or by stealing.

Those who do not work, disguise it in whatever pretty language we please, are doing one of the other two. The practical necessities must take precedence of the intellectual. A man, if he would not be a mendicant or a rogue, must learn to stand upright upon his own feet, to respect himself, to be independent of charity or accident." The richer a nature the harder and slower its self-preparation and development. Two boys were in the same class in the Edinburgh Grammar school. John was quick, smart, and a *dux*; Walter was slow, dull, and a dolt. In due time John became Bailie John, of Hunter Square; and Walter became Sir Walter Scott, of the World. Bailie John's self-preparation was over within a few years; Sir Walter was planning his greatest works after he was forty-six years of age. Carlyle was forty-two when he published the "French Revolution"; and the first two volumes of his "Frederick the Great" did not appear until he was sixty-three and the last until he was sixty-nine. Swift was sixty-nine when he gave to the world "Gulliver's Travels" and conceived the plot only two years before. Macaulay's "History of England" came from the publishers when he was fifty-five; Milton's "Paradise Lost" when he was fifty-four; Bacon's "Novum Organum" when he was fifty-nine; and Cowper, Defoe, and George Eliot wrote best after they were two-score and ten. After many years of heroic self-preparation, Longfellow, Prescott, Motley, Racine, and Victor Hugo gave us their ripest and richest fruit. To-day the noblest figure in Europe stands erect under the snows of eighty winters; and because of his rigid, righteous self-preparation through all these years, the "grand old man" is the freshest in thought and the maturest in wisdom of all who meet in the parliaments of men. Patient preparation is permanent power. If the mulberry leaf were impatient, it would never become satin. In an age that lacks composure, men are apt to mature too quickly and decay too soon. Reserved power should ever be greater than spent power. An act is never great unless there is a greater something behind it. What a man is should be greater than what he does. The master must be greater than the masterpiece. Self-preparation is more important than self-projection.

III. THE HEROISM OF SELF-CONCENTRATION.

The rays of the sun, spread like a cloth of gold over the floor of the autumn woodland, do not scorch the fallen and scattered leaves; but let these arrows of light concentrate upon the crystal face of yonder bit of glass, and they become a rod of fire whose magic turns the leaf into ashes. A life often fails to make a lasting impression because of its disposition to spread itself. To shine and play over a wide expanse of territory is much more beautiful and brilliant than to turn all the weight and fire of your life in a given direction and upon a specified spot ; by the one you may dazzle and delight during to-day, by the other you may leave the imprint of a golden influence after the sun is set. Persevering concentration converts weakness into power, spreads fertility over the barren landscape, bids the choicest fruits and flowers spring up and flourish in the desert abode of thistles and thorns, and opens to poverty the world's wealth. Men whose lives were not distracted, but whose life-work was contracted, have impressed the age in which they lived, and have brought things to pass. To attempt everything and to accomplish nothing is a fatal folly, encouraged too often by our educational system and by our professional and commercial life. " The objects of knowledge have multiplied beyond the powers of the strongest mind to keep pace with them all. We must choose among them, and the only reasonable guide to choice in such matters is utility. The old saying: '*Non multa sed multum*' becomes every day more pressingly true." If our lives are to mean the most we must take one line and rigidly and sternly confine our energies to it. Never lift the weight of your head and heart and hand from a thing until you have become its master. The higher and more unselfish the end toward which we would direct our lives, the greater is the demand for intense and ceaseless concentration of our noblest powers. The pursuit of your purpose may lead you over rugged mountains, across rolling seas, through fierce flames; but others have conquered these and so may we. Clearly does history echo the truth that the life worth living is the life worth suffering for; and the end proposed by a human being may put honor upon self-dedication and self-sacrifice.

> Oh, fear not in a world like this,
> And thou shalt know ere long,
> Know how sublime a thing it is
> To suffer and be strong.

On the skirts of the town of St. Andrews, Scotland, in the sixteenth century, a slave in a French galley was one morning bending wearily over his oar. For nineteen long months he had done his work faithfully in the galleys; and, unused to such labor, his body was wasted, but his spirit was unbroken. "The day was breaking, and rising out of the gray waters, a line of cliffs, the white houses of a town, and a church tower were visible. A companion touched him, pointed to the shore, and asked him if he knew it. 'Yes,' he answered, 'I know it well. I see the steeple of that place where God opened my mouth in public to his glory; and I know, how weak soever I now appear, I shall not depart out of this life till my tongue glorify his name in the same place.'" That galley slave was John Knox; and we know that he came back to that same place, and from it and through him the glory of God went forth over the hills of Scotland and filled the land with new light and life. Many, to-day, who slumber in nameless graves or wander through the tortures of wasted lives, are those upon whom nature has poured her richest gifts, but whose powers are dissipated rather than directed. What we fondly call genius is often but the child of application. Focus your best powers upon the details of your life-work. In explaining his work upon a statue to a visitor at his studio, Michael Angelo said: "I have retouched this part—polished that—softened this feature—brought out that muscle—given some expression to this lip, and more energy to that limb." "But these are trifles," remarked the visitor. "It may be so," replied the sculptor, "but recollect that trifles make perfection, and perfection is no trifle." The eye must long be fixed upon the ideal before the hand can touch it. Like the fabled bird in the oriental legend which slept on the wing, learn to rest in your labor, but never rest from your labor. Contemplate! Concentrate! Consecrate!

> If what shone afar so grand,
> Turn to nothing in thy hand,
> On again! the virtue lies
> In the struggle, not the prize.

IV. THE HEROISM OF SELF-PERPETUATION.

The truth has been urged that, "the great men of the earth are the shadowy men, who, having lived and died, now live again and forever through their undying deeds. Thus living, though their footfalls are heard no more, their voices are louder than the thunder, and unceasing as the flow of tides or air." Truly great and good men are not half living when they are alive! Their best and truest life on earth, comes after they walk no longer on earth. The prophets of the Most High God seemed almost useless in their time; but when you look at the life they have lived since, they appear to be the world's pilots, guiding amidst the perils of the ages. Their enemies could kill them then; but the arrow from no archer's bow can strike them now. Martin Luther was mighty when he lived. But the shadowy Luther is mightier than a regiment of fleshly Luthers. When he was on earth, he in some sense asked the pope's leave to be; he asked the stream and the wheat to give him sustenance for a day; but now that his body is dead, now that that rubbish is out of the way, he asks no leave of pope or elector or emperor, but is himself a ruler of thought and a deathless defender of truth. Truth, like a seed, does not bear its fruit in a day; the richer the truth and more precious the seed, the slower the full fruition. Great principles, like great bodies, move slowly. Twenty centuries elapsed before the principle of the conic sections, set forth by Apollonius Pergæus, was made the basis of the science of astronomy. Every life in this church to-night is enriched by the mellow fruit of seed-truths planted by unknown hands in the dim, distant past. A man's self becomes a part of the truth to which his life is wedded, and as this truth, which he introduced or merely advocated, passes beyond the limit of his visible existence and takes its endless course through the ages, the strongest and best part of the man's self advances with it, and is perpetuated, it may be, cycles of centuries after his bones are rotten and his name is forgotten. The great men of the past never lived so really and intensely as they do to-day. The momentum of their words and work has been added to by the accumulated force of other words and other works; and, unconscious to themselves and to the mass of mankind who are their beneficiaries, their lives are increasingly forceful as the years come and go. Each life is a contribution to history; but few lives have their historians. Only one Johnson ever had a Boswell. Heroic lives are oftentimes written anonymously upon the tablets of time; and coming ages never recall by name their greatest benefactors. Live so that your life shall not bear its best fruit until after you have passed from the ground in which the seed was sown. Strive not for present praise, but future fruition. Earnestly covet that all men may be your heirs. The fame of your name may soon perish; but what you are, the sum-total made up of the items of your beliefs, purposes, affections, tastes, and habits, you can bequeath to men who shall never know or be known by you. Some are dead while they are living; others are living while they are dead. Think much of your postmortem life among men. Make the earth richer and the sky brighter by having lived on the one and under the other. Maintain an uncompromising enmity toward the false, an invincible friendship toward the true. Cultivate a practical faith in the living God. Accept the Christ as your Redeemer and ideal. This fertilizes the whole field of man's being, and is the hidden spring of self-heroism. It makes man's business safer, his scholarship wiser, his life manlier, his joy brighter; and when the veil is lifted, he shall stand erect in the undimmed light of a glorified manhood.

G. A. NUNNALLY was born on his father's farm in Walton County, Ga., and attended country schools until he was eleven years of age, and was then sent first to an academy in Madison and afterward to one in Marion. He graduated from the State University at Athens, taking one of the highest honors of his class. He also enjoys the distinction of graduating at an earlier age than any other student at this university. He was teacher, and pastor of country and village churches for several years, and then filled successful pastorates at Rome, Ga., and at Eufaula, Ala.; organized the church at Anniston, Ala., and laid the foundation and secured the funds to build the present elegant house of worship at that place. Was elected president of Mercer University, and after presiding over this institution for nearly four years, accepted a call to his present pastorate at the Central Baptist Church, Memphis, Tenn.

G. A. Nunnally, D. D.

IX

THE DIVINITY OF JESUS CHRIST [1]

BY G. A. NUNNALLY, D. D.

"What think ye of Christ? whose son is he?" Matt. 22 : 42.

MAN is a thinking animal. God treats him as a rational being. All revelation and accountability, all vice and virtue, all rewards and punishments are based upon the idea that man is capable of thought. Grand themes are presented for his meditation in government, in nature, and in revelation. The expansion of an idea often produces a great life. Thoughts develop and decide and declare character. They kindle desires and control conduct and fix habits. They measure the man and settle the standing and determine the destiny of the individual. "As a man thinketh in his heart so is he." The greater the theme, the greater the force of thought. "What think ye of Christ?" is the all-important question to the human soul. You must think, and your thoughts will determine your relation to him. As the mariner scans the sky and discerns his relative position to the star in the north, and thereby learns his latitude and longitude, so you turn the telescope of thought toward Jesus and learn your relative position to the Star in the East, and discover the latitude and longitude of your soul. And knowing this, we can tell whether we are on safe waters or near the breakers— whether or not we are on the way to a haven and a

---

[1] Preached in Massachusetts Avenue Methodist Church, Washington, D. C., during the Jubilee Session of the Southern Baptist Convention.

port that we desire to reach. Thoughts are the bell-buoys that ring the danger signals, or are the beacon lights along the shore that guide into the harbor.

God by his revelation and by his providence and by his creation and by the movements of man, would provoke us to think of Christ. The first disciples had the prophets and the unique character and powerful presence and miraculous display of the Wonder-worker to make them think of Christ. In addition to these, we have the testimony of the apostles and the continuous, abiding, and growing miracle of his living kingdom, and the transformations and forward movements of eighteen centuries to arrest our attention and fix our thoughts on Christ. Every power of man has been subsidized and utilized in the world's evangelization. The achievements of genius, quickened by thoughts of him, have all become evangels to declare him to mankind. The galleries of art, from Florence to Washington, are filled with paintings—visions transferred to canvas, which men, inspired by Christ or by scenes in his life, have portrayed. The brush of the artist, from Raphael to Gustave Doré, has been busy through the centuries depicting the world's thoughts of Christ. The sculptor's chisel, from Michael Angelo to Madame Howe, has been at work giving form and body in brass and bronze and marble to the conceptions they had of the Man of Galilee. Musicians, from Ambrosius to Wagner, have made the cathedral and church and chapel and concert hall and field and fireside resonant with melodies, upon whose waves there floated into the minds of choir and congregation thoughts on the life and love and light and liberty of Christ. The author's pen, in book and magazine and paper and tract, in poem and prose, in broken language and polished words, has been inditing for eighteen hundred years thoughts of Christ. Great libraries have been filled with ponderous or less pretentious publications, produced by the best minds of two hemispheres presenting the claims and character of Christ. Unnumbered tongues, burning with live coals from off the altar, have been speaking in pulpit and grove and tent—tongues from Paul to Spurgeon, from Jerusalem to London, from Ephesus to Paris, from Corinth to New York, from Rome to Washington. All along the line of the march of humanity this voice has kept pace with the procession of the generations, and in eloquence has thundered or in broken sentences has stammered thoughts of Christ. Indeed, so fully and vividly has he been presented to the human mind—tongues of canvas, tongues of stone, tongues of melody, tongues of fire everywhere declaring him—it seems strange that any intellect should be devoid of thought and conviction concerning him. In the midst of such a display, in the light of such a revelation, in the face of such cumulative evidence, and in the presence of such monumental testimony, "What do *you* think of Christ?"

"Whose son is he?" is the question of this life, of this age and of every age, of this country and of all countries. It rises above all the questions that try the wisdom of statesmen. The relations of capital and labor, of what is anarchy and what is liberty, are questions of minor moment. The problems that perplex the professor in his laboratory and defy all solution by the test-tube and crucible and alembic, are insignificant when compared to this: "Whose son is he?" A little fame or gain or promotion may be won in this life by the proper solution of the questions of government and finance and science; but eternal issues depend upon the correct answer to that question propounded by the Saviour, which silenced all caviling for the rest of his ministry, "Whose son is he?"

This question becomes more fearful when we remember that every man must answer it for himself.

There is a Sanhedrin in every community, and every man at some time in his life belongs to this high tribunal. There is a Pilate in every breast, and a judgment hall everywhere. Jesus Christ is always on trial. The investigation never ceases. An appeal is always being taken from one generation to the next. Ancestral decisions will not, cannot be accepted by the tribunal of posterity. The consensus of mankind does not relieve any man of individual and personal responsibility. Face to face every man must be brought with this question, "Whose son is he?" Your reply will determine the estimate you place upon his atonement, the faith you have in his promises, and the share you expect in his inheritance.

Then let us convene a court, impanel a jury, examine the witnesses, and try to reach the truth. You be the judge and jury, and I will introduce the witnesses and plead the cause of him who, I believe, is my Advocate to-day with the Father.

The first witness we would bring before the court is Jesus of Nazareth, the son of Mary, the Man of Galilee, that One who was born in Bethlehem and died on Calvary. Mark you, it is the man, Christ Jesus, not the Son of God, whom we are about to place on the stand. But before calling him to testify, allow me to say that this historic person has been and is still regarded by all men as a man of exceedingly high character. His friends and his foes agree that he is truthful and reliable and trustworthy. They all hold that he is humble and pure and blameless, that he is a perfect man, a model man, a faultless example worthy the imitation of all men. The witness is on the stand, and is ready for examination.

The first question we ask is: "Jesus, what do you claim for yourself more than any good man might claim for himself?"

He replies: "'I am the light of the world' (John 8:12); 'I am the bread of life' (John 6:35); I said:

'I am the way, the truth, and the life' (John 14 : 6); I said: 'I am the vine, ye are the branches' (John 15 : 5); I said again: 'Without me ye can do nothing' (John 15 : 5); I declared: 'I am the resurrection'" (John 11 : 25).

How silly and puerile and repulsive would such expressions seem if spoken of one and by one who is simply human. But the man Jesus is truthful; he would not set up a claim which could not be substantiated.

Again we ask: "What relations do you claim to exist between you and the Father?"

He replies, "I assert that I am the 'only begotten Son' (John 3 : 16); I declare that, 'I and the Father are one' (John 10 : 30), and 'He that hath seen me hath seen the Father'" (John 14 : 9).

Would this meek and humble and truthful Nazarene claim such divine kinship and identity if it did not really exist? Such pretensions are not compatible with his established humility unless the declaration be admitted as true.

But we ask further: "Jesus, what promises have you made that would be utterly worthless and only tantalizing mockeries if you were only a man?"

He replies, "I promised: 'Whosoever drinketh of the water which I shall give him shall never thirst' (John 4 : 14); I spoke out so that all the world might hear: 'Come unto me all ye that labor and are heavy laden and I will give you rest' (Matt. 11 : 28); I promised: 'Whatsoever ye shall ask in my name that will I do' (John 14 : 13); I stood up before my disciples and said: 'I go to prepare a place for you, and if I go and prepare a place for you, I will come again and take you to myself' (John 14 : 2, 3); and just before taking my departure from them I declared that, 'All power is given unto me in heaven and earth . . . and lo, I am with you alway, even unto the end of the world.'"

Would Jesus, an honorable man,—and all men say he was the soul of honor,—would Jesus, as a truthful, reliable man, as a merciful man, make promises that he could not fulfill and excite expectations he could not meet? And can any one who is only a man do what he promised to do? The clearing houses of earth cannot handle such checks, only divinity can cash such drafts. We must reject the promises and condemn the man, or accept them and admit the Sonship of Christ.

But before dismissing this witness, we ask: "Jesus, have you any witnesses to testify in your behalf?"

He replies: "'Search the Scriptures, . . . they are they which testify of me,' and Moses and the prophets wrote concerning me. Here are my disciples; 'they are of age, ask them.' Demons also said to me, 'I know thee who thou art,' and my Father 'beareth witness of me.'"

Time will not allow the introduction of all these witnesses, but we will take a word or two from some of them. David had special advantages, was often in communion with God and was "a man after God's own heart." He is a truthful and competent witness.

We ask: "David, what have you to say touching the question, Whose Son is Christ?"

He replies: "One day I was lifted up and was striking a grand song of praise from my harp, and I heard the Father say: 'Thou art my Son; this day have I begotten thee'" (Ps. 2:7).

Let us wake up Isaiah, the old gospel prophet: "Tell us, Isaiah, what have you to say on this question?"

He replies: "I wrote: 'Unto us a child is born, unto us a son is given: and the government shall be upon his shoulder: and his name shall be called Wonderful, Counsellor, The Mighty God, the everlasting Father, The Prince of Peace'" (Isa. 9:6).

Isaiah wrote this at the risk of his life, and it is

not probable that he would have declared a fraudulent vision with such danger impending.

Daniel, the victim of Nebuchadnezzar and the hero of the lions' den, unmoved by royal wrath and unswerved by gods of gold and unfrightened by flaming furnace, what is your testimony?

His answer comes in clearest tones, above the roar of lion and rage of king: "Lo, I see four men loose, walking in the midst of the fire, and they have no hurt; and the form of the fourth is like the Son of God" (Dan. 3 : 25).

But let us consult men of later date who were eye-witnesses. Call in that brave man, John the Baptist, whose loyalty to truth was written in his own blood.

"John, what do you know of this case? Whose Son is Christ?"

The voice in the wilderness replies in tones that sweep down the Jordan to the sea and across the sea to every land and is still echoing over the continents: "I said: 'Behold the Lamb of God, which taketh away the sin of the world! . . . and I bare record that this is the Son of God'" (John 1 : 29, 34).

Here is another witness: "Andrew, what do you think about him?" He modestly replies: "I met him and knew him, and I ran and told my brother Simon, 'We have found the Messias, . . the Christ'" (John 1 : 41).

And Philip speaks: "We have found him, of whom Moses in the law, and the prophets, did write" (John 1 : 45).

And Nathanael, "an Israelite indeed, in whom is no guile," is ready to give his testimony. He declares, "Rabbi, thou art the Son of God" (John 1 : 49).

The timid and frail but reclaimed woman of Samaria,—her name is not given in the book, but she met him at the well,—what is her opinion?

She replies: " I was convinced, I forgot everything.

I went running and crying aloud, 'Come see a man which told me all things that ever I did; is not this the Christ?'" She was impressed that she had met the Divine One.

But let us call some good women whose hospitality Jesus often enjoyed. "Mary and Martha, tell us what you think?"

Here is their reply: "In John 11 it is recorded that our brother had been taken sick and had died, and we sent for Jesus and said to him when he came, 'Lord, if thou hadst been here, my brother had not died.'"

They knew that men could not save him from death, but they believed that Jesus was more than man and that he could have saved him.

But let us place some of the apostles on the stand. The first one we would call in is that skeptical, doubting Thomas.

We ask: "Thomas, you were often with Christ, but was absent at the first meeting after his resurrection; but after a rigid and satisfactory examination of the Risen One, what did you say?"

And Thomas, no longer doubting, but without mental reservation or equivocation, says: "I am on record in John 20:28, and I said then and I repeat it now, 'My Lord and my God.'"

Now we come to Peter, the rock, the converted and confirmed disciple, the follower of many experiences, one of the specially chosen who constituted his body guard. "Peter, whose Son is he?"

He says: "I assert, 'Thou art the Christ, the Son of the living God'" (Matt. 16:16).

But let us call in some of the evangelists, and we ask: "What opportunity did you have for knowing and understanding Christ?"

John speaks for them all: "That which was from the beginning, which we have heard, which we have seen with our eyes, which we have looked upon, and our hands have handled, of the Word of life; . . . declare we unto you" (1 John 1 : 1–3).

Well, let us place Matthew, the publican, upon the stand. "Tell us, Matthew, in a word, what did you think of Christ?"

His reply is: "Emmanuel, . . God with us" (Matt. 1 : 23).

Call in Mark. "What is your testimony?"

He says, "I wrote: 'The beginning of the gospel of Jesus Christ, the Son of God.'"

And John, the beloved disciple, who knew more of the inner life, the God-life of Christ than any other of the disciples: "What is your testimony?"

Here is his reply: "In the beginning was the Word, and the Word was with God, and the Word was God. . . . All things were made by him; and without him was not anything made that was made. . . And the Word was made flesh and dwelt among us; and we beheld his glory, the glory as of the only begotten of the Father" (John 1 : 1–14).

Surely John, who was so close to him, could not be deceived; and being so much like him, he could not deceive us.

What more is needed to establish the claims of Christ to Divinity?

But we would have some old documents we would place in evidence. In many references the testimony is incidental, and is all the stronger because incidental. Paul's letter to the church at Rome begins with these words: "Paul, a servant of Jesus Christ, called to be an apostle, separated unto the gospel of God . . . concerning his Son, Jesus Christ, . . . declared to be the Son of God with power," etc. Again, in this same letter, he says: "Christ came, who is over all, God blessed forever" (Rom. 9 : 5). In Philippians, speaking of Christ, he writes: "Who being in the form of God, thought it not robbery to be equal with God." And again, "That every tongue should confess that

Jesus Christ is Lord, to the glory of God the Father." In Hebrews, it is written: "God, who at sundry times and in divers manners spake in times past unto the fathers by the prophets, hath in these last days spoken unto us by his Son."

Paul was a lawyer. He had learned to be careful in his words. He was too well skilled in investigation to be misled, too well trained in logic to be imposed upon by sophistry, too impassive to be misguided by sentiment, and too pure and true to stoop to deceive and mislead others. His testimony cannot be shaken.

But let us look at another old document. There are blood stains upon the pages, for while he wrote the author was dying, and among his last words are these: "Blessed be the God and Father of our Lord Jesus Christ" (1 Peter 1:3).

In another old, tear-stained scroll in trembling handwriting—for John was old and feeble and was closing his ministry, and getting ready to stand before the judgment seat of Christ—it is written: "These are written, that you might believe that Jesus is the Christ, the Son of God." It is preposterous to think that this aged servant of God and friend of humanity would for a moment, by a single word or allusion or suggestion, mislead any man. This lover of Christ and God, loved man too well to deceive him. Wherever you find John, in Ephesus or on Patmos, leaning on the Saviour's bosom or, according to tradition, in the caldron of boiling oil, running with the ardor of love to the sepulchre or bending with benedictions over his children in the faith, it matters not where you find him, in the church or in the prison, alone or with the multitude, his testimony is always the same: "This is the Son of God."

But there is another class of witnesses I would introduce. They are his enemies; those who rejected and despised and persecuted him. Let us call from the pit of despair some of the demons who are locked in prison, and as they know they are beyond the reach of hope, they can expect no relief by turning State's evidence.

We ask: "You doomed and damned and lost ones, you met Jesus here on earth; whose Son is he?"

And here is the reply of the legions: "Jesus, thou Son of the Most High God." And now they believe and tremble.

Again, the thief on the cross, who, guilty of great sins, and perhaps at the first joined with his fellow in railing, lifted up his voice at the last, and recognizing in the sufferer at his side the Son of God, exclaimed: "Lord, remember me when thou comest into thy kingdom."

Let us call up the old Roman soldier, whose profession cherishes truthfulness as a cardinal virtue. What is the testimony of the centurion?

Here is his reply: "I was there with others at his crucifixion, watching Jesus and those things that were done, and I was convinced, and I said, 'Truly this was the Son of God.'"

But once more. He has some friends whose testimony is valuable. Their character and opportunity and motives make them unimpeachable. Their words were taken for truth by the patriarchs and prophets, and history and providence have confirmed all that they ever said. I mean the angels, those blessed spirits who fell not, neither rebelled, but have always served about the throne that is set in truth and righteousness. What have they to say as to the divinity of Christ?

Their reply sweeps down the starry slopes in heavenly melodies: "We sang his praises, 'Glory to God in the highest'; and when the Father said, 'Let all the angels worship him,' we fell down before him and bowed in his presence, and magnified his name."

Once more. There is yet one other witness; one who cannot lie; himself is truth. Sooner the heavens would fail and hell become a place of bliss than one word of his could fail. Reverently, with bowed head, we come before his eternal throne and ask: "Heavenly Father, whose Son is Jesus?"

Be silent, O earth, and hushed every voice in heaven, and let the demons keep silence below. Here is his reply: "Twice while he was here in the world, at his baptism and at his transfiguration, I came down through the clouds and declared in tones that rang through the universe and across the eternities, 'This is my beloved Son, in whom I am well pleased.'"

Surely with such testimony, coming from the lips of men and demons, of angels and of God, coming from the cradle and the grave, from the earth and the skies, emphasized by the bowing heavens and the quaking earth, tempered with the love of friends and accentuated by the hate of foes, surely we are ready to fling doubt away and join with that disciple who was reclaimed and say, "My Lord and my God."

Then, inspired by such a faith, let us live in his service, die to his glory, and go up and join in the song:

> All hail the power of Jesus' name,
> Let angels prostrate fall.
> Bring forth the royal diadem
> And crown him Lord of all.

A. G. McManaway was born in Bedford Co., Va., August 19, 1852. He was educated at Richmond College and Southern Baptist Theological Seminary. His pastorates have been in Blacksburg, Va., and Lewisburg and Franklinton and Charlotte, N. C., and Little Rock, Ark. He is now the Financial Agent and Secretary of the faculty of Ouachita Baptist College, Arkadelphia, Ark. Dr. McManaway has been for several years intimately and officially identified with the work of the denomination in his State and the South, and has always discharged the responsibilities placed upon him with credit to himself and satisfaction to his brethren.

A. G. M. Manaway, D. D.

X

UNANSWERED PRAYERS

BY A. G. MCMANAWAY, D. D.

"For God is my witness, whom I serve with my spirit in the gospel of his Son, that without ceasing I make mention of you always in my prayers; making request, if by any means now at length I might have a prosperous journey by the will of God to come unto you. For I long to see you, that I may impart unto you some spiritual gift, to the end ye may be established; that is, that I may be comforted together with you by the mutual faith both of you and me. Now I would not have you ignorant, brethren, that oftentimes I purposed to come unto you, (but was let hitherto,) that I might have some fruit among you also, even as among other Gentiles." Rom. 1 : 9-13.

I READ to you, in the opening service, from the Sermon on the Mount, some of the Saviour's remarkable promises concerning prayer. At first glance it would seem from these that one might have the eloquence of a Beecher, the wealth of a Vanderbilt, the power of a Gladstone, or anything else he might desire, simply for the asking. Is that what is meant when we are told to "Ask, and ye shall receive; seek, and ye shall find; knock, and it shall be opened unto you"? And if not, in what sense are these promises true? Your first answer to my question would be that in the very promises themselves the Saviour has limited himself to the giving of good gifts. If a hungry child, deceived by the pone-like appearance of a stone, should ask for it to satisfy his hunger, would any earthly father give him stones for bread? Or if, supposing it to be a fish, a child should ask for a serpent as a plaything, would any earthly father heed such a request? If we then, being evil, know how to give good gifts to our children, and to withhold from them the things that would harm them, how much more will our Heavenly Father give only good things to them that pray to him? So, if I should ask for anything that would harm me, or not be for my highest good, my Master has kindly promised not to bestow it. Then, you would answer me in the second place, that through the Apostle James our Lord has still further limited his promises to those who do not ask amiss. So if I should ask for a good thing, and ask in a spirit of selfishness, rebellion, or carelessness, he would not encourage such a spirit by granting my petition, but would withhold the gift until I came into a better spiritual frame.

But do these two limitations explain all the multitude of unanswered prayers? Have you not asked for good things, such as an outpouring of God's Spirit, an ingathering of souls, the spread of the Redeemer's kingdom, and, so far as you could tell, asked with a good motive and in the proper spirit, and yet received no answer? How are these experiences to be reconciled with the promises read? Can you find another precept still further limiting the promises so as to cover such prayers as these? Or, if you cannot find a precept, can you find a Scripture example furnishing such limitation? All Scripture is profitable, and the example is as authoritative as the precept. Let us see if the text does not supply you with the example for which you ask.

The writer was a good man. He could say of God, "whom I serve with my spirit in the gospel of his Son." Not only did he turn away from sin when he heard that voice on the way to Damascus, but he consecrated himself fully to the work of his new Master. In labors, as well as in sufferings, he was more abundant than any others. In the case we are now considering, he was impelled by a good motive. He wanted to visit Rome, not that he might satisfy an idle curiosity by a sight of the world's metropolis, nor that he might secure places of power and profit for himself or his friends, but that he might "impart a spiritual gift," the very thing for which he had been ordained an apostle. Now this good man, under the influence of a good motive, had been inserting in each one of his prayers a petition that by any means he might at length be permitted to accomplish this praiseworthy object, and had also added his efforts to his prayers, having purposed oftentimes to make the journey. But he tells us in the text that prayer and efforts alike had proved unavailing, and his purpose was still unrealized. What may we learn from such a notable example?

I. That in addition to the limitations already noted, *God reserves to himself the right to DELAY the answers to prayers that may be all right in substance and spirit.* He did that with Paul, and then inspired him to put the fact on record, that the lesson might be handed down to all generations. So too, in the cases of Simeon and Anna, who with fastings and prayers had waited to see the consolation of Israel; the answer did not come until both were old and ready to die. And who has not sympathized with the cry of those, who having given their lives in martyrdom to the Christ, look up from under his throne for vengeance upon their persecutors, while their prayers are unheeded, until at length they are represented as crying out, "How long, O Lord, holy and true, dost thou not judge and avenge our blood on them that dwell on the earth?"

But let me hasten to say that God ordains these delays, not for his own good, but ours. The text furnishes an illustration in point. Paul could not see any satisfactory reason for his disappointment, but we can. When we remember that his greatest letter, the Epistle to the Romans, was occasioned by that disappointment, and then consider how much more good the epistle has accomplished and will accomplish in building up the kingdom of God than the conversion of every soul then in Rome would have done, we can begin to see that God was really answering the spirit of Paul's prayer more largely than he would have done if he had answered immediately and literally. Paul's great desire was to glorify God by extending his kingdom. In his short-sightedness, he thought that could best be done by a visit to Rome, and so he prayed for that, but he has seen ere this how much better it was to have the answer delayed until the letter was written. So it may be with your unanswered prayers. God is delaying that he may give you a better answer than you have dared hope for. God is

> Supremely good when'er he gives,
> Nor less when he denies.

When the due season came, Paul received his answer and went to Rome. So shall it be with you. The due season is known to God and is in his hands. Wait patiently until he sends it.

II. God also *reserves to himself the right to CHANGE the answers to our prayers.* In this case the writer was praying for a "prosperous journey." We know what he meant by that. He was weary with many labors, so he hoped, when the time came for his journey, that he might take passage some pleasant day in a well-appointed vessel, and then, under cloudless skies and over quiet seas, he might be wafted by pleasant breezes from the harbor on the one side to the harbor on the other, rested, refreshed, invigorated by the delightful voyage. This is what he asked. Do you remember what he received? He embarked as a prisoner in chains, he endured two weeks of fearful buffetings in a storm that was phenomenal; at last he got to the shore of a barbarous island just in time to escape the fate of the unfortunate ship. He went on to Rome, finally, chained to a soldier, and so distressed and disheartened that the thoughtful kindness of some nameless ones in coming a day's journey to meet him was enough to make him "thank God and take courage." What a contrast between this all and the prosperous journey for which he prayed!

So too, Moses, after he had promised his people a land flowing with milk and honey and had encouraged them through forty years to follow him on toward that land, when he asked that he himself might go over into it, was given something else.

And our apostle, on another occasion, when he found himself hindered in his blessed work by some affliction which was a thorn in the flesh, asked three times that it might be removed, but it remained.

There was one other who could say, "I knew that thou hearest me always," and there came a time when he prayed three times, "If it be possible let this cup pass from me," and it did not pass.

But let me hasten again to say that when God changes the answer to the prayers of his people, he does it that he may give them something better. We may well rejoice that Paul did not get the sort of journey he asked for. He had written much of God's sovereignty, election, foreknowledge, and predestination, and had so greatly magnified these doctrines that many have turned away from his writings with the idea that man is the mere creature of a fate that is entirely beyond his control. The answer to such is that Paul himself did not so understand the principles he taught. And the character of his voyage furnished him an occasion to illustrate that fact. While in the teeth of that fearful storm it was made known to him that God foresaw the result of the storm, and had foreordained that Paul should survive it, together with all who were in the ship, so that not a life should be lost. No stronger illustration of the truth of the principles he had inculcated could have been given. But he did not understand that God's sovereignty, foreknowledge, predestination, and election relieved those concerned of all responsibility for the safety that had been foreordained and declared. On the contrary, when he saw an unwise and dangerous thing about to be done, he did not hesitate to say: "Except these abide in the ship, ye cannot be saved." It was worth all that Paul suffered, and a great deal more, to have from his own lips such an interpretation of his writings. If no other purpose had been subserved, this would have been sufficient to justify the changing of the answer.

Moses too received a better thing than he asked. If he had gone through the land he would have seen only a few acres on either side of his pathway, but as it was, he was permitted "to view the landscape o'er"; and, as it would seem from the account, see the whole of it in panoramic vision.

Paul's thorn was not removed, but he was given grace to bear it, and so became an illustration of the greatness of God's grace to all generations.

The cup of the Sufferer in Gethsemane did not pass. If it had done so, all that had been suffered and accomplished up to that time would have been lost, and the work of salvation would have proved a failure. But instead of that, an angel came to strengthen him, and he went forward to complete his work and win his final triumph. And so in every case, when God changes the answers to the prayers of his people, he does it that they may be benefited more than they thought or dreamed. You may not see now why you received something else instead of the thing for which you plead, but you shall see hereafter, and from the scene of that final revelation you shall go singing:

> Great and marvelous are thy works,
>   Lord God Almighty;
> Just and true are thy ways, thou King of saints.

HENRY WILSON BATTLE belongs to the distinguished and honored Battle family of North Carolina, Georgia, and Alabama. He is the son of Gen. C. A Battle, and was born at Tuskegee, Ala., July 19, 1856. He was admitted to the bar at the age of nineteen, and practised law about three years. He began his ministry at Columbus, Miss., in 1878, and has been signally successful in attracting large congregations, promoting denominational interests, and winning souls. Inheriting the oratorical temperament, Dr. Battle uses the pen but meagerly in preparing for the pulpit, and, therefore, to be fully appreciated must be heard. Great audiences are often mightily swayed by his oratory, but in the pulpit he ever exalts the Cross and humbly trusts in God for results. Mrs. Battle is the daughter of Rev. (and Hon.) J. L. Stewart, of North Carolina, and by her rare personal attractiveness, beautiful character, and devotion to the service of Christ, greatly enhances her husband's usefulness. Wake Forest College conferred upon him the honorary degree of D. D. As pastor of the First Baptist Church, of Petersburg, Va., he is successor to a long line of distinguished and honored men in the Baptist ministry of the South.

XI

CONSTRAINING LOVE [1]

BY HENRY W. BATTLE, D. D.

"For the love of Christ constraineth us." 2 Cor. 5 : 14.

THIS is the great apostle's triumphant answer to his accusers. Paul under open and severe censure from members of a Christian church, strikes us as furnishing a situation so painfully incongruous that an explanation would be the most natural thing in the world. But for the present it is enough for us to bear in mind that the First Epistle to the Corinthians had only fomented the Judaistic elements in the already faction-torn church at Corinth, until at the date of this epistle they were clamorously challenging the authority of Paul and the truth of the doctrines he was preaching. Timothy and Titus brought news of the condition of things at Corinth (after the church had received his first epistle), and if we only had the letter Paul dispatched from Ephesus by Titus, written in the heat of his righteous indignation, what a piece of invective we would have! The Holy Spirit suffered that letter to be lost, but it accomplished its mission. It caused the church to do some much-needed thinking, and thus prepared the way for the Second Epistle to the Corinthians, intended, in turn, to prepare the way for the apostle's personal visit.

More persons than Paul have found that it is not easy to maintain one's equanimity under unjust criti-

[1] Preached in Washington, D. C., during the Jubilee Session of the Southern Baptist Convention.

cism, especially when the aspersions relate to the fondest attachment and the supreme ambition of life. Such an ordeal reveals the man, and in its fierce light graces or defects stand forth in sharpest outlines. If Paul never appeared more human, neither was he ever more manifestly great, than when pouring out his mighty heart in these rushing sentences, often made obscure by their very intensity.

Is Paul ambitious? Does he desire by talking about bonds and imprisonments, or dreams and revelations, to exalt himself above his brethren? Does he wish by his unsparing anti-Judaism, in ideal demands on the Christian life, to make himself the judge of conscience and the infallible interpretation of the Divine mind? or has he gone quite beyond himself and is he mad? All this—and much more—his enemies openly charge. To one and all his answer is: "The love of Christ constraineth us." I am quite confident that Paul meant the love of Christ *for us*,—it is so like Paul to look Christward for the source of power,—that love which prompted the Christ to die for us, "That they which live should not henceforth live unto themselves, but unto him which died for them and rose again." But it is a love that generates love: "We love him because he first loved us." Paul says this love-producing love *constrains*. It constrained him. It made him brave; it made him zealous; it made him gladly bear all things for Christ, and count them *gain*.

But somebody will say, "I do not wish a constraining love; I wish a love that will revel in a world above the exactions of law." You do? You are sighing for a love that melts away into a rosy cloud of sentiment, without form, substance, or power? Pray, where will you find it? Love, genuine love, on earth or in heaven, disdains your vapid dream, and answers you back: "I must, I must!" Mark you, it is a *must* which has no despotism in it: "Perfect love casteth out fear; because fear hath torment." Listen to the Christ: "I must do the will of him that sent me"; and again, "My *meat* is to do the will of him that sent me." The glory of the new covenant is not found in that there is now no law,—no constraint,— but the rather that "the fleshy tables of the heart" have been substituted for "the tables of stone." "I will put my laws into their minds, and write them in their hearts, and I will be to them a God, and they shall be to me a people." They will not need in that day to take up their abode close by Sinai; Calvary—ever present—will prove the safest guarantee of the law's performance. "If a man love me," said the Saviour, "he will keep my words." He *will*, he cannot help it, *if he love me*—from what Archbishop Leighton calls "the inward bent of the mind." "As it should not be a compulsive or violent motion by necessity from without, so it should not be an artificial motion by weights hung on within, . . . but a natural motion like that of the heavens in their course." The love of Christ for me, appropriated and interpreted by my responsive love to him, creates through the mysterious operation of the Holy Spirit a new nature, whose highest law and chiefest joy is to do his will. *Christ's* love and *man's* love! where and how do they meet and blend? One has beautifully said: "Like burnished mirrors that face each other, they flash the sunbeams to and fro. And thus as we live near God we are filled with love, not ours, but his—his love we reflect back on himself, his love flung forward to men." Liberty! talk of liberty! here is the noblest sort of liberty—"the perfect law of liberty," because glad conformity to the conditions of the new life. "I will walk at liberty; for I seek thy precepts." We need it, we must have it. A poet has said:

> Unless above himself he can erect himself,
> How poor a thing is **man**!

But man needs something more than that. Men are constantly erecting themselves, by forces within themselves, above their ordinary selves. It is this that gives to literature its poetry and to history its charm. Thus does the common man of yesterday become the hero of to-day. We need more than a mighty impulse, cradled in an emergency and sepulchered in a day.

> O Henry! always strivest thou to be great
> By thine own act—yet art thou never great
> But by the inspiration of great passion.
> The whirl-blast comes, the desert-sands rise up
> And shape themselves: from earth to heaven they stand,
> As though they were the pillars of a temple
> Built by Omnipotence in his own honor!
> But the blast pauses, and their shaping spirit
> Is fled: the mighty columns are but sand,
> And lazy snakes tread o'er the level ruins!

Thus begins, and thus ends, man's vaunted resolutions! The world needs something more. Humanity needs the stability of an abiding principle, blended with the fervor of the heart's purest and best emotions. Where can you find it? I answer, *Nowhere in all the universe but at the* CROSS! "Other foundation can no man lay than that is laid, which is Jesus Christ!"

"The love of Christ constraineth us." Go to the cross and learn how Christ loved you! In the light of the cross, many a word in the text of life's hard lesson, which you have been spelling over through blinding tears, will put on supernal beauty, and affliction will lose its sharpest sting. If the ecstasy of an earth-born love could make a pagan smile on the dagger reeking with her blood, and exclaim while dying, "My Pœtus, it does not hurt!" ought not the joy of this love to make a Christian glory in tribulation? If love, "of the earth earthy," can boast its illustrious examples of sublime self-sacrifice, esteemed priceless privilege though made at any cost, shall not this love awake in the breasts of its votaries a spirit of heroism purer, nobler, and more passionately earnest than any other beneath the stars? Was not this the Saviour's meaning when he said, "If any man come to me and hate not his father, and mother, and wife, and children, and brethren, and sisters, yea, and his own life also, he cannot be my disciple"? Oh, friends, we do not love him as we ought; and we love him in such a beggarly way because we meditate so seldom and so coldly on his love for us. We hardly half believe that he bore each of us in his heart from Bethlehem to Calvary. We hardly half believe that love, and not the Roman's nails, held him to the cross. Oh, if I could only have you go from this place to-day saturated with the thought that Christ Jesus loves you, and gave himself for you! Then would you go out to a new life, a life with the Christ at your side. I plead for more love to the personal Christ. A love that shall be fervent and constraining; a love that will make a man whisper, in the soul's most secret chamber, "Dear Lord, for thee," and then flash a joyous radiance over the face and through the life; a love that will make a woman break the alabaster box, nor think of the sensuous pleasures its price might have bought; a love more than earthly, because mixed with a love divine. And yet, the love of a mind alert to learn, and of a life made strong for service. I repeat, the world cannot do without it. The age, with all its magnificent attainments in material things and vast acquisitions of knowledge, cannot afford to forget that, "The knowledge of Jesus is the most excellent of the sciences." Imagine the stupendous loss this world would sustain if that sweet Personality, to-day enshrined in innumerable human hearts, could be changed into an abstraction, so that for the devotion of the lover would be substituted only the zeal of the student. I tell you, take Mary's "*Rab-*

boni!" and the trembling disciple's "*My Lord and my God!*" out of Christianity, and humanity turns wistfully from it with the cry of the prisoner of Machærus, "Do we look for another?"

Finally, the work to be done for the world, the work needed and promised, is possible only for those who love the Christ and have caught his spirit. It is a blessed partnership work. "And, lo, I am with you alway, even unto the end of the world." "I can do all things through Christ which strengtheneth me." If we would save men we must love Christ and live near the cross. We are safest when, sitting down, we watch him there. "The Mediterranean is ever losing by evaporation, and yet it is always full, because it draws by the Strait of Gibraltar on the Atlantic." The cross is our Strait of Gibraltar, and our Atlantic is God's infinite love. We are best fitted for service when "bearing about in the body the dying of the Lord Jesus." To-day shall we not consecrate our powers afresh in love's sacred cause?

After all, love's work is the best work. I have somewhere read of an old cathedral, upon one of the arches of which was a sculptured face of exquisite loveliness. It was long hidden, but one day a slanted window flung a ray of sunlight full on the wondrous face and revealed its almost divine beauty. Ever after, year by year, when for brief moments the angel in the stone looked out, multitudes gathered eager to catch but a glimpse of that face. It had a strange history. When the cathedral was being built, an old man, with face plowed by tears and form bent with age, came and besought the architect to let him, somewhere on the noble pile, execute the commission of his heart. Out of pity, but fearing lest his failing sight and trembling touch might mar some fair design, the master set him to work in the deep shadows of the vaulted roof. One day they found the old man cold in death, the tools of his craft resting beside him, the cunning of his hand gone, and his face upturned to this other wondrously beautiful face which he had wrought—the face of one loved and lost in early manhood. And when the artists and sculptors gathered there, gazing on that face, they exclaimed, "This is the grandest work of all; love wrought this!" Working amid the great world-shadows bodying forth without what love has enshrined within; working it may be unheeded by human eye; working, we fear, so poorly, but working out the heart's sweet and blessed behest—one day (what matter if the worker be still!) a slanting ray from God's cathedral window will fall on the work, and then shall the Master say, "*This is the grandest work of all; love wrought this!*"

XII

GOD'S UNSPEAKABLE GIFT [1]

BY REV. MALCOLM MACGREGOR

"Thanks be unto God for his unspeakable gift." 2 Cor. 9 : 15.

A VERY noticeable characteristic of the great apostle to the Gentiles is his devout habit of ejaculatory prayer and praise. Even in the rush of his arguments, counsels, exhortations, and entreaties, he finds a brief breathing space for sudden supplication and thanksgiving. These isolated gems of devotion are very precious to the hearts of all spiritual people. They are thrilling and sweet as the music of melodious bells rung in the momentary silence of the band. They captivate and charm the heart, like some wondrous voice pouring forth a song of unearthly sweetness, while for a time the stormy harmony of the orchestra is hushed.

On land or sea, in labor or at rest, in solitude or in society, in prison or at liberty, unfolding a truth or enforcing a duty, in all employments and under all circumstances, the devout soul of the apostle breaks out frequently into fervent flame-like jets of devotional feeling, into sudden upliftings of prayer and praise.

In a very natural way, the brief ejaculation of the text sprang forth from the heart of the apostle. He had been urging upon his readers the great duty of Christian liberality, particularly to the poor saints at Jerusalem who had been sorely impoverished by

---

[1] Delivered in Grace Baptist Church, Washington, D. C., during the Jubilee Session of the Southern Baptist Convention.

Rev. Malcolm MacGregor

MALCOLM MACGREGOR was born in Osgoode, Ontario, Canada, November, 1842. He was baptized by Rev. W. R. Anderson, in Breadalbane, Ont., June, 1854; under the ministry of Rev. Daniel McPhail, experienced a call to preach the gospel; completed the prescribed course for students for the ministry in Woodstock College under President R. A. Fife, in the spring of 1868, and in June of that year was ordained. For twelve years, in his native province, he did pastoral work in the Kemptville, Smith Falls, and Georgetown churches, and evangelistic and fostering work in connection with the Convention East. From the spring of 1880 to the close of 1890 he labored in the State of New York, first as pastor of the Baptist church at Fredonia, N. Y., and then of the Riverside Church, New York City. He has been for four years pastor of the First Baptist Church, Jacksonville, Fla.

widespread dearth, by prolonged persecutions and by extreme self-sacrifice in behalf of the people and cause of Christ, in a season of great emergencies. While thus employed, the apostle came naturally to think of the insignificant and trivial character of all human giving when contrasted with the marvelous, boundless grace of God in giving the Son of his love to be our Saviour; and thus the apostle was led to exclaim with all his heart and soul, "Thanks be unto God for his unspeakable gift."

I. The unspeakableness asserted of God's gift.

1. The gift of God is unspeakable by reason of the greatness of its worth. The strong expression "unspeakable gift," used here with such emphasis by the apostle, necessarily refers to that gift of gifts, God's Son, for our salvation. God gave his only begotten and well-beloved Son, the brightness of the Father's glory and the impress of his substance, *for* us as an atoning sacrifice to eternal justice, and *to* us, as our personal Saviour and Lord. He gave him to become united to our humanity, to become burdened with our transgressions, to make expiation for our guilt, and to deliver us from our sin and doom. The deity and dignity of Christ's personality, the perfection of his humanity, the glory of his character, the power of his atoning and intercessory work, and the riches of his grace and love are of unutterable and inestimable value.

In and with Christ, God freely bestows on all who by faith receive the Saviour all kinds of blessings, all manner of precious gifts. How could it be otherwise? "He that spared not his own Son, but delivered him up for us all, how shall he not with him also freely give us all things?" Through Christ he delivers us from legal condemnation and from bondage to Satan, the world, and sin. Through Christ he bestows upon us divine sonship, likeness, heirship holiness, comfort, and love, with all the riches of his grace here and of his glory hereafter. In Christ himself, we have a Saviour and helper, and through him we have, in God the Father, a Father and a friend, and in the Holy Spirit, a comforter and guide. The supreme and all-comprehensive gift of God is unspeakably great and precious. Christ and the benefits coming to us through him are "unsearchable riches." In view of the vastness of the chief divine gift and its varied and gracious implications, one may well exclaim, with Addison:

> When all thy mercies, oh, my God,
>   My rising soul surveys,
> Transported with the view, I'm lost
>   In wonder, love, and praise.
>
> To all eternity, to thee,
>   A joyful song I'll raise;
> But oh, eternity's too short
>   To utter all thy praise.

2. The gift of God is unspeakable on account of the mystery of the giving. The giving is as unique and wonderful as the gift. To whom did God make this unspeakable gift? To sinful men, foes of his character and government, unholy, unthankful, hell-deserving. Why did he give his Son to die for his enemies? That we, "his enemies," might live through him. "Herein is love, not that we loved God, but that he loved us and sent his Son to be the propitiation for our sins." "Scarcely for a righteous man will one die: yet peradventure for a good man, some would even dare to die. But God commendeth his love toward us, in that, while we were yet sinners, Christ died for us."

The mystery of this divine giving is marvelous and inscrutable. We are enriched with the Saviour and his salvation, not because of any merit present or foreseen in ourselves; but for reasons hidden in the infinite heart of God. Rightly considered, there is something profoundly impressive and awe-inspiring in the mystery of grace. No one adequately understands and appreciates the gospel who does not recognize and adore the sovereignty, and therefore the mystery, of the divine mercy. But to those who know it and bow to it, the sovereign and mysterious mercy of God in Christ is unutterably solemn, precious, and sweet. Once in a long while the heart of the civilized world is made to throb with admiration and wonder at some rare instance of self-sacrificing friendship; but the noblest gift ever made by man or the noblest deed ever done by man, deserves not to be named in the same breath with God's great gift of his Son, nay, his sacrifice of himself for the salvation of his enemies. To all eternity, the vastness and mystery of the divine mercy will be to the redeemed and to the angelic inhabitants of heaven a fountain of solemn and reverential joy.

The prophet Hosea, in describing the ultimate rescue and return of the apostate tribes of Israel back to the mercy and love of God, after all their wanderings and sin, says of them, that, in those latter days, "they shall fear the Lord and his goodness"; that is, they shall humbly, wonderingly, and tremblingly reverence the great goodness of God in accomplishing their restoration and salvation, despite their stupendous unworthiness and guilt. When Moses, standing by the burning bush in Horeb, was about to be divinely intrusted with the commission to accomplish the deliverance of Israel from the Egyptian bondage —a deliverance foreshadowing and preparing for the great deliverance through Christ—he was commanded to reverently take his shoes from off his feet, because, in view of the divine majesty, faithfulness, and mercy there revealed, he stood on holy ground.

The utter unworthiness of the recipients of the supreme gift of God and the inexplicable goodness in its bestowment—for he has loved and redeemed us we cannot tell why—should fill and melt our hearts with loving awe and trembling joy.

Every soul that has had a true experience of divine love and grace might well exclaim:

> Why was I made to hear thy voice
> And enter while there's room,
> When thousands make a wretched choice
> And rather starve than come?

> 'Twas the same love that spread the feast
> That sweetly forced us in;
> Else we had still refused to taste
> And perished in our sin.

3. The gift of God is unspeakable because of the inadequacy of language. Limited as are our comprehensions, our souls may, nevertheless, have thoughts too large for utterance, too deep for tears. The poet Tennyson, standing on a cliff on the rock-bound coast of England, gazes upon the sea; and his soul is filled and overwhelmed with its immensity, its majesty, its mystery. So, in lines now long familiar to all, he strives to express the inexpressible within him:

> Break, break, break,
> On thy cold, gray stones, oh sea;
> And I would that my tongue could utter
> The thoughts that arise in me!

But the subject before us presents to the gaze of our souls an ocean of divine love and mercy, without bottom and without shore; an ocean, the immensity, the majesty, and the mystery of which infinitely transcend those of all earthly seas, and the contemplation of which should inspire every human soul with adoring gratitude and overpowering awe.

The power of the chief languages of the world, notably that of our composite English tongue, is, when one comes to consider it, something wonderful. Think of the vast number and variety of terms, with their endless capabilities of combination, possessed by each great language, and the consequent capacity of each of these tongues for expressing great, manifold, and diversified thoughts and innumerable shades of feeling! But no language, whether natural or artificial, or both combined, can adequately express the great gift of God's love in Christ Jesus to a ruined world. Each human pursuit forms for itself peculiar facilities for expressing its own ideas; but none of them can fully express, or, at best, do more than hint at, the greatness and the mystery of the gift of God to men.

The gift of God is unspeakable in *commercial* terms. In our day, there is a strong tendency to reduce all values, moral as well as material, to the dollar standard. But there is no ratio between material and moral values; between the worth of property and personal worth; between the importance of the things of nature and of the things of grace. The work of spiritual and holy character, the value of the love of God, the preciousness of the Saviour and his salvation cannot be estimated in financial terms. We are not redeemed by such things as silver and gold; nor can gold and silver express, or even competently symbolize, the price of our redemption or the worth of God's great gift to men.

The gift of God is unspeakable in *philosophic* terms. Philosophy grapples grandly with great problems, and more than any other secular pursuit, unlocks, liberates, strengthens, and sharpens the powers of the mind, and while doing so, furnishes it with a powerful, flexible, and keen vocabulary especially adapted to the philosophic aim and method. But it does not express the greatness nor expound the mystery of the supreme gift of God. Devout philosophers, such as Bacon, Newton, Pascal, though they have habitually and earnestly brought their powerful minds to bear upon the theme, have ever felt themselves to be but children picking a few pebbles on the mighty shore of truth, to be but neophytes learning the rudiments of the science of salvation. They have ever felt themselves unable to express or to compute the worth of God's great gift of the Saviour.

The gift of God is unspeakable in *theological* terms. Theology is the noblest of the sciences. It deals with the greatest and most important subjects; and it constantly enriches and refines its vocabulary, laying nature, society, philosophy, learning, science, and art, under contribution for exact and illustrative terms with which to express the lofty and spiritual thoughts of God and the infinitely comprehensive and precious gift of God's grace. The advantages of thorough theological training and study are unquestionably very great. Theological systems have highly valuable uses; but no theological system has yet succeeded in embracing all religious truth, or in exhausting the subject of divine salvation. Doctrinal studies and discussions are profoundly important; but no man, and no body of men, have ever yet put the whole of God's great gift into exact doctrinal form, or even exhausted any one great truth of the divine word, whether it be the Trinity, the incarnation, the atonement, regeneration, Christian ethics, the future life, or any other prominent Christian theme.

> Our little systems have their day;
> They have their day and cease to be.
> They are but broken lights of thee;
> And thou, O Lord, art more than they,

The gift of God is unspeakable in *artistic* terms. All art is, in some sort, language. Art is nothing if not expressive. Oratory, with its richest resources, its most golden tongues, its Chrysostom, its Massillon, its Robert Hall, its Spurgeon, and its hosts of others, ancient and modern, whose names have become household words throughout the world, does not fully utter, does nothing more than faintly lisp the unspeakable gift of God. Poetry, with its mighty, magic gift of utterance, with the glowing, sacred epics of Milton, with the enchanting sacred lyrics of Bernard, Wesley, and Cowper, has striven in vain to give full expression to the wondrous theme. Music has expended its highest creative powers, its most massive combinations, its most ethereal influences, its most captivating enchantments, its sublimest strains, as witness the "Passion Music" of Bach, Handel's "Messiah," Gounod's "Redemption," and Liszt's "Christus," all in the vain endeavor to do more than suggest the overpowering majesty, mystery, and sweetness of the theme. Painting, with its brightest lights of genius, its Raphael, its Michael Angelo, its Munkacsy, has depicted, and can depict, only a few gleams from the glory of God's unspeakable gift.

Thus all earthly methods and forms of expression—commercial, philosophic, theological, artistic—fail to give adequate utterance to the great and gracious saving truth, fail fully to express even such fragments of it as may now be apprehended by human souls. Nor even in heaven itself can the unspeakable gift ever be fully uttered. The most flaming tongues among the redeemed in glory, or among the seraphic hosts before the eternal throne, can never give full expression to God's unspeakable gift; but these intelligences must ever find new conceptions, new aspects, new applications of it, for speech and for song, through all the rolling cycles of eternity.

II. The thankfulness demanded for God's unspeakable gift. "Thanks be to God for his unspeakable gift."

1. The thankfulness demanded for God's unspeakable gift is an imperative obligation. The numerous analogies of gratitude in the natural world forcibly

suggest to the thoughtful and sensitive mind the duty of thankfulness to the gracious Giver of all good. Throughout the material universe we see a bounteous and constant giving of benefits, and a ceaseless and gladsome returning of them again. The planets and their satellites cheerfully reflect the light bestowed upon them by the sun. The sea sends up her unbounded exhalations in acknowledgment of the rain-gifts of the clouds, and the consequent inflowing of the streams. In grateful response for the air and light and rain of heaven, the earth sends up her offering of fragrant flowers and savory fruits. The vegetable and animal kingdoms, in their mutual giving and returning of benefits, acknowledge their mutual indebtedness. In joyous recognition of the glorious gift of the sunlight, the feathered songsters make the fields and forests resound with their tributes of grateful praise. In all these beneficent reciprocities, and in numberless other ways external nature is a suggestion and a symbol of the highest truth—the unspeakable gift of God and the deep thankfulness due him from man.

The duty of gratitude to God is firmly maintained by the law of nature, which plainly declares that benefits and favors received impose upon the recipient the duty of grateful regard and acknowledgment to the benefactor. Hence it is that all moralists and casuists whatsoever, heathen and Christian alike, treat the duty of gratitude under the general head of justice; and they teach, with manifest truth, that gratitude for favors received is founded upon, and demanded by, absolute justice. Indeed, in some ages and by some nations, instances of flagrant ingratitude to great benefactors were severely punished by law as odious crimes. How criminal and odious in the sight of God must be ingratitude to him who is the greatest and the best, the most loving and merciful, from whom we derive life and breath and all things, and who, in addition to all his earthly benefits, seeks, notwithstanding our unworthiness and sin, to bestow upon us his unspeakable gift! Yet what is more common on the part of men than flagrant and persistent ingratitude to God?

That God attaches great importance to the duty of thankfulness to him for all his benefits in general, and especially for his gift of a Saviour, is manifest from his high favor toward those who gratefully receive the Saviour, his salvation, and providential benefits; and it is equally manifest from his severe displeasure toward those who impiously refuse the gifts of his saving grace, while thanklessly consuming the temporal gifts supplied by his providence.

The duty of thankfulness to God for his unspeakable gift is sanctioned by the law of nature; it is commended by the example of the truly good in all the ages; and it is rendered absolutely binding by the frequent and express commands of God, recorded in his holy word.

2. The thankfulness demanded for God's unspeakable gift is a regenerate impulse. Such was the thankfulness of the apostle. It sprang from a nature regenerated by the Spirit and truth of God; and it was awakened by the sweet consciousness of possessing a sacred and saving interest in God's unspeakable gift. Though the gift of God is unutterable, yet every truly regenerate heart, every heart that has tasted that the Lord is gracious, instinctively strives, in various ways, to express its deep and ever-increasing sense of the greatness and preciousness of the gift; and, on every account this gracious desire and tendency should, by every one, be assiduously cultivated and developed.

Profound thankfulness to God for the gift of the Saviour, of which the Apostle Paul was a shining example, is one of the surest evidences of regeneration and of a saving interest in Christ; and it is equally true that only by spiritual regeneration of the heart and heart-experience of God's unspeakable gift, can man's deep, hard, black ingratitude toward God be broken up and abolished, and the human soul be made to throb with love and thankfulness toward him, and with all gracious and evangelical affections.

On an ancient German castle, between its widely separated towers, strong wires were strung on the principle of the Æolian harp. No gentle zephyr, no ordinary summer breeze, no average wind could stir a note from this unique musical instrument. But in the autumn, when the storm-king came down from the mountains and, with his strong tempestuous hands, smote those mighty harp-strings, they resounded with a harmony so grand, so weird, so awful, as to shake the inmost souls of the listeners and to produce upon them impressions never to be effaced. So, only the breath of the blessed Spirit of God can evoke from cold, dead human nature, the rich, full soul-harmony of devout gratitude and praise.

3. The thankfulness demanded for God's unspeakable gift is a practical acknowledgment. If the true Christian's grateful acknowledgment of God's great gift of a Saviour be analyzed and compared with God's word, it will be found that there is in it much more than the outward service of the lips. Our English word "thank," when its close relationship to the kindred words "thing" and "think" is remembered, becomes particularly suggestive. The word "thing" indicates an object present to the mind, as a subject of thought; the word "think" expresses the action of the mind upon the thing, the subject of thought, before it; and the word "thank" represents the pulsating and practical response of the heart when the "thing" upon which the mind is "thinking" is a benefit received. So, in true thankfulness, both mind and heart and will are profoundly active. The text is indicative of a state of mind and heart in which

the unspeakable gift is clearly perceived, personally appropriated, and gratefully acknowledged.

True thankfulness for God's unspeakable gift involves, at the very outset, a *hearty acceptance* of it. Without this there can be no true thankfulness for it. It is no part of gratitude to refuse or postpone acceptance of the great gift of God freely offered in the gospel. On the contrary, it is black ingratitude *not* to accept, and that promptly and gladly, the mighty benefit. Rejection of Christ is an evil and a heartless return for the goodness and mercy of God in freely providing and proffering so glorious a Saviour. Unless you heartily accept Christ, you are chargeable with the blackest ingratitude to God and with the willful ruin of your own soul.

True thankfulness to God for his unspeakable gift demands *entire consecration* to him on that account. Think not of thanking God with what costs you nothing, with the mere remnants of your life, with the mere dregs and rinsings of your self-indulgence. Give him yourself, give him your all. As the recipient of the Saviour and of his salvation, you are bound to give yourself and all that pertains to you to him, humbly and gladly, as a perpetual thank-offering for those benefits.

Christian, if you would render true and acceptable thanks to God for his unspeakably precious gift, you must lay your soul and body, your talents and time, your possessions and pursuits, your powers of service and your powers of endurance, on the altar of God. He having not only created and preserved you, but having also redeemed you by his blood, renewed you by his grace, and enriched you with his love, he has the profoundest conceivable right to yourself and to all that pertains to you. To consecrate yourself unreservedly to God will enable you to more fully and more joyfully to appreciate and appropriate the Saviour.

True thankfulness to God for his unspeakable gift should prompt every recipient of it to *imitate the divine character.* The great design both of our creation and of our redemption is likeness to God. What, in the essence of it, is godliness but God-likeness? Unless the unspeakable gift, by being received and incorporated into our hearts, produce in us, sooner or later, what might be called a speaking likeness of Christ and of God, that gift is in no sense ours. Out of profound gratitude to God for the Saviour and for salvation, there should be in every redeemed soul practical, self-sacrificing and holy love to God, to Christ, to his people, and to the unsaved for whom Christ died, and the greatest readiness to serve God and to do good to men for his sake.

True thankfulness to God for his unspeakable gift requires *faithful effort to win souls* to Christ and salvation. If our own souls have been rescued and enriched through the redemption of Christ, we should, from love of God and love of men, strive diligently, tenderly, prayerfully, to win others to him, that they may become partakers of his salvation and evermore be trophies of his grace. With such practical acknowledgments God is well pleased.

Let us therefore, with all our hearts, accept the unspeakable gift, consecrate ourselves and all we possess to the service and glory of God, striving daily to become like him in character and life, and for Christ's sake try to bring many souls to be saved by his grace. Let us endeavor ever to maintain in our private and social life, in our work and in our worship, a devout, thankful, and joyful spirit. Then hereafter in the realms of glory we will "behold the King in his beauty" and join in the mighty chorus to his praise: "Worthy is the Lamb that was slain"; "Thanks be to God for his unspeakable gift."

C. S. GARDNER was born in Gibson County, Tenn., February 28, 1859. He was educated at the Southwestern Baptist University, Jackson, Tenn., Richmond College, and Southern Baptist Theological Seminary. He has had the following pastorates: Trenton, Tenn., 1884-5; Brownsville, Tenn, 1885-6; Edgefield Church, Nashville, Tenn., 1886-94; First Church, Greenville, S. C., 1894—; in all of which he has been successful and popular. Still a young man, the future has bright promise for him.

XIII

THE HISTORY OF A SIN

BY REV. C. S. GARDNER

"And in process of time it came to pass, that Cain brought of the fruit of the ground an offering unto the Lord. And Abel, he also brought of the firstlings of his flock and of the fat thereof. And the Lord had respect unto Abel and to his offering: but unto Cain and to his offering he had not respect. And Cain was very wroth, and his countenance fell. And the Lord said unto Cain, Why art thou wroth? and why is thy countenance fallen? If thou doest well, shalt thou not be accepted? and if thou doest not well, sin lieth at the door: and unto thee shall be his desire, and thou shalt rule over him. And Cain talked with Abel his brother: and it came to pass, when they were in the field, that Cain rose up against Abel his brother, and slew him. And the Lord said unto Cain, Where is Abel thy brother? And he said, I know not: Am I my brother's keeper? And he said, What hast thou done? the voice of thy brother's blood crieth unto me from the ground. And now art thou cursed from the earth, which hath opened her mouth to receive thy brother's blood from thy hand. When thou tillest the ground, it shall not henceforth yield unto thee her strength; a fugitive and a vagabond shalt thou be in the earth." Gen. 4 : 3-12.

WE have the history of a sin recorded here, and I ask you to trace with me the successive stages of its development.

But first, it is worthy of note that Cain lived and acted under circumstances very different from those which condition our lives. We live in the midst of an organized society, under the restraint of many institutions and influences which curb our impulses. We have our sheriffs, our court-houses, our jails, and our penitentiaries. We live under the daily, hourly pressure of a powerful public sentiment. And speaking generally, we have two classes of sinners among us: those whose evil dispositions are partially repressed and largely modified in their expression by their social environments, and those who desperately defy the restraining forces that would hold them in check. Cain represents neither of these classes. So far as we know he did not live in the midst of social institutions that were a terror to evil-doers. If there were such institutions they were in a crude and incipient state. It is true that after he had murdered his brother and received the divine sentence of banishment, he expressed the fear that he would be killed and the fear was accentuated by a guilty conscience. It probably does not indicate that he lived under social conditions which acted as a great deterrent force upon sinners.

The history of his sin may therefore be regarded as the normal development of sin, undisturbed by outward and counteracting influences. It is the revelation of the essential nature of sin. Sin does not always manifest its essential character naturally and truly in our lives; and so it happens that sin often does not seem so hateful to us as God's word depicts it; and so it is that many of us come to think better of ourselves than we deserve.

1. Let us look at the origin of this sin. Cain and Abel had come to present their offerings to God. Each brought that which represented his labor, and was, therefore, the best expression of self-dedication to God. So far as the formal action was concerned both men were equally devout and equally obedient. But God looks beyond the form of actions, and he saw in Cain the spirit of pride and self-importance. It had not occurred to Cain that there might be anything wrong with him or his worship. He presumed as a matter of course that God would find no fault with his sacrifice or with his life. Abel might be wrong; that was quite within the bounds of possibility, as Cain saw it. But the idea that there was anything in himself to which God could object, he

would have scouted. He came to the altar with a high countenance and waited with presuming confidence for the manifestation of the divine favor. It did not come. He saw the divine favor bestowed on Abel's offering, and observed with surprise and indignation that his own was neglected. His countenance fell and he was wroth. He left the altar with wounded pride rankling in his heart.

The root of his sin was the wrong attitude of his heart toward God. This is the origin, the potency of all sin. This is the flowing fountain of evil. And it is the fundamental truth which is overlooked by many men. Who of us has not seen the manifestations of this same spirit of Cain? Are there not men here, who because their lives are formally correct, or at least approximately so, have presumed that they are right with God, and fancied that they are ready to abide the test of the divine judgment? If the attitude of Cain's heart as he approached the altar had been expressed in words, I am sure that many men among us would be startled to find that they had adopted the very same self-righteous phraseology as the first murderer. The same painful and humiliating surprise awaits them as awaited Cain. They will be rudely awakened from the repose of their self-confidence and self-complacency by the rejection of their lives. And why? Not because they are formally incorrect, but because their spirits are wanting in humility and self-distrust and dependence upon the mercy of God. To be without the consciousness of unworthiness is the strongest possible evidence of the lack of worthiness, and also of the moral vision to perceive the lack.

2. The rejection of his offering awakened in Cain a feeling of jealousy and hostility toward his brother. That was very irrational and foolish. Abel had nothing to do with the rejection of his sacrifice. But none the less the acceptance of Abel's sacrifice and

the rejection of his own made him very angry with his brother. Sin is illogical. It is the negation of reason, the very essence of folly. Righteousness alone is rational both in principles and development.

The fact is that Cain's heart being wrong in its attitude toward God from the first, was wrong also in its attitude toward his brother. And the rejection of his sacrifice was merely the occasion for the development of this double iniquity of his soul. The only reason that can be given for the hatred of his brother, which now burns within him, is that he has never loved him before, has always been cold and selfish toward him. The fuel of hatred has been in his heart all the time, and this spark has simply ignited it. It is impossible to be right with man so long as we are wrong with God. To be out of harmony with God is to be out of right relations with everything and particularly with our fellow-men, who next to God are the most exalted beings who claim our respect and love. The humanitarianism that does not have its root in religion is only an artificial flower.

At this point in the history of Cain's sin, God meets him with a warning. He seeks to call back the foolish, passionate, angry man to reason, "Why art thou wroth?" He calls upon him to stop and think, to analyze and account for the strong feelings that rage within him. The excited man ought, on peril of his soul, to heed this divine call to calm reflection. A moment's sober inquiry into the state of his mind would reveal to him its utter irrationality. And God adds the solemn warning, "sin lieth at the door." Be careful. You are in a dangerous state of mind. With a heart so charged with unholy passion you are likely to do a rash, reckless, desperate deed. Surely this call to reflection and this warning need to be taken to heart by every man in whose breast jealousy, anger, hatred, have gained the sway. If your heart is bitter toward your fellow-men, remember that bad feeling is only latent crime. You do not know when nor where you will be ushered into a set of circumstances which will bring to combustion all the inflammable material stored away in your soul, and then all the restraints of disused reason may be forgotten in the rush of unregulated impulse, and the hidden wickedness of the heart may register itself in a deed whose shadow shall darken your pathway to the very end of your days. The man of ill-will is a potential criminal.

3. But Cain did not heed God's call to reflection or his warning. He did not dispossess himself of the bad feeling engendered by his disappointment. He did not keep a watchful eye upon the lion of sin, that crouched at his door. He went back to his dwelling with his heart surcharged with evil feelings, inwardly vowing that he would yet get even with his brother. And behold, the next development of his sin. He met Abel in the field. That which was uppermost in his heart must come out. He talked with Abel about the occasion of his chagrin, and being in no amiable mood, picked a quarrel with him. It was unfortunate that he did not hold his tongue; but he had not learned the lesson of self-control. Words led to blows; in a fit of passion he dealt his brother a fatal stroke. And the first victim of murderous hate fell and gasped and died, and the first murderer felt the prick of that impenitent remorse which became the nemesis of his life. Not till then had he known the real nature of the passion which he had harbored in his bosom when he had become the typical example of the truth, "He that hateth his brother is a murderer." The murder was probably unpremeditated, but it was no more than the sudden translation into deed of the disposition which he had cherished in his heart. Looking stealthily around to see that there was no witness to the foul work of his hand, he drew his brother's body into a covert place,

and with throbbing heart and stinging conscience crept back to his dwelling place, and strove to wear the air of innocence and unconcern. The wretched man seems to have forgotten that All-seeing eye which read and judged the secret contents of his spirit when he came to make his offering, and did not realize that all the events and incidents of life are pictured upon that infinite retina. His brother's blood cried into the ears of God from the earth, which felt the eternal shame of that red stain upon its fresh and innocent soil.

4. But follow his sin to the next stage of its development. God met him again, not this time with a timely call to reflection, nor with the merciful warning, but with the probing question, "Where is thy brother?" In the memory of Cain there was no scene so blazingly distinct as the spot where he had hidden the body of Abel. Every detail of the tragedy and its surroundings was burned into his mind forever. At this question it flashed upon his mental eye with startling clearness. But he said, "I know not." The lie was the natural sequence of the murder. Oliver Wendell Holmes says: "Sin has many tools, but the lie is a handle that fits them all." There was an awful directness in this lie. "I know not," said the guilty man. But in fact there was nothing in all the world that he knew so well as what had become of his brother. There was a more brazen boldness in it. It was a lie to God. It has in it a solemn warning to us all. If you have sinned, the next step in Satan's programme for you is to lie. And he would have you lie not only to your fellow-men, but to your own conscience, the voice of God within you. He will impel you to deny your guilt to your own heart, and no falsifying is so depraving as that. The lie is the Satanic suggestion as to the way to disentangle one's self from the meshes of a sin. Cain thought thus to free himself and escape the conse-

quences of his deed. And the temptation is always for sinners to follow him in this effort. But oh, what a pitiful shield is a lie to lift between one's self and the flaming dart of justice.

A falsehood does not cut the cord that ties the sin and its consequences to the guilty soul; it is another bond that binds it faster. Confession is God's method of getting rid of a sin; denial is Satan's. Will you follow God or the adversary? "If we confess our sins, he is faithful and just to forgive us our sins and to cleanse us from all unrighteousness." All the falsehoods with which a man may delude himself and elude his fellow-man do but multiply the threads with which to entangle his feet and ensure his downfall. Confess your sin and you are no longer identified with it, and you escape the fearful catastrophe which it is preparing for your soul.

5. But this was not all of Cain's answer to God's searching inquiry; he boldly put a question to God in return, "Am I my brother's keeper?" It was a further development of his sin. It was a crude attempt to formulate a theory of life that would justify him. Poor wretch! had he not assumed to be more than his brother's keeper? Had he not assumed to dispose of his brother's life? And now he seeks to take refuge from the bitings of his guilty conscience and from the withering gaze of God in a formulated conception of human relations which would divest him of responsibility for his brother. Is it my business to look after him? If he comes to misfortune, is it not his own lookout? Why call me to account for him? Have I not the burden of my own life to bear?

Certainly in this matter Cain proves himself beyond all doubt to be a typical sinner. What has the world of sinners been doing since his day but following in his footsteps in this matter? Does not every debauchee in this city, every thief, every whisky seller, every hard-faced swindler, every shrunken-hearted son of avarice, every rich exploiter of the poor man's earnings, every proud social pharisee, reason Cain-wise about his relations with his fellow-men? After these thousands of years it would seem wonderful indeed if men had not made some refinements upon Cain's crude suggestion; but it is only too evident whence they have derived the substance of their social philosophy. Alas! that this Cainism has so much colored the thinking of the world upon this subject. Being a direct denial of our responsibility for one another, it has given to selfishness the dignity of rationality and the complacency of self-respect; and it has played a great role in history. It has been a great principle in the social conduct of individuals and corporations and States, and not infrequently has shaped the conduct of the church of God. Out of it has come the larger part of the social wrongs and oppressions and sufferings which, like Abel's blood, have cried to the God of heaven for vengeance.

Are we our brothers' keepers? Of course; that is precisely what we are. Every man's life must have a self-regarding aspect, but so profoundly true is it that we are our brothers' keepers that only in the faithful fulfillment of this great mission does a man really take care of himself. Selfishness is self-destruction, and love is life. Cain far more effectually destroyed his own life than he did Abel's. The real enemies of social life and progress and prosperity are the men who to-day are living in the spirit of Cain; the men who in things material and spiritual, in the sacred or the secular spheres of life, in church, society, or business, deny their responsibility for their fellow-men.

The life of Cain teaches us that the wrong attitude of the spirit toward God is inseparably connected with iniquity in our social relations, and this expresses and justifies itself in a false philosophy of life. It therefore gives us a hint as to the right method of procedure in the regeneration of society. It is primarily a religious task. The first step is to set the hearts of men right with God. But this must be, and inevitably will be, followed by efforts at the readjustment of social relations, and this will be accompanied by the revision of social theories. And the more active, aggressive, thoroughgoing, is the religious movement, and the more intense and pervasive the religious spirit becomes, and the more rapidly and radically the hearts of men are set right with God, the more momentous will be the social movements and the more general and earnest will be the thinking on social subjects. But the social movements which do not proceed clearly from a religious basis can never come to good. Their success would be but a farther step in the progress of organized sin. In these times of agitation and counter-agitation in society, which we believe to be the ferment created by the active leaven of Christianity, we need to keep a critical eye upon the would-be reformers, and to carefully discern whether the men who propose to be casting the demon of Cainism out of the body of society, are themselves proceeding in the spirit of Cain. To begin the reformation of society by a denial of God looks to me much like adoption of the first principle of Cain; and it seems clear that such doctoring of the sick social body as these men will do will only amount to a fresh injection of the deadly poison. The humble, obedient acknowledgment of God must be the cornerstone of the new society.

But let us turn from these general inferences, to look at Cain again before the curtain falls and the wretched sinner passes from our view. The divine curse falls upon him. He is cast out from the presence of God; and he cries in bitter despair, "My punishment is greater than I can bear." There is remorse, there is despair, but there is no penitence.

As we see the sad, blasted man turn to walk away

in the deepening shadows of the eternal night which now settled about his spirit, we cannot help uttering the cry, "Oh, that he had repented!" If instead of the lie and the evasive self-justification, he had confessed the sin that burned like fire in his soul, if he had said: "O Lord, I killed my brother. See, these hands are red with his blood, see this heart that is panting under the pain of its guilt. O God, I hate myself; wash my hands of this blood, purge my soul of this intolerable guilt. O God, forgive, forgive!" Then instead of the fiery curse, God's pardon, like gentle dew, would have fallen upon his soul, and a humbled, forgiven sinner, he would have gone about to serve his God and love his fellow-men in the joy of sweet gratitude.

R. T. VANN was born in Hertford County, N. C., in 1851. He was converted in his twelfth year. One month later he suffered the painful accident of having his hands crushed in a cane-mill which deprived him of both of them. About the very hour his fellow-converts entered the baptismal waters, he was on the operator's table undergoing the amputation of the right arm above and the left just below the elbow. Soon afterward he experienced a call to preach the gospel, and began preparation for his life-work. After two years in Buckhorn Academy, he entered Wake Forest College and took his degree. He then entered the Southern Baptist Theological Seminary and spent one year. The following year was spent in reorganizing the Scotland Neck Baptist Church. He then returned to the seminary to complete his course, but, after another year, ill health compelled him to forego this ambition. His most important charges have been Wake Forest, Edenton, and his present pastorate at Scotland Neck, where he began his ministry. His preaching is sound, original, and abounds in striking metaphors.

R. T. Vass, D D

XIV

THE DECEITFULNESS OF SIN

BY R. T. VANN, D. D.

"The deceitfulness of sin." Heb. 3 : 13.

WHAT is the origin of sin? Has evil always existed, or did some being originate it? Who was that being? If Satan, must not God have created sin in him? How could God ever have allowed sin to enter the world? On questions like these men have bestowed profoundest thought, only to realize after all their study that they know as much about them as when they began, and no more. What time have creatures like us to waste in such idle speculations? The enemy is upon us; shall we stop to guess who invented his arms? Where is the wisdom of waiting to analyze the poison of the serpent that has bitten us, when we should be hastening to a physician? What sin is, in its origin and first history, we do not know. One thing we do know, it entered the world and ruined the race by deception. One of the saddest pictures in all Scripture is given in the third chapter of Genesis. It is in three parts: First, we have a sinless pair of human beings, fresh from their Maker's hands, in the beauty of innocence, and gazing upon a serpent at their feet; next, a shameful pair in conscious guilt, shrinking away from the Maker's face to hide among the garden trees; lastly, a wretched pair taking their sorrowful way from their first and best home with a flaming sword behind them. Do you ask the meaning of the picture? The woman's answer to the inquiring Judge shall explain it: "The serpent beguiled me." It is to this deceiver and his terrible work that I would turn your minds to-day.

I. I must crave your patience while seeking to impress the doctrine that sin deceives.

1. While the text seems to refer to the sin of unbelief, the writer to the Romans, speaking of sin in general, declares that it deceived him and slew him. Indeed, it is difficult to conceive of any man's sinning without some kind of deception. Men do not violate human law without a perverted view of the law itself or of the deed contemplated, or some hope of escaping the penalty. Can it be possible for one in open view of the wrath of God to persist in a course that he knows must incur such wrath? Nay, there must be some sort of deception and a vast amount of it in the matter.

But are not men depraved, and do they not naturally love sin? To be sure; but as I take it, they do not love sin because it is sin, but because it gratifies some appetite of their nature. It is safe to say that all of an ungodly man's actions look toward his own pleasure. Does he steal? He does not do so because the law says "Thou shalt not steal," but because theft promises gain. Does he give alms? It is not because of God's blessing upon him that hath pity on the poor, but his own gratification.

Satan would have been dangerous if the fall had only made him our adversary. But now he comes with double power. To the strength of the lion is added the subtlety of the serpent. His native force is joined with matchless strategy. Every blow has a heightened effect; every movement a hidden design.

2. This deceptiveness will still further appear if we remember that, as all sin deceives, so all men are liable to this deception. Some one has said that sin deceives the Christian but forces the unbeliever. This cannot be true. Exposed to the same temptation

and by the same tempter, all men fall by the same process. Being crafty, sin catches them with guile. Of one thing you may be sure, no human being was ever forced to sin. One essential of sin is freedom: Deeds under compulsion are guiltless. God condemns no man for what he cannot avoid.

But are we not blinded by Satan and led captive at his will? Yes, but by our own consent. We are not driven into sin, but drawn. We are not forced, but fooled. And yet, while sin does not compel, how well-nigh absolute is its power. It throws a spell over its victim, and charms him to death. There are two forces in every human being: The power of conscience, which persuades to righteousness; and the power of sin, which makes for iniquity. Man consents to the law of God that it is good. At his best moments he serves the law of God; but sin intervenes, persuades, deceives, and he goes on to serve the law of sin.

> I see the right and I approve it too;
> Condemn the wrong, and yet the wrong pursue.

You have felt the charm in that fine stanza:

> Go ask the infidel what boon he brings us;
>   What charm for aching hearts he can reveal
> Sweet as the heavenly promise hope sings us,
>   Earth hath no sorrow that heaven cannot heal.

You know too, that in all your acquaintance, there is hardly a man who in life and character is farther from heaven than was the author of that stanza. Poor fellow, I think he could not have sung so sweetly of heaven if his soul had not sometimes looked heavenward and sighed for a better life. But why will men thus awakened still follow the old life to their own undoing? In the text lies the answer: "The deceitfulness of sin."

But it was to Christians that the text was addressed. Says Spurgeon, "If any man thinks he is perfect he is perfect in folly." Says a greater than Spurgeon, "If we say that we have no sin we deceive ourselves and the truth is not in us." I am speaking of the two forces within us. In the believer these forces are reversed.

The power of sin is weakened and the power of conscience strengthened by the grace of God. But both are still mighty, and sometimes painful is the conflict. We are not yet free from the effects of the fall. If you fancy that Satan abandons the fight when once he is defeated, you have much yet to learn about him. He never yields until the gates of heaven have closed behind the soul. And if we were absolutely sinless, there would still be vast meaning for us in the warning of the text. Our first parents were perfectly pure, and yet they were deceived and ruined by sin. But if we were more than human, we should still need to guard against our crafty foe. Angels, once lustrous in the glory of the skies, lost all their thrones and splendor through sin's deceptive arts. "Take heed, brethren, lest there be in any of you an evil heart of unbelief, in departing from the living God."

But can the elect be deceived? Who are the elect? Are you one of them? Has the Father ever handed down to you a fee simple title to heaven? Nay, the only sure proof that one is elected is his holding out to the end. And besides, in electing to save his people, God chose to do so through their watchfulness. Moreover, the bulk of what we know about election comes from Paul, and yet the man who had heard from the lips of Christ that he was a chosen vessel, said, "I keep under my body, and bring it into subjection: lest that by any means, when I have preached to others, I myself should be a castaway." When a man says, if I knew I was one of the elect I

THE DECEITFULNESS OF SIN

would sin as much as I liked, there is grave reason to fear that he of all men is not one of them. He is no child, seeking the Father's table and the Father's face, but a miserable tramp begging stale bread from the kitchen door.

Yes, all men are open to sin's deception. "Watch ye, therefore; . . and what I say unto you I say unto all, Watch."

II. It may be well now to observe some of the methods of sin's deception.

A common practice of evil is to hide itself wholly from view. It begins as secret sin. All sins start in this way, as all fruitage is the result of planting, and Satan is willing for the seed to lie buried long for the sake of a certain harvest. The crime that shocks with startling horror is but the eruption of a long diseased heart. So does the cancer shoot its deadly fibres through the system for years before it breaks the surface.

You are not aware of this evil presence within you. True, and therein lies your danger. You had rather fight six armed men before you than a single unarmed foe behind you. In secrecy lies much of Satan's power. Secret sins! They hide away in the heart's chambers, ashamed of the light. Secret sins! They paint those dark life-pictures over which we blush even in dreams. Secret sins! They skulk in the dangerous darkness, waiting for our blood. Secret sins! A nest of vipers unperceived till their fangs of death have poisoned the life. Secret sins! Slumbering volcanic fires that shall roll over the soul a sea of flame.

And when its presence is revealed sin begins to argue how small the evil is. But there are no little sins. We say there are, forgetting that the mere tasting of a little fruit lost paradise to our first parents and heaven to so many of their children. Little sins are sent to introduce greater ones. Why is one end of the wedge small but to make way for the larger end? Let Cain but cherish that secret grudge, and ere long Abel's blood shall flow for it. Let Judas harbor that devilish greed for gold, and you shall see him betray the Son of Man with a kiss. Up yonder in the mountains is a tiny stream oozing between the sheltering leaves. Now it meets a kindred streamlet. Still a little child at play could turn their course. But by-and-by these meet a third, and thus a rivulet is formed, and then a river, till at last you behold the wild cataract breaking its resistless way to the sea. This is the course of your little sins.

Another method of Satan is to paint the pleasures resulting from the evil course proposed. "Your Master would not deny you pleasure. He himself is called the happy God, and he 'giveth us richly all things to enjoy.'" Yes, God delights in your happiness, but take heed, good friend, lest the apples of pleasure turn to apples of Sodom and become dust on your lips. Beware, lest you wake from your dreams of pleasure in a land where dreams and pleasures come no more. I know you will pardon the reference. It was years ago, but I remember it well. They gave me the soothing narcotic and my sleep was sweet. I awoke to find my best physical strength forever gone.

These are not all of sin's devices. Their name is legion. Now the deceiver quotes the example of some good man, as if any man were perfect Now he exhibits the good to be accomplished by yielding, as if we might do evil that good may come. Sometimes one command is destroyed by magnifying another. Thus, if one has been baptized he fancies that all is well, though he has never put forth a hand to help the needy, nor given a dime to spread the gospel. Another thinks that it matters little whether he is ever baptized if only the heart is right; as though the heart could be right that refuses to obey the last command of the Lord Jesus. A pleasing performance of sin is to step boldly forth in the garb of humility, as the spy in the enemy's camp wears the enemy's uniform. Thus, one says, "Alas, I am too vile to be saved by the mercy of God," fancying that he is magnifying God's justice while he is really making him a liar. His promise is: "Him that cometh to me I will in no wise cast out," and I honor him by believing. Another tells us God is too merciful to punish a soul forever. But he hath said, "The soul that sinneth it shall die," and who art thou that gainsayest what God hath declared? I think that some such method as this was pursued with Adam and Eve. God had warned them that eating the fruit meant death. "Oh, no," said Satan, "you shall not surely die." They believed Satan; they disbelieved God; they ate the fruit. The result—oh, the mournful result!

III. But why make such ado about deception? You have often been deceived, you say, and yet with no serious results. But look to the end of sin's deception and you will see reason enough for keenest solicitude. Sin is no idle worker. It proceeds with sure and steady aim. It seeks nothing less than the death of its victim.

I am not sure that physical death is the result of sin. It may have been that bodies like ours must, after a while, have wasted away from their own weakness. But I am sure that sin has invested death with all its terrors, for "the sting of death is sin."

But there is another death outlined in Scripture, the moral death. "In the day that thou eatest thereof thou shalt surely die." Man ate and died right there. He instantly lost his finest life. When the preacher mentions death as the outcome of sin, men at once begin to think of the future. They forget that doom follows guilt as promptly as peal follows flash. Death treads hard upon the heels of sin.

You spend a round of years in sin and call it life. It is not life. It is but a wretched skeleton with the soul all gone. Sin pulls the tap and your best life runs gradually out. You are dying hourly and by inches.

And then that other death—the final death, the deathless death. "The wages of sin is death."

> There is a death whose pang
> Outlasts the fleeting breath.
> Oh, what eternal horrors hang
> Around that second death.

It is not my purpose to picture those horrors. I would not if I could. I only want to remind you that eternal death is the outcome of sin's deception. How many of the ills in your life are traceable to mistakes! One step, you thought, and my fortune is secured. You took the step and realized too late that it was a blunder. It is melancholy, it is mournful, to hear the fallen emperor saying in reference to his crime against Josephine, "I thought I was treading on a bed of roses, when a fearful abyss yawned beneath and engulfed me." I have sometimes tried to imagine the utter dismay of a lost man when first he realizes whither sin has brought him. I can only fancy him wailing out in bitter despair, "Oh, blinded madman, oh, wretched idiot, not to have seen through sin's deceitful veil and have chosen a better way!"

Is this the power of sin? Am I thus exposed to so fearful a foe? Who then can be saved? Who shall deliver me from the body of this death? Do you fear sin? Would you be free from its damning dominion? Then I thank God, through Jesus Christ our Lord, I have a message from the King for you: "Call his name Jesus, for he shall save his people from their sins." Yes, from their *sins*. "But, alas! that does not cover my case, for I am not one of his people." Well, here is something that does cover your case: "The blood of Jesus Christ, his Son, cleanseth us from all sin." Apply to him, prove the efficacy of his blood, test his power to save, and then if you are turned away, go and tell it in the regions of the damned that there is no balm in Gilead and no physician there. But that shall never be, never.

> Thou dying Lamb, thy precious blood
> Shall never lose its power,
> Till all the ransomed church of God
> Be saved to sin no more.

Dear old stanza, sing it over and over again. It sounds like a song from the upper temple. I do not love the thorn bushes, but I love the roses that they bear. I do not love the freezing winter winds, but I love the music that they make. I do not love the darkness, but I love the stars that it reveals. I do not love to be a sinner, but I do love to think of the sinner's Redeemer, who "is able also to save them to the uttermost that come unto God by him." And sometimes my soul stands upon the verge of gratitude for sin in rapturous view of God's amazing redemption from sin.

But you mean to turn from sin, you say. When? "Not now; some other time." That is Satan's great soul-soother which lulls to everlasting sleep. God says, to-day; you say, no, to-morrow. That is unbelief, the devil's first-born, and by it he shall lead you on till the gates of mercy have swung to and death has barred them fast. But are you longing to turn now? You need not wait, for the Father is calling to-day. The preacher was standing on the steps of a cottage, just leaving for a Western State, and the woman was showing him a picture. "You remember him," she said. "Poor Rob, he fell into sin and ran away, ashamed even to come and bid me good-bye. If you see him, tell him to come right home, for his mother loves him yet." Oh, child, famishing in the far country, come back home to-day, for the Father loves you yet.

But you sometimes hope that you have been delivered from sin, and yet you fall so often, and your life is full of tears. Well, you shall have many more falls, I fear; but they shall not be final nor fatal. Tears, yes, showers of them; but the sunshine of grace shall turn them into rainbows about you. And so it may ever be until there bursts upon your astonished vision the glory of the rainbow around the throne. Jesus says: "He that endureth to the end shall be saved." Anybody can tell me how I ought to live. The vilest wretch in the gutter can deliver me a fair lecture on morals. Thanks be to God for the wonderful, wonderful Teacher, who not only tells me how I ought to live, but helps me to live in that way.

JAMES CONWAY HIDEN was born at Orange C. H., Va., Nov. 5, 1837. His father was a member of the Legislature of Virginia. His mother was a niece of Governor James Barbour, and of Philip P. Barbour, Speaker of the House of Representatives of the United States, and Justice of the United States Supreme Court. He was educated at the Virginia Military Institute and the University of Virginia. He was professor of ancient languages in Chesapeake Female College, and was ordained to the ministry in 1859. He served as Confederate chaplain 1861-5. He has served as pastor in Portsmouth, Va., Wilmington, N. C., Greenville, S. C., where he taught homiletics in the Southern Baptist Theological Seminary; was pastor in Charlottesville, Va., Lexington, Ky., New Bedford, Mass., Eufaula, Ala., and now serves as pastor of Grove Avenue Church, Richmond, Va. Dr. Hiden is a man of broad scholarship, wide reading, and refined literary taste.

XV

CHRIST CRUCIFIED[1]

BY J. C. HIDEN, D. D.

"We preach Christ crucified." 1 Cor. 1 : 23.

THERE are certain forms of speech which, in brief phrase, sum up whole systems of thought —political, philosophical, religious. If two men are discussing the principles of government, and I hear one of them say, "The best government is that which governs least," if he is not mouthing, but knows what he is talking about, I know where to rank him as a politician. He is a straight-out, old-fashioned, States-rights Democrat.

If two men are discussing philosophy, and I hear one of them utter solemnly the words, "Know thyself," if he understands himself historically, I know where to place him. He is a disciple of a philosophical school, founded by an old Greek more than two thousand years ago, a school whose doctrines have been expounded by Reid, and adorned by the genius and learning of Sir William Hamilton, in his "Philosophy of Common Sense."

And when two men are talking about religion, and one of them utters reverently the words, "Christ crucified," I know that he holds the New Testament view of Christian doctrine, that he is an evangelical Christian. "Christ crucified" is Christianity. It is our religion. What sort of a religion is it?

---

[1] Preached at Vermont Avenue Christian Church, Washington, D. C. during the Jubilee Session of the Southern Baptist Convention.

1. IT IS A HISTORICAL RELIGION.

Christianity is no mere "theory of moral sentiments." It implies, and is based upon a history. However high an opinion a man may have of the personal character of Jesus; however highly he may praise the Sermon on the Mount, if he does not accept the historical facts of the gospel—if he does not believe in Christ crucified—how can he be called a Christian? If I reject Christ crucified, my religion is gone.

This religion does not depend upon any theory, nor even upon the fact, of inspiration. If Matthew, Mark, Luke, and John have given us real, honest histories; if Jesus said the things that they say he said, and did the things that they say he did, then there stands our doctrinal Christianity historically vindicated, inspiration or no inspiration.

Nor are we absolutely dependent upon the evangelists for our history. Tacitus tells us that during the reign of Nero, the Christians became numerous in the city of Rome; that the sect was founded in Judea by Christ, who was executed under the administration of the Roman Governor, Pontius Pilate; and that this superstition spread itself even to the city of Rome. Tacitus did not like Christianity. He called it a pest. But then he was writing a history, and there the Christians were.

Pliny, a judge in the province of Bithynia, in a letter to the Emperor Trajan, tells him of the Christians, who had become numerous in Pliny's province. He describes them as innocent in their lives, and says they were accustomed to meet together and sing hymns of praise to Christ as God. Now there stands a historical statement of the doctrine of the divinity of Christ, as held by the Christians of the first century. What are you going to do with it? I once heard a learned professor of Greek speak contemptuously of what he was pleased to call "the slipshod Greek of the New Testament." What would he say of the classic Latin of Tacitus and Pliny? But

II. IT IS A RATIONAL RELIGION.

I mean what I say; for I do not admit that the infidels have a monopoly of the reason of the world. In the strict sense of the term, I am a rationalist; that is, I do not believe anything that seems to me unreasonable; and I do believe historical and doctrinal Christianity, because I see good reasons for believing it. When the so-called rationalist charges me with professing to believe what I do not understand, I flatly deny the charge. It is impossible for me to believe an unintelligible statement.

"But," says the skeptic, "don't you believe in the doctrine of the Trinity?" Yes, and I understand all that I believe about it. I believe, from various statements made in the New Testament, that the Father, the Creator and Governor of the universe, is God. That is a perfectly plain statement. I understand it, and so does that eight-year-old boy, sitting there before me. Then I believe that the Son, Jesus Christ, the Redeemer of the world, is God—another perfectly plain statement. Finally, I believe that the Holy Spirit, the Comforter and Sanctifier, is God—still another plain statement. I have no difficulty whatever with the meaning of any one of these statements.

"But," says my antagonist, "how do you reconcile these statements? How can three persons constitute one God?" Well, I don't understand anything about the "*how*," and I don't *believe* anything about it. I have no revelation on that subject. The Bible says nothing about it; and I have no creed, and not even an opinion about it.

"But, how about miracles?" Well, I believe in them. "But you don't understand them." Yes, I do understand them exactly as far as I believe them. I believe that Jesus plastered up the eyes of the man that was born blind; that he sent him to the pool to wash; that the man obeyed, and that his eyes were opened, so that he could see; and I understand every one of these statements, and so can any average child of eight years.

"But," says the unbeliever, "you do not understand how that was done." Certainly not; and I don't *believe* anything about the how. If I knew *how*, probably I could do it. Why not? When I am prepared to tell *how* miracles are wrought, I expect to work some. If I know how a thing is done, then that thing is no longer a miracle to me. Jesus Christ explained many of his parables; but he never explains one of his miracles; and the preachers who explain them nowadays always explain them away. As soon as the explanation comes, the miracle is gone.

"But how about the sovereignty of God and the free agency of man?" Well, I believe in both. I believe that the Creator works all things in this universe according to the counsels of his own will; and then I believe that I am responsible to him for my conduct. And if I did *not* believe that he is sovereign, then I could not believe that I am responsible to him.

Thirty-five years ago a strong party in this country held that the paramount allegiance of the citizen was due to the sovereign State in which he lived; and this *because of* the sovereignty of the State. Another strong party held that the allegiance of the citizen was due to the Federal government, because *that* government was possessed of sovereignty. Both parties held that responsibility followed sovereignty; and so we fought for years over the question, "*Where* does sovereignty reside?" I hold then, that my responsibility grows out of God's sovereignty.

"But," says the objector, "you do not know how

to reconcile the two doctrines." **No; I don't** pretend **to** "reconcile" them. The Bible says nothing about **it, and I** have no creed on the subject—no, not **even** an opinion.

But there **is** *no* subject on which thorough **investi**gation will not bring us to the point at which we **are** obliged to say, "We don't know." We say, "**As** plain as a, b, **c**." But a, b, c will become an insoluble problem, if you only go deep enough. If any of you school children want to puzzle your teacher, ask him **where** a, b, c came from, and **he** will be "turned down." The world does not contain a scholar who knows the origin of the alphabet.

But

III. IT IS A PRACTICAL RELIGION.

I was once sitting on a car, at Gordonsville, Virginia, reading the "Westminster Review," the organ of British infidelity. A skeptic came to my seat and said, "Do you read that sort of literature?" "Yes," I replied, "I want to see the devil's latest dodge. How can I hit him if I don't know where he is?" And then we entered upon a discussion of the evidences of Christianity. I called his attention **to** a man whom we both knew; who had been a notorious profligate, had become a Christian and a most excellent and useful man. The infidel did not even try **to** answer that argument.

If you ever knew a very **bad** man **who** became a Christian and a good man, then practically **this religion** holds its own until the infidel produces a **real** Christian who was a bad man, and who **was** converted **to** infidelity and became a good **man. Did any** one ever hear of such a man? And **yet infidelity** is logically bound to produce him or **else quit the** field.

Now, I can **produce** *my* **man.** I was preaching in a protracted **meeting at a country church in Tide-**

water, Virginia. A man present was **notorious for** his wickedness and his opposition to religion. **His** wife had been converted, but he would not allow **her** to be baptized. His niece,—a member of the family,— a girl of sixteen, had been converted and wished to be baptized. He told her that if she was baptized he would turn her out of the house. She was baptize**d and** he did turn her out, and she was obliged to go **to a** neighbor **for** shelter. During the service that day I saw this man rise from his seat, fall upon his knees, **the** tears streaming down his cheeks. After kneeling a minute, he arose, walked down the aisle to the seats on the right of the pulpit, and began to shake hands with the deacons and other members of the church, saying, " My friends, you know what **sort** of life I've led ; you know how I have hated religion. **But** I can't stand it any longer. I must go with you. I **must be a** Christian." Just across the church sat his poor wife, her face all bedewed with tears of joy; and the next Sunday they went down together into the water and were buried with Christ in baptism. Years afterward, I learned from the pastor of the church that this man was living a consistent Christian life. Now, if you should ask that man why he so changed his course of life, *he* would tell you that it was the religion **of** "Christ crucified" **that** wrought the change. **Don't** you think *he* ought to know what was the matter with him ?

Ungodly man ! the very charges which you bring against Christians for doing what you do **not** pretend to abstain from, are clear proof that you *do* believe in the practical power of Christianity to help a man in his life. *You* do not hesitate to do what you would condemn me for doing. Why ? Because you really believe that a Christian **has, and** ought to have, a higher standard of life and **conduct than have the** ungodly around him. But if there **is no practical power** in his religion to help **him to do right, and to** restrain him from doing wrong, what right have you to require a higher standard for him than you have for yourself? On merely natural principles you are just as much bound to do right as I am.

Now, here is this world full of wickedness. We Christians are struggling against the power of darkness, and striving hard to make the world better. And there you stand, looking on indifferently at their hand-to-hand fight with sin and the devil, and criticizing the plan of the campaign! Man! it is neither sense nor decency. If you are of any account, stop your foolishness and take hold like a man and *help* in the fight.

XVI

THREE STEPS UP[1]

BY J. B. GAMBRELL, D. D., LL. D.

"And this I pray, that your love may abound yet more and more in knowledge and in all judgment; that ye may approve things that are excellent; that ye may be sincere and without offense till the day of Christ; being filled with the fruits of righteousness, which are by Jesus Christ, unto the glory and praise of God." Phil. 1 : 9-11

THAT is a wonderful prayer, isn't it? The prayer sprang out of the apostle's heart, as he exclaims above, in behalf of the church which he evidently loved very much—one of the churches to which he wrote against which he could lodge no complaint at all. This letter to the Philippians is a beautiful love letter—warm, sweet; ranging from beginning to end on a high plane of thought and feeling. And yet, as good a church as this one was, it was capable of being a better church. The apostle wanted them to get up higher, to see things from a higher standpoint; in other words, to grow in grace, that growing in grace they might burst out like the full sap in the trees, into buds, and flowers, and fruits.

There is a suggestion in the very way in which the apostle comes to the matter of getting this church on the up-grade. He laid the foundation of his whole effort in his prayer for them—an excellent lesson for us. Our brethren pain us often. Some of them are perverse; some of them are so narrow; some of them are so weak. They vex us, and we fret, scold, and talk;

---

[1] Preached in Trinity M. E. Church, Washington, D. C., during the Jubilee Session of the Southern Baptist Convention, and stenographically reported.

J. P. Campbell, D. D., LL. D.

J. B. GAMBRELL was born August 21, 1841, in Anderson County, S. C., and was taken by his parents to Mississippi the next year, where he "grew up with the country," spending the years of his growth alternately between the country school and labor on the farm. From an academy he went into the war at nineteen, and for most of four years was captain of scouts. It was while scouting he met Miss Mary T. Corbell, of Nansemond County, Va., to whom he was married inside the Federal lines on January 13, 1864, at one o'clock at night. After the ceremony he drove across the Blackwater, twenty-five miles, before nine o'clock the same morning. He was ordained to the ministry in 1866, and after completing his education at the University of Mississippi, was chosen editor of the "Baptist Record," which position he filled with great and growing distinction for fifteen years. He was elected president of Mercer University in 1893, without seeking the place. Furman University, S. C., gave him the degree of D. D., and Wake Forest, N. C., LL. D. Dr. Gambrell is an energetic and incisive writer, an entertaining, popular, and effective speaker.

they get worse and we get worse. The suggestion of the apostle's method is this: When our brethren are weak, are in any way short of what they ought to be; if they are living on a lower plane than they ought to live on, we should put under them the arms of our prayers and lift them up. I have in my thought at this moment a sister who had been in a great deal of trouble over a succession of inefficient pastors; and after a while one worse than all the others came. She betook herself to earnest prayer for the weak man in the pulpit. Her account of it was that she had never seen any one improve as he did, and I doubt not that she was wonderfully improved herself by her own prayers.

Brethren, let us approach the initial thought—the uplifting power of prayer in the life of a church and in the life of an individual. Might I not say with propriety that what we really need in these troublesome times is a great, swelling undercurrent of prayer in all our work to lift us up. We have great trouble in our Christian work, and a great many of our enterprises are like vessels on the Mississippi River; when the water gets low they go on the sand-banks, and can't be gotten off until the water rises. We want a great rising tide of heartfelt prayer to God throughout the land.

The apostle gives us three distinct stages in this upgrade movement. And they are logically connected; very plain, very simple, they come to my experience and to yours. In the first part of this prayer the burden of the supplication is that the love of these brethren might abound more and more. Our religion, brethren and sisters, is a religion of love. It is no use talking about doing things religiously in cold blood. Love is the manifestation of the divine life in us. It all began in love—"God so loved the world." Christ loved us and gave himself for us; and if we do not love Christ we have missed the whole secret and the whole power of the Christian life. We must put away the idea that people can live a Christian life and not have a Christian life to live; unless we have the life in us we cannot live it out. But some of us who began to love the Lord years ago—and I am satisfied we love him this morning—do not love him as we started out to love him. Might not some of us be compelled to own that some of the old love has gone? We must get the idea of growing in love, not simply the idea of growing in the efficiency of doing things, but primarily of growing in love. I think it ought to be like the love that married people have for each other—the well-married. How fresh, how exuberant is the love of a newly married couple! How sentimental! People laugh at it. Yet it is very beautiful to think on. I am sure that no two people who have ever walked through life in this relation to the end have ever loved each other too much. It is a pity that they sometimes grow cold in love. You know our Lord speaks of our relations to him under the form of marriage; and it is a good figure, a good illustration. People who are just married think that there are no other people in the world who love as they do, and that they will never be able to love so much any more. Yet, if they live as people may and should, this is only the beginning of a constant, widening, mighty current of love. It seems to me it is like a mountain stream which comes down the mountain side, laughing, sparkling, dancing, making a good deal of noise; after a while it gets more to a dead level, and the banks widen, the current deepens and broadens, and other streams flow in from right and left until, away down yonder, the little mountain brooklet that leaped out of the mountain gorge has become a great river, bearing on its majestic bosom the commerce of the nations. So married life, fresh, exuberant, a little noisy, a little showy at the start, deepens with the years, as it is tested and tried, and the one is close to the other through the long weary hours of sickness and when they stand together and weep over little coffins. Now they are gray-headed and old. Oh, the height and depth, the length and breadth of that love! Deep as the sea;—eternal as God, is love, for it is heavenly.

My brethren, it is a great pity if we who are old to-day, after thirty or forty years of experience, do not love more than we used to. If we have not increased the breadth of our Christian love, the depth and strength of it, then we have greatly neglected our privileges. If we are not better for the experiences through which we have passed, let us look again, just a moment, at the marvelous tokens of divine love that have come to us since our conversion.

Some of us have passed through deep waters; and as we went down into them and the great waves of affliction rolled over us, and the storm was upon the mighty deep, our hearts quaked. But there came to us through the waves and walking on the sea one who is Lord of land and sea, and he stilled the waves, and great peace came to us in our afflictions. This is not a passing dream or speculation, but the blessed experience of those who have attempted to walk with God. The old saint, scarred and weather-beaten, who put to sea forty years ago, did not understand many things then that he understands now; he did not appreciate then the words, "I will never leave thee nor forsake thee," but now he knows it is all true. The heart is stronger now and fuller of love.

I will not forget this morning that I am talking in a city church. I have great concern for our city churches, for they need to be strong, surrounded as they are by the strongholds of worldliness. Oh, brethren and sisters, what we want back in our city churches to-day is the great heart and patience of Jesus Christ and of his love for men and women. We cannot fiddle people into the kingdom, and we cannot beguile them by worldly methods into the love of Jesus Christ. We want something you Methodists had—the zeal of John Wesley; and we Baptist people want the rugged earnestness of John the Baptist. We are compelled to live; we are compelled to fight; and ever-growing love, which is a part of experience, should feed itself day after day upon the ever-increasing number of divine blessings bestowed upon us, and so shall we be stronger to live aright and fight valiantly.

I was in a place somewhat north of this some years ago at a prayer meeting. I heard a great many things said that were not particularly edifying to my thinking—fanciful, flowery, and secular. After a while there was a lull, and a girl stood up and said, "I was converted a year ago, and from the day that I was converted I have made a practice of stopping quietly for a time every day, and thinking of what new blessing God has given me." And then she mentioned some new blessing or experience she had received that day. It was a good suggestion, this of stopping to think of the blessings that God gives us; for those blessings nourish our love, they broaden it and strengthen it.

I am not to dwell much longer on this point, but I cannot leave it without enforcing it. I wonder if there is here this morning somebody who is trying to serve God without love? There are such people in the world; they are all about us. Such service is perfunctory; it has a form of godliness, but it lacks power. If there are any such before me this morning, let me say that the idea is a mistaken one. Be done with it; be done with it! If you have never loved, seek now to love the Lord Jesus Christ. Men and women, throw yourselves down at the feet of the Christ until you are caught up by the great, swelling tide of Jesus' love; and don't try to serve God without love. I wonder if there is anybody here this morning who is trying to serve God under the old love—whose religious love is a recollection, a bright spot in the past? Let your love catch up with your years. You need it to help you to-day. I notice that people who are quick at cultivating a good many other things, and do not cultivate love, get into a bad state of mind. They are hard to please. The preacher cannot please them; nobody else can please them; not even God himself, not even the blessed adorable Christ can please them; and they never will get pleased until there comes back to them as a present experience the blessed love of Christ that passeth all understanding. Brother, sister, do not let this day go out until you have renewed your vows and come back into touch with the loving Christ.

But to the next point. This love is to be in knowledge. Love is a great force, comparable to a river sweeping on, blessing and making fruitful everything that it touches. Love that is thoughtless, indiscriminate, and degenerates into mere sentimentalism, wastes itself like a stream broken from its banks, burying itself in the sandy plain. There is a great deal of difference between the dignified and manly love of Jesus Christ and mere religious sentimentalism. I wish we could note the difference this morning. We have some in the world who go about with their mouths full of soft words. They love God and they love the devil; they love God's people and they love the devil's people, and they love them all the same way. They don't know any difference between right and wrong. They think God is so full of love that he would take the Apostle Paul to heaven, and the chariot would catch Judas in his downward descent and take him there too.

Let us understand that love does not necessarily make people foolish. Knowledge! knowledge! growing in knowledge! We ought to know the quality of the things we are going to love. There are some things to be loved, and there are some things not to be loved. A good thing is to be loved; a bad thing is not to be loved. I never was in a theatre but once; that was in the days of my ignorance. I went not knowing the guile in there; but I soon saw the difference between the theatre and the prayer meeting. I found things all about me which a church-member had no business to love. There are many people who need to know things! And yet, they will not have knowledge. They will not let you talk to them. They go out on the streets and talk to infidels, and catch all sorts of loose notions; but they will not let God's people touch them—never.

Not a great many months ago a cultured woman came to me. Her face was the picture of intense suffering. She said, "I have come to consult with you about my boy." "Well," I said, "madame, tell me about your boy. How old is he?" "Twelve years old," she said. "What is the matter with him?" She said, "I cannot control my boy at all. He goes down town all the time, and he gets into all sorts of mischief, and now he is in the lock-up. The mayor has just sent me a note that if I will be responsible for his punishment I may take him out. What am I to do with my boy?" I said to her, "Madame, you go down there and take your boy; and when you get him at home shut him up in a room, and you go in there with him with a heart full of love and a bundle of switches, and stay with him a week if necessary, stay there with that boy until he is thoroughly conquered and thoroughly submissive to your will." She said, "I love my boy; I cannot whip him." "Oh," I said, "madame, you don't love your boy with any common sense. Your love is not a love that has any knowledge of boy nature in it. You are raising your boy for the gallows. You had better stay with him in that room a week, and wear out on him all the switches you can get your hands on rather than let him go to ruin. Solomon was not the fool many modern people think he was on that subject." Yet, she did not do it.

Now, brethren, we want love, but we want love according to knowledge. This church needs to love the Lord Jesus Christ, and to love the souls of men, but you do not want to run about after all sorts of worldly ways. Think you that you can save men by encouraging them in their worldly lives? Oh, how we need sound knowledge! How much we need knowledge in our religious work and in our individual lives!

And then, not only abound in knowledge, but in judgment also. There is a great difference between knowledge and judgment. Judgment is that sense which enables us to make the right use of knowledge. A wise man, having all the facts before him, will know what to do. He will not know what to do unless he has the facts, for his judgment must have something to work on. He must have knowledge and then judgment to tell him what to do.

Now Christians ought to be wise people. We need to be harmless—as harmless as doves, but as wise as serpents. We want to be very wise in our church methods. We should so adjust our church methods as to reach out as far as we can to help people; but we want to be very wise, that when we reach out to take the world the world does not take us.

It ought to be a matter of profound study all the time how to be wise; how to be wise in the management of a definite case. The father wants to be wise with his boy. I have in the school where I am, a strong, resolute boy, at that critical period in his life when it is hard to say which way a boy is going. His father took hold of that boy with a strong grip, but with a grip that was flesh and blood, with warmth and tenderness. It saved the boy.

What I am insisting on now is wisdom—practical

wisdom in our Christian lives. There are a great many people who seem to think that as soon as a man gets converted he must give up common sense entirely. We do not put into our religion the common sense we put anywhere else. Christianity is a monumental miracle because it has lived against the folly of people who have had it in hand. To illustrate: you have a congregation that wants to build a church house. They go to work to build the church, but don't know anything about the money. After a while they find themselves deeply in debt. Then they wonder how it all happened, and they go to praying for assistance, and try to pray the money out of somebody's else pocket to pay their church debt. If you intend to build a church you ought to know that you have to build it out of common material, out of wood and stone or bricks; and you want common sense in it; wisdom, practical judgment.

Now let us go back and come up these three steps rapidly. The prayer began with love, that it might abound more and more in knowledge and in all judgment—three great steps upward, landing us on a higher platform; a heart full of love, a mind well informed, a judgment well balanced. The result of it is most excellent—" That ye may approve things that are excellent."

The Bible is not given on the plan of telling us everything we must do and everything we must not do. There are great principles laid down, and we must have judgment to apply these principles. There are new tendencies coming up constantly that are new; and there is nothing specific about them in the Bible. But if a man's heart is right with God, and if his knowledge is as it ought to be, and his judgment is right, he will not have any great trouble to find out on which side of any common question of the day he ought to stand.

A great many of our people are greatly pestered by

theatres and dancing and card-playing, and the like of that. They say in their confusion and in their anxiety, "Where is there anything in the Scriptures against these things?" Well, they are in a greatly unseasoned condition spiritually. Nobody doubts when he gets on the platform where Paul wrote this letter to the Philippian church. Nobody doubts which way the theatre is going: it is of the earth, earthy; and there is not a spiritually minded man or woman between the seas that doesn't know it. Nobody doubts where the ball-room stands: it is of the earth, earthy; it is of the flesh, the world, and the devil. Every spiritually minded person knows where it stands and what stands for it. "That ye may approve things that are excellent." It is not excellent, is it?

I recall that some years ago I was interviewed by two ladies on this very subject. One of them was a church-member; the other was not. They were both very elegant ladies. This very question of the ball-room was brought up, and my opinion asked. I can sum up what was said in a very few words. The church-member said she did not feel that it was wrong. I said to her, "All right; but the next time you get dressed for a ball, while you are waiting for your escort, you open your Bible at the twelfth chapter of Romans and read that chapter right through: 'I beseech you therefore, brethren, by the mercies of God, that ye present your bodies a living sacrifice, holy, acceptable unto God, which is your reasonable service. And be not conformed to this world: but be ye transformed,' and so on. Then get on your knees and ask God to bless you and bless the ball, and bless the ball to you, and to everybody there." The other lady, who was not a member of the church, broke out laughing. She said afterward, "I was not laughing at you; I was laughing at how ridiculous Cousin Dona would look, on her knees, asking God to bless her and bless the ball." They are things that do not go together, and will not hold fellowship with each other.

Thousands of questions are coming up all the time, and a man ought to be elevated enough in his spiritual life to discern the quality of things and to approve the things that are excellent.

Then we are to be sincere. That is a very fine quality for the Christian. To tell the truth; to be honest enough not to say, "I am not able to give" when he is; not to say, "I cannot go to prayer meeting," when he just does not want to go; not to say, "I cannot do this or that," when the real reason is, he does not want to do it; but to be perfectly sincere and open before God, being filled with the fruits of righteousness to the praise and glory of God.

It was one of the first thoughts in my spiritual life that I should be saved. Of course, we cannot help it—nobody can help thinking about that. I think now I am going to be saved, and my heart is resting on that. I know one thing for a certainty; I am not going to be saved because I am worthy to be saved. But my feet are on the rock, and I expect to stand there. I am not thinking now so much about being saved; I am thinking about heaven. I feel that I am going to a city, now only a little way off. I can see the spires yonder, I am so close; and I am not sorry it is close, not sorry at all. Brethren, the thought in my mind now is, that I shall fill up all the remaining days of my life with the fruits of righteousness, living the life of service that God will help me to live, so that when I come into the presence of my divine Lord and Master, I may be like a transplanted tree borne down with fruit, and not like a tree with leaves and no fruit.

I may not see you again until we meet before God's great throne. May the Lord Jesus preserve your souls, and sanctify you, and help you, and fill you with his Spirit. For Jesus' sake I ask it. Amen.

LANSING BURROWS, son of J. L. Burrows, D. D., was born in Philadelphia, Pa., April 10, 1843. He was taken while a young child to Richmond, Va., and there at the age of fifteen years he joined the First Baptist Church, of which his father was pastor. He entered Wake Forest College in 1859, and though prevented by the war from graduating in 1862, was graduated by the faculty when the institution reopened. In 1867 was married to Miss Lulie S. Rochester, of Stanford, Ky., and the same year was ordained to the ministry. In 1872 Princeton and Madison Universities gave him the degree of A.M., and Bethel College, Ky., that of D. D. in 1882. He has held important pastorates North and South, and is now pastor of the First Baptist Church, Augusta, Ga. As secretary of the Convention since 1881, he has won great praise by the promptness and proficiency with which he, together with his associate, Dr. O. F. Gregory, has each year issued the Minutes of the body. He is also the skillful editor of the Baptist Year-Book, the most valuable statistical handbook possessed by the denomination. Few men among us preach more of the gospel, or the gospel with more power, than does Dr. Burrows.

Lansing Burrows, D. D.

XVII

UNBELIEVING BRETHREN [1]

BY LANSING BURROWS, D. D.

"For neither did his brethren believe in him." John 7 : 5.

THAT must have been a great sorrow to Jesus. While he came to be "despised and rejected of men," it would seem peculiarly hard to be despised and rejected of his own kindred. The family tie among the Jews was always very strong. It is now; the Hebrew is a model of family affection. He may follow the instincts of his father Jacob in his dealings with you on the street, but in his home he is tender and true and loving. His wife and his children are always the handsomest and best, and he delights to shower benefits upon them. The kindred of the Lord ought not to have been exceptional in this virtue.

But they did not believe in him. So the Master became identified with the chief sorrow of many people. There is many a good man whose heart is sore over the waywardness of his children. The sweet and holy schemings to persuade unto like precious faith all go for nothing. Prayers are unavailing, and exhortations, like those of just Lot, only awaken cruel mockings. It is a heavy burden to bear, with the world looking on amazed and wondering what hidden sin has brought forth such nauseous fruit; inquiring with the old short-sightedness as to who the

---

[1] Preached in Foundry M. E. Church, Washington, D. C., during the Jubilee Session of the Southern Baptist Convention. This discourse was delivered in the main without notes, and cannot, therefore, be considered an exact reproduction of what was said on the occasion.

sinner was, **that** such blindness and hardness should follow. With a quiet meekness, **He** who bore **our sorrows,** bore even this mighty sorrow too; among **his own** kindred, those who knew him best, those in **whose** veins flowed the same blood, those were found who gave no heed to him or seemed to care for him.

They knew much about him. They **were** not strangers. His doctrine was no new thing to **them.** He was always full of gentle admonition, and sometimes addressed them with great plainness of speech; **as** when he says to them in this connection, "Your time is always ready; the world cannot hate you." There was so much in common with them and the world, that the caviling, persecuting spirit had no fault to find with them. They could go to feasts or anywhere else, and nobody would trouble them. But all those years, the history of which is hidden from us, they **had** been with him; they had seen his sweet childhood and his guileless youth and the majesty of his budding adolescence, all marked by patience and unrestrained piety—the richest piety of all, that of the home and in the family circle. Then they had seen the beginning of his wonderful works; the marriage at Cana of Galilee was probably **a** family affair; at least, they were all with him, and saw what he did. They saw his wonderful works, for they urged him to go and show what things he could do to other people. They were very astute with their advice. They said in effect: "What is the use of doing these things **in a** corner; go out in the wide world and let people **see** what a great man you are; you have impressed some folks; **you** have disciples in Judea who ought to see **more** of you; go to them and make sure of them, lest they waver in their faith in you."

All this is very surprising **to** us. They must have heard the **talk** concerning the wonderful happenings attendant upon his birth; the song of angels and the adoration of wise men; **and the** testimony **of** their aged kinsman, Zacharias, and that of Anna and Simeon and Elisabeth and their cousin John, the ascetic preacher of the wilderness. Now all these things that are strong evidences to us were supplemented by his blameless life, his earnest ministry, his just and perfect character, his unfailing power of wonder-working. How could it be that they failed to believe in him? It was most surprising, was it not?

I. These "brethren" have their counterpart to-day. I suppose that a strict exegesis would not permit us to trace a similarity between these kinsmen of the flesh and us, who are his brethren because given power to become the sons of God through faith in his name. I do not insist on such interpretation, although "brethren" is a title of his own choosing. He has taught us to say, "Our Father," and for him "the whole family in heaven and earth is named"; and the chief distinction he confers on us is in the fact that "he is not ashamed to call them (us) brethren."

But we are in such a position to him as were these brethren according to the flesh. If anything, the position is better. Once a woman blessed the mother who bore him, and he said that they that heard the word of God and kept it were more blessed. Once his kindred sought him and a superserviceable person interrupted his discourse by telling him that they were without desiring to speak with him; and you recall how with impassioned eloquence he bent his hands over his disciples and exclaimed, "These are my mother and my brethren." It is a greater thing to believe in Christ than to be merely allied to him by ties of kinship. What is outward is not so much as that which is inward.

The important matter is this: you are brought into very close contact with him. You know him, you see him, you understand his word with less difficulty of understanding than men have ever experienced.

All the light of the centuries clusters about him and his mission and his doctrine. He has been attacked by the learning of all ages, and the truth still stands. There has not been a single opposition that has not been met. There can be no new argument against him. The latest forms of doubt and unholy criticism are but borrowed from men that died a hundred years ago. We know more about him than those who saw him with their eyes and heard him with their ears. The accumulation of testimony is simply amazing. The numbers who have been converted by the power of his Spirit, the rough, unlikely natures that have been changed, the trophies won by the power of the cross, the millions who say, "Thou art the Christ," where once a single voice proclaimed him, all of these are occasions of belief that even his own kindred failed to possess.

And yet, with this richness, the difficulty of yielding him an implicit trust is great. We believe him and do not the things that he says. We hear him and yet doubt. We listen to his command and yet follow not, or with halting and uncertain steps. We know his power and yet fail to lay hold of the arm of his strength. In the midst of his unfailing supply we go wretched with hunger and paralyzed with fear and barren when we should be abundant with fruit. Faith in him is still the pressing need of discipleship. The want of faith in him is the occasion of the church's somnolence, and is the secret of whatever inefficiency may be justly attributed to her. The absence of thrilling testimony, the self-satisfied languor in view of opportunity, the insidious thought of self-ministry, all spring out of the fruitful matrix of unbelief. Like his brethren, we desire that he shall show yet other wonders, while we leave untried the victorious power of a faith that overcomes the world and makes us the workers of wonders.

II. The occasion of the unbelief of his brethren is

the occasion of our unbelief. I mean by that we have, as had those brethren, mistaken conceptions of his work. You have often heard in what great error they were concerning his Messiahship. What pictures of temporal grandeur they drew! a restored Israel, a rebuilt temple, a majestic kingdom! They wanted him to go to Judea; for what? To set up a kingdom that should outstrip the world for greatness. What was the use of his miracle-power if he could not do something great? Miracles? He was using his power only to heal people and to feed them and calm them. Why not take the rule from the oppressor? Why not blast the intruder? When they saw he would not do this, they did not believe in him. Ah, if they only had a kinsman who would do as they wished. If their ideas could be carried out, why, they would be princes and dukes, and live in palaces, and roll in luxury and abound in wealth. This was what they wanted. In place of power and grandeur and wealth and luxury, he was giving them self-denial and service. So they did not believe in him.

You may trace a resemblance. Men compliment Jesus, they speak of his wonderful works, they admire his character, they even profess his name and become of the body of his disciples and pay some regard to his institutions and ordinances. But some of his plainest commands are disregarded, some of his doctrines are pronounced uninviting, and some others are said to be out of date. Too much stress is laid upon self-denial, too much said about charity, too much importance attached to non-essential matters. It is folly to attempt so much as the gospel declares; the Sabbath must not be too strictly kept; the tithe is a matter of an exploded system; the evangelization of the world is a ridiculous impossibility; to say nothing of separation from the world, or of laying down life for men, or of bearing injustice and persecution with meekness, or of answering not again the voice of detraction. Oh, **we are** very much like his brethren.

Do you say there is **no** such resemblance? **Let me** ask you, what is your conception of his **work and** mission? No, not **to** the *world*, but to *you?* **Is** it that you shall be saved? Yes, but not all. It **is** not enough to be saved. His thought **is** to create within you his own image. What he intends you **to** be is **a** reproduction of himself. How shall he do that? By setting you up in palatial grandeur, and ministering to your comfort and ease? No, no. He begins by a process of excision. Before he builds up he must tear down. Before he fills you with himself, he must empty you of yourself. When he lays you down upon a bed of suffering, when he darkens your house, when he brings to you **a** cup of bitterness, when he destroys **the** fond idol **of your** life, when he breaks **your** heart and **covers you with** gloom, you cry out in the despairing tones **of** unbelief. Has he not told you, " In the world ye shall have tribulation"? Has he not shown you the patent of heavenly nobility, the mark of divine sonship, not **in** sorrow, but in *scourging?* Because you have not an unruffled joy, **an** abiding comfort, an unfailing prosperity, an answer to every temporal craving, the consummation of every heart-wish, shall you turn upon him as did his brethren, and say to him: "Thou art not what we thought, thou hast not fulfilled the measure of **our** hopes"?

Suppose he did give you the **wish of your** heart, **what** manner of men would you be? **It** is easy to say that you wish to be holy, undefiled, like unto him. The way to this **is** the path **he** trod. For you to be **what** you **say** is your wish, **demands** the denial of Capernaum **and** caviling Jerusalem, and the experiences of Gethsemane with its bloody sweat, and Calvary **with** its unspeakable agonies. Had you his

power, what would you do with it? He never used
it for himself. He went hungry while he fed thousands, and while preparing a mansion for you in his
father's house, had no place whereon to lay his head.
Had you his power you would exert it for yourself or
for those you love. Whose dead would you raise?
Whose hunger would you first appease? Whose eyes
would you open? He raised Lazarus, but Joseph he
did not raise; and while his last thoughts clustered
around his mother he gave her into the hands of loving charity. He never thought of self; really, do we
ever think of much else? With the demolition of
self, with the shattering of hopes, with the crown of
suffering, recognize his faithfulness to his promise,
and perceive the stately steppings of the King coming
to his kingdom, set up in your own hearts.

III. The remedy for this sad condition is an apprehension of the fullness of the gospel. There is one
text that gives me an immense comfort. It is in
Acts, the first chapter and the fourteenth verse. When
the Saviour's expiation for sin was made, when he
had won his victory over the grave, after that he had
ascended on high, then we read how the disciples,
waiting for their enduement at Jerusalem, "continued
with one accord in prayer and supplication, with the
women, and Mary, the mother of Jesus, *and with his
brethren.*"

Ah, then they did believe at last! After Gethsemane and Calvary and Olivet they found their
hearts broken and they believed. Let us keep on
with our preaching and let us be faithful in our testimony, and let us be not weary in our effort, the
time will come when he that goeth forth with weeping will return rejoicing, bearing his sheaves with
him.

Understand the Christ of Calvary, and go and see the
place where the Lord lay. That is the key of belief
in him. So long as these brethren heard his sermons

and saw his works, they found it not to their purpose to believe in him. But when they saw the cross, that was too much for them. My hope for you is in the cross. I do not wonder at your being confused and undecided so long as you think of his teachings, matchless as they are. These sayings of his do trouble ; they amaze, they invite to disputations, and they tempt to explanations, that the keenness of their edge shall be somewhat dulled and be so fitted to our understanding. When there comes to you some saying more forceful than usual, you say, "This is a hard saying, who can understand it?" and you keep quiet until you think you can understand it. When there comes to you a pointed exhortation, you say, "No one is able to do such things," and you lay it aside until you think you can. The result is, a belief of a general sort, with much misgiving and with little power and with less joy and peace. But when following him, though like Peter, "afar off," you see him uncomplaining, pierced through and uplifted as a spectacle of shame, with death creeping over his features, and the head that was always an invitation to trust, bowing into unconsciousness, with eyes no longer mellow and tear-wet, and lips no more opening with gracious words, you find another train of thought quickened within your minds. Do you remember that while he was teaching his disciples, men said "Rabbi," or "Master"? That meant Teacher. But afterward men said "Lord." That meant Ruler, King. Once in a while, under some strong experience, when drawn into a foretaste of what was coming in its fullness, and when the emotions were strongly stirred and the spiritual became dominant over the fleshly, they said "Lord." As, when under its subtle influence the desire to know how to pray took hold upon them, or as when they felt the power of the ever-living bread, they addressed him as Lord, and begged to be taught how to pray, or to be filled with such bread. But after the ascension it was "Lord" all the time, and strengthened as the "Lord Christ" or the "Lord and Saviour Jesus Christ." Oh, Calvary was a great illumination to men's intellects!

If you are content with him as a teacher only, it is not surprising that you will reserve your opinion upon some things, or counsel about them, or desire further light. But if he is to you a Lord, a King, you will do what he says. If he appoints to you sorrow and disappointment, it is the Lord, and he may do as he lists. He bids you follow no different path from that he himself has trodden. He makes you a partaker of his own sufferings. Where you began as an endorser of his maxims, a student of his philosophy, you end as a servant doing his will. He who can die for you, can be more easily obeyed and followed than he who came to teach you of mighty and wondrous things. He who has bought you is more than he who has taught you.

So what you want, brother, is not more information, not more argument, not more explanation. You want your heart broken. Oh, we go about seeking and digging up the remains of buried centuries, and exhuming treasures of learning out of accumulated piles of ruins, and with pride point to them and challenge doubt and unbelief. We have enough. The heart is not going to melt before these silent and unimpeachable witnesses to the truth of the Son of God. No preacher can melt the heart. No witness can do aught but condemn the flinty nature. The cross breaks down our opposition. The cross breaks up the stony indifference. What the world needs is not more knowledge about the Christ of God; it needs to look upon him dying for its sin and misery. That is the antidote for all unbelief in its varying shades and forms. Especially is it the antidote for unbelief where it creeps into the hearts of those who know him best. "Behold the Lamb of

God that taketh **away** the **sin** of the world"; and takes away no **sin so** effectually as that one great damning sin, the sin of unbelief. It was that which our Lord himself declared the source of condemnation, and taking away that he removes all.

Z. T. LEAVELL was born in Pontotoc County, Miss., on the 30th of August, 1847. Attended the University of Mississippi. Was three years a student in the Southern Baptist Theological Seminary. Has preached in Dalton, Ga., Murfreesboro, Tenn., Columbus, Ky., Oxford, Natchez, and Clinton, Miss. Was two years financial secretary of Mississippi College, and five years president of Carrollton Female College, Carrollton, Mississippi. Mississippi College conferred upon him the degree of D.D. in 1895. He is a man of singular piety and fraternal spirit.

XVIII

THE TRIAL OF FAITH[1]

BY Z. T. LEAVELL, D. D.

"That the trial of your faith, being much more precious than of gold that perisheth, though it be tried with fire, might be found unto praise and honor and glory at the appearing of Jesus Christ." 1 Peter 1 : 7.

SURELY there is not a blessing which we receive at the hands of our Heavenly Father that is less appreciated by us than the trial of our faith. It comes to us like the rainy day. There is no one of us who likes the rainy day, with its cloud above and its discomfort beneath. But we all rejoice in the effects of the showers, as they make the earth "bring forth and bud," and give "seed to the sower and bread to the eater." So of the trial God makes of our faith, it has much that is disagreeable, but we all rejoice in the fruitage it may bring. We may come out of it in every way purer and stronger in the Lord.

In the trial God makes of our faith we should see the manifestation of his goodness. He would have us understand that he is simply purposing our welfare, and that he does not chastise us in anger. He says, "Our light affliction, which is but for a moment, worketh for us a far more exceeding and eternal weight of glory"; and "we know that all things work together for good to them that love God." In this connection it is said, "Though now for a season, if need be, ye are in heaviness through manifold temptations." More tenderly it would be impossible

---

[1] Preached in Trinity Methodist Church during the Jubilee Session of the Southern Baptist Convention.

to speak. The loving kindness of our Lord, declared in these and kindred passages, may be discerned by all whose faith he puts to the test.

There are many ways in which God tries the Christian's faith.

He sometimes does this by permitting us to go our own way. Most people get obstinate now and then, however meek their natures may be. They become weary of the performance of duties that follow each other in dull routine, or they are tempted to seek those things not for their good. Our desires are often exceedingly hard to control. Some bright, dazzling object, alluring and fascinating, is beheld by us. It seems to be the one object above all others that would gratify us. More ardent grows the desire until we are permitted to have the object, which we find fire in our possession. Happy are we if thereby we are purged of the dross which was the cause of our temptation.

Sometimes God tries the Christian's faith by more severe means. The trial is not simply a permission to go into the fire; he puts us into it. By a gradual process it may be we become so much enamored by the things of time and sense, as to lose interest in spiritual things and the things that make for our peace. The soul woos and sometimes weds that which God hates. It goes like Samson into Philistia, seeking pleasure rather than worshiping God. The Lord our God is a jealous God and can suffer no such wandering from himself without using the necessary means to bring us back to our first love. We are told that gold is exceedingly fond of quicksilver. When the two come together there is nothing that can separate them but extreme heat. So our souls become so intermingled with the things of time and sense, that God must turn extreme heat upon us that we may be severed from our sordid attachments and return to him.

God sometimes tries our faith by disappointments. There is a constantly recurring pain in a series of disappointments. Everything we attempt fails of the measure of success we wished and had expected. Insignificant, trifling circumstances persist in coming between us and the realization of that for which our soul longs; and this state of things goes on until our patience becomes exhausted, and our hearts grow sick of our fruitless search after gain, and we turn to God for solace. They tell us that in every ton of sea water there is just one grain of gold. By putting a ton of sea water just at the boiling point, the water becomes vapor, and the grain of gold is left. So God sometimes extracts the one grain of gold in the Christian's nature. He is subjected to the heat, and the foreign matter vanishes and the golden grain is left in his presence.

God tries the Christian's faith again by prosperity. This is the severest test. There is nothing harder for a Christian to endure. It is far more damaging to Christian character than affliction or loss. He who can stand with folded arms in mute resignation by the pale form of a loved one and lift his tear-bathed face to heaven with the silent prayer to God in his heart, "Thy will be done," is overthrown at once by prosperity. Prosperity naturally puts one in the ways of the world, and he readily takes to them. Gold earth is sometimes washed in a little rocker like a child's cradle. It is an easy swinging process; noiseless and sleep-provoking. There is a bar in the rocker over which the dross passes and against which the gold gathers. So God sometimes gets at the gold in his people. They are rocked back and forth in the cradle of prosperity. Thanks be to his name, there are some who can endure this test. We have many noble-hearted ones whose piety suffers no diminution by the enlarged prosperity God awards them, and who feel that they are but the trustees of the Lord, holding the means put into their hands for the advancement of his glory.

But why does God try the Christian's faith? Why not let his children go to heaven "on flowery beds of ease," instead of subjecting them to constant trials? There must be good reasons for the tests to which he compels their faith. Not only does God afflict for our profit, but for the strengthening of that within us that is most profitable for the life here and hereafter. He tries us that "the proof of our faith may appear more precious than refined gold that is tested by fire," as the Syriac translation puts it. The proof of our faith, or our tested faith, is more precious than refined gold. It will be very difficult to make the world see this, but it is true. Some men contemn Christianity because it lays so much stress on faith. But strong, tested faith is basal in human happiness and usefulness. Such a faith gives no room in the mind for distrust. Faith in the soul gives what no external circumstances can bring. You have doubtless read that beautiful little poem written by Mrs. Hemans, which portrays the King of England after his only son was drowned:

> He sat when festal bowls went round,
>   He heard the minstrel sing,
> He saw the tourney victor crowned
>   Amid the mighty ring.
> But a murmur of the restless deep
>   Was blent on every strain,
> A voice of wind that would not sleep;
>   He never smiled again.

His external circumstances were perfect, and yet so indescribably sad was he that not even a smile was seen upon his face after his great bereavement.

But faith is a fundamental principle in the happiness of the many as well as the individual. It gives cement to the compact of society. Let us see how this is. Conceive of a community of people living together in neighborly proximity utterly destitute of faith in each other. Neither man, woman, nor child has any faith in any other of the entire population. The conception puts before us a condition of extremest anarchy. You might take all the gold of Ophir and empty it into the laps of that people, and it would not produce happiness. A tested faith in the affairs of life and much more in religion is as an element so basic that naught can surpass it in value.

Again, a tested faith has an absolute intrinsic worth which gold has not. The lack of established intrinsic worth in gold and silver gives the problem with which statesmen have to grapple in settling the question of the day. How can a parity of coinage be secured so long as the metals fluctuate in amount and so in value? This question of parity between the metals is a question that might be settled if their intrinsic worth could be determined by their amount being constant and known. But a tested faith has an absolute intrinsic worth. Its value is inherent, independent of outward conditions. Large increment of it not only does not depreciate its value, but increases it. The more of it there is the more it is worth. Let it be multiplied till countless multitudes possess it and its worth has been magnified in that God's praises are sung over all the earth and the best of happiness is insured for his people.

Once more, a tested faith is eternal, and gold is not. Let it be known that the discovery of America was a financial necessity. At the time America was discovered there was only a sufficiency of gold gotten from the mines of the Old World to repair *the loss* in handling and manufacture. There was no increase in the amount of gold in the world because of the natural waste of the precious metal. There is no waste in the using of a tried faith in God. On the contrary, the more it is used the larger it is. Nor will the fires of the last great day melt it nor depreciate its value. It will go beyond the things of time and sense into the world of unfading light and shine with undimmed lustre after the earth has dissolved in fervid heat.

But this is only a subjective view of the worth of a faith tried and tested by the Lord in the ordeals of life. Our text paraphrased, says that the proof of our faith may appear more precious than refined gold that is tested by fire unto glory and honor and praise at the manifestation of Jesus the world's Redeemer. We are told that he is coming a second time to manifest his glory. When he comes the tried faith of his people will appear to his praise and honor and majesty. In our happiest spiritual moods we wish to do something to show our gratitude to our Saviour for what he has done for us. This is the spiritual outgoing of the generous soul. Much may be done in many lines of effort to show this gratitude. We are blessed with a broad field over which we may perform the labors of love. But in nothing can we glorify our Master better than to submit to the purifying, polishing tests that are made of our faith. When Christ shall come to make up his jewels our proven faith will appear to his praise and honor and glory. It is not so much what we do, as what we are, that heaven takes delight in. It is the development of the soul gotten in labor that Christ wants more than the labor itself. Before the angels our Saviour shall have praise and adoration not for what we have done, but what we are, standing in the grand review with a faith so shaped by the discipline of human life as to elicit their admiration. Then let us kiss the rod that smites us and patiently wait till the coming morn of the resurrection to glorify our Saviour with a faith that is perfect and complete.

Our tried faith shall be to the praise of our Saviour. It is to the praise of the United States that we do not have our currency in gold ore and bullion. Our gold eagle has passed its ordeal of heat and the die, and comes forth most shapely current coin of the realm. And it shall be to the praise of our Lord that we do not appear at the last day in a crude state, but that we have passed our ordeal, and have come through it shapely and with the image of our adorable Lord stamped on us, so that when he shall appear we shall be like him.

At the last great day our tried faith shall be an honor to Christ. It is an honor to the refiner that he takes the gold in its original condition, with sixty per cent. of adulteration, and brings it out twenty-four carats fine. And before God's assembled hosts it shall be to the honor of Christ that he has taken humanity with all its adulterations, "dead in trespasses and in sins," and made it meet for an inheritance in the world of light. It is said that the question shall be asked of some who shall appear in that day of accounts, "Who are these?" The answer shall be given, "These are they that have come up through great tribulation, and washed their robes and made them white in the blood of the Lamb."

Finally, the proven faith of the Christian shall in the judgment day be the glory of Christ. What is England's glory? It is not in the fact that the sun never sets on its broad empire. It is not in her great bank, though it is true that there is nowhere else such wealth. England's glory is in England's purified, refined intelligence—in England's Disraelis and Gladstones, her Miltons and Tennysons, her Spurgeons and Wesleys.

In the day of assize the glory of our Saviour will not be in the fact that he is one with the Father and was present when our world was made, when the morning stars sang together; but his glory will be in the purified ones who stand ready to enter a world of unfading light and unbroken love.

What a support is such a faith in the trying emergencies of life. It is a staff on which the soul may lean; it is an anchor when tempests rage without. And how dark is death without it. How dreary the last moments of life to one who cannot rest his weary head by faith on the bosom of his God! How sweet and cheerful its presence to the departing Christian! I have stood and looked at the evening star as it has sunk beneath the western horizon. I have seen it as it has gone down in darkness, and left the world in deeper darkness, and have thought, how much like the death of the one who faces the last issue of life without faith in God through Christ. It is a going down in darkness to leave the world with no ray of light cast back for those left behind. I have taken pleasure in looking on the morning star. I have seen it as it has risen over the eastern hills. I have seen it as it has faded away in the brighter light of the glorious sun of day, and I have thought, how much like the death of the Christian. No going out in darkness to leave the world in gloom, but a fading away in the light of the Sun of Righteousness. God grant a saving faith to all whose eyes fall on these printed pages, as a support in life, a solace in death, and as a watchword at the portals of eternal bliss.

M. B. WHARTON is a native of Virginia, and was converted in Alexandria at the age of eighteen. He is a graduate of Richmond College. The degree of D. D. was conferred upon him by Washington and Lee University. Dr. Wharton has served some of the largest churches of the Baptist denomination South, and has throughout been identified with its general work. With a bright intellect, fine oratorical power, rich imagination, extraordinary memory, and a good degree of energy, he has always succeeded. Wide reading, close study of men, and extensive travel, have made him a man of varied gifts. Besides conspicuous success as a preacher and pastor, he has achieved distinction as an author. He is at present pastor of the Freemason Street Baptist Church, Norfolk, Va., the largest Baptist church in that growing seaport city.

M. B. Wharton, D. D.

XIX[1]

THE RESURRECTION OF CHRIST

BY M. B. WHARTON, D. D.

"Then were the disciples glad when they saw the Lord." **John 20 : 20.**

SOME years ago, while spending the summer at Tallulah Falls, Georgia, amid scenery as grand and picturesque as any to be found this side the Alps, I had descended to the "Grand Chasm," fifteen hundred feet deep, through which flows Tallulah River with its wonderful cataracts. Lying down upon one of the large flat rocks so common on the sides of that stream, and looking upward through solid granite gorges and over lofty and frightful precipices, I asked a skeptical companion, "Who made all this?" My friend responded, "God made all this; only God could make it; and if you will only convince me of the resurrection of Jesus Christ I will be a Christian. That is the tunnel which, once cut through these granite formations that speak so eloquently of God, every train of Bible thought and doctrine could pass successfully through. Do not preach of God; the whole earth is full of his glory, but preach of the resurrection of Jesus Christ."

He was right as to the importance of this subject. The resurrection of Jesus Christ is the pivotal truth of Christianity, the basal principle around which all its doctrines resolve. The word of God declares this in no uncertain language. Preaching is important,

---

[1] Delivered at Calvary Baptist Church, Washington, D. C., during the Jubilee Session of the Southern Baptist Convention.

and the congregations of Washington are all aglow to-day as representatives of our Convention are holding forth to them the word of life. From the time of Christ to the present moment the world has been swayed by earnest preaching, and to take away preaching is like robbing the world of light which enables men to know each other, work, and live. But "if Christ be not risen then is our preaching vain." Faith is important, indispensable to our happiness, enables us to overcome the world; millions have died in it, and millions would die for it; but "if Christ be not raised your faith is vain." Sin is an awful thing, the author of all the woes burdened with which the whole creation groaneth and travaileth in pain together until now; but if Christ be not risen "ye are yet in your sins." So that the most important question we can consider this morning is the resurrection of Christ. And I think I am prepared to show that he did arise, that our preaching is not vain; your faith not vain; you are not in your sins; but may joyfully exclaim, "Blessed be the God and Father of our Lord Jesus Christ, which according to his abundant mercy hath begotten us again unto a lively hope by the resurrection of Jesus Christ from the dead, to an inheritance incorruptible and undefiled, and that fadeth not away, reserved in heaven for you who are kept by the power of God through faith unto salvation." I do not know a more appropriate text to guide in the discussion than the one announced: "Then were the disciples glad when they saw the Lord." Just two questions are suggested:

1. Did the disciples see the Lord?
2. Why were they glad when they saw him?

First, we have in proof of the resurrection of Christ, presumptions arising from the empty grave. While infidels deny the resurrection of Christ, they have never denied that he died; on the contrary, they have thrown it up to Christians as an opprobrium that their divine leader had to die. They cannot see how it was that he was compelled to die to save a lost and ruined world, and say his death was a refutation of his claim. Neither do they deny that his grave was found empty on the third day. Had it not been empty his enemies would have produced the body to show that the story of the resurrection was false. The fact that the grave was empty gives a strong presumption in favor of his resurrection. If he did not rise his body must have been stolen by his disciples. Men do not rob graves without some selfish purpose in view. The body of A. T. Stewart was stolen that a large sum might be obtained for its restoration. But why should the disciples have wished by stealing the body of Jesus to perpetuate an imposture which was costing them their property and their lives? They cannot be supposed to have been so foolish as that course would indicate. But if, in order to palm off a false story, thus expensive to themselves, they had wished to rob the grave they could not have done so. They were a weak and timid set, one denying the Saviour before a servant girl, and all forsaking him in presence of his enemies. Would those men have attempted to face a guard of Roman soldiers when they knew that death would be the consequence? But the story went out that the body was stolen while the soldiers were asleep. Roman soldiers never slept on their posts. When in Pompeii, my guide at the Herculaneum gate showed me a sentry box in which the skeleton remains of a Roman soldier were found. He was placed on duty on that ever-memorable night, and while the flood of lava was pouring on the city, while men and women were flying, he kept his post, and more than seventeen hundred years afterward was found, one hand over his mouth to keep out the dust and ashes, and the other grasping his rusty sword.

No, these Roman soldiers did not sleep on their posts. Augustine well says, "If they were asleep, how could they testify that the disciples stole the body?" for no man can testify to what happens while he is asleep.

But we are not left to presumptions but have the testimony of the apostles. This testimony is of the most incontrovertible kind, whether we consider the nature and number of the witnesses, the facts they testified to, the places where they deposed, or the time when their statements were made. Who were these witnesses? Not scholars, theorists, and philosophers. Not men of such great ability as to be able to make "the worse appear the better reason," but unlearned Galilean fishermen and tentmakers, who had never been known to advance an idea they had not received from some one else. How many of these witnesses were there? The principle has been laid down that in the mouth of two or three witnesses every word may be established. We have here not two or three, but many hundreds. He was seen of Mary Magdalene, of the two disciples whose hearts burned within them as they conversed with him on the way to Emmaus. He was seen of Cephas, then of the twelve; after that, he was seen of above five hundred brethren at once; ... after that he was seen of James; then of all the apostles; "and last of all," says Paul, "he was seen of me also, as of one born out of due time." We can think of not less than ten occasions when Christ was seen by different persons after his resurrection from the dead, all of the witnesses testifying to the one simple, unvarnished, tangible fact, that Christ had risen from the dead.

Where did they tell this story? Was it in a foreign land? Was it among a heathen people who might be willing to believe a fanciful report, and who had no means of investigating its truth or falsehood? No, they told this wondrous story at Jerusalem where the terrible deed of the crucifixion had taken place.

They told it on the very spot where he had been condemned, where scribes and Pharisees had hounded him to death; they told it over the empty grave in which his body had been deposited.

When did they tell it? Did they wait until the popular mind had turned to other subjects? Shrewd lawyers ask for time when they have a bad case on their hands. Grant them time enough, and they can save almost any one from the gallows, for they know that

> As from the wing no scar the sky retains,
> The parted wave no furrow from the keel,
> So dies in human hearts the thought of death.

These witnesses might have waited for five or ten years and had a better chance of palming off upon the people the story of a resurrection that never occurred. But they did not wait to tell the truth. They told it as soon as he had risen, within three days of the time that he was buried, while the people who slew him were still filled with rage against him, and while the cruel cross was still stained with his blood.

To whom did they tell it? To peasants, to strangers not interested in the wondrous details, to each other? They told it to all who listened—to Jews, heathen, to magistrates before whom they were summoned, to governors, to Cæsar himself. They told this story when they knew they would be despised, imprisoned, tortured, and crucified for its telling.

Could it have been anything else than a true story? Was such testimony ever rejected in an earthly court on any other subject? One day in Montgomery, Ala., I was approached by a prominent lawyer who said, "If you will prove to me that Jesus Christ rose from the dead, I will become a Christian and join your church." "What sort of evidence do you wish?" I asked. He replied, "I will take any good evidence such as would be admitted by our courts." "Very well," said I; "who is your greatest authority on evidence?" He replied, "Greenleaf." "If Greenleaf should pronounce the evidence good, you will be satisfied, will you?" He responded, "I will." "Then I must tell you," I said, "that Greenleaf not only wrote his great work on 'The Law of Evidence,' but in 1846 he published an 'Examination of the Testimony of the Four Evangelists, by the Rules of Evidence as Administered in Courts of Justice, with an Account of the Trial of Jesus,' in which he says that the testimony in behalf of the resurrection of Jesus is so conclusive that no twelve sane jurors in the world could do otherwise than pronounce in favor of it." Still he did not yield, for,

> Convince a man against his will
> He's of the same opinion still.

We have still further in favor of the resurrection of Christ what may be styled demonstrations. The Holy Spirit came down to assist the apostles in preaching the doctrine of the resurrection. Behold that great assembly on the day of Pentecost, an audience of many thousands, consisting of Jews and strangers. This vast audience was addressed by men unlettered and unknown. What did they say? "You think we are fanatics and madmen; that we are endeavoring to palm off an imposture upon you all; that we are liars, who say we have seen a man whom we have not seen, eaten with a man with whom we have not eaten, touched and handled a man who has no existence. You think we are such fools as to tell these stories at the expense of our fortunes and our lives; but we are going to convince you to-day. Bring forth your sick and afflicted and we will heal them in proof of the resurrection. We will give hearing to the deaf, sight to the blind, life to the dead. We, illiterate mechanics, who cannot speak our own mother tongue correctly, will talk to all of you, Medes, Elamites, Mesopotamians, Cappadocians, Phrygians, Pamphylians, Romans, Cretes, Arabians, in your own tongues; we will speak to you in the polished and polite languages of the earth." And thus they did, when three thousand of the very men who had taken and with wicked hands slain the Saviour were cut to the heart and converted. The evidence is so irrefragable that the great wonder is that all did not believe in the resurrection of Christ. But there are still people who do not believe the world is round, but flat. Multitudes believe that the sun moves. Why is it that men do not believe in the emblematic resurrection—immersion? This liquid grave was ordained as an emblem of the place where the Lord lay. "Know ye not, that so many of us as were baptized into Jesus Christ were baptized into his death? Therefore we are buried with him by baptism into death: that like as Christ was raised up from the dead by the glory of the Father, even so we also should walk in newness of life. For if we have been planted together in the likeness of his death, we shall be also in the likeness of his resurrection." Why do not men believe in the monumental resurrection? Here is a grand monument on the banks of the Potomac, one of the tallest shafts in the world, commemorative of the man who won the proudest and the finest of all earthly titles—Father of his country. His name is not on it, but you know it is Washington's monument. But in the holy Sabbath we have a tall, white, graceful monument to the resurrection of Christ; his name is on it; it was changed to and called "the Lord's Day," because Christ rose on it. And yet there are millions who do not believe in it, and millions more who do not keep it holy. Oh, it is true, gloriously true, forever true, that the disciples saw the Lord; but

2. Why were they glad when they saw him? (1) They were glad just as you and I would be glad in

meeting a dear friend whom we had supposed dead. I was at Monteagle, Tenn., a few years ago. A lady received a telegram that her brother was dying; how great was her distress! She sped to his home in anguish and tears. On reaching the spot she was glad to see him restored—not dead, but living. I was standing at a railroad depot in the South, just after the war, conversing with one who had been a general in that hard-fought struggle. As the train drew up, a young man stood upon the platform who, as soon as he saw the general, leaped into his arms. The general exclaimed, "Oh, William, my son, I am so glad to see you," and he wept tears of joy. Turning to the crowd he said, "This young man was on my staff, and I saw him killed, as I thought, on the field of battle, and now to think he is alive." He was glad when he saw him. The disciples, many of whom did not know that Christ would rise, had seen him laid in the grave; the three days had been days of sorrow and gloom. Now that he had come forth no words could express their joy at seeing him whom they loved with all the devotion of their ardent natures.

But they were glad because Christianity had stood the severe test to which it had been subjected. Christ was frequently asked to give a sign to the people, which he refused to do. "He answered and said unto them, An evil and adulterous generation seeketh after a sign; and there shall no sign be given to it, but the sign of the prophet Jonas: for as Jonas was three days and three nights in the whale's belly; so shall the Son of man be three days and three nights in the heart of the earth." All this had come true. He had entered the mansion of the dead, "and struggling there and in his grave clothes with the tyrant had wrested from his brow his black diadem, wrenched from his hand his cruel sceptre, shivered at a blow his skeleton empire, and rising brought life and immortality to light."

They were glad for another great reason. They saw in the resurrection of Christ an earnest of their own resurrection. We love our bodies, though they may not always be lovable to others. We are fond of these tenements where our immortal spirits dwell, these caskets which contain the precious jewels of our souls. We love the bodies of our friends and loved ones here. Sad indeed is the moment when we put them into silence and darkness; sadder still the thought of their moulding to decay and dust. But Christ's resurrection gives us the assurance that these bodies will be ours again and as immortal as our souls. "Christ the firstfruits and afterward they that are Christ's at his coming." We look with pity on those who have no such hopes.

> Alas for him who never sees
> The stars shine through his cypress trees,
> Who hopeless lays his dead away,
> Nor looks to see the breaking day
> About the mournful marble play;
> Who has not felt in hours of faith,
> The truth to flesh and sense unknown,
> That life is ever lord of death,
> And love can never lose its own.

They were glad because now the sting of death was forever taken away. Up to that moment he was the king of terrors. Henceforth he could be welcomed as a friend, and all because of this conquest of Jesus. The thoughts henceforth which a Christian should indulge in his expiring moments would be not those of dread of this ghastly monarch, but of praise to the heavenly Conqueror who had delivered him from his power. No wonder he shouts: "The sting of death is sin; and the strength of sin is the law. But thanks be to God, which giveth us the victory through our Lord Jesus Christ." A lady visiting the Paris Exposition lay dying in her hotel far away from her home and the friends of her youth. Watchers stood around anxious to catch any word which might escape her lips. At last they heard her whisper, "Bring." They placed her child by her side. She still said, "Bring." They brought her flowers and refreshing water. They were puzzled to know what she meant. At last summoning all her strength, while a smile played over her face, she exclaimed:

> Bring forth the royal diadem
> And crown him Lord of all,

and so expired in the arms of him who died for her and rose again.

They were glad because heaven was assured to them. Had that stone not been rolled away from the door of the sepulchre, there had been no admittance through the gates of light; had Christ remained in the grave, no human soul had ever entered heaven. The heavenly inheritance is a reward for his rising. Standing by his grave he said: "Touch me not; for I am not yet ascended to my Father: but go to my brethren, and say unto them, I ascend unto my Father, and your Father; and to my God, and your God." And he did ascend, escorted by a company of angels to the right hand of the Father. Where our Forerunner has gone we shall go. He has gone to make ready for our coming. He says, "In my Father's house are many mansions. . . I go to prepare a place for you, . . that where I am, there ye may be also."

Lastly, they were glad because now they might look forward to the universal triumph of the gospel. With such a doctrine as that attested by such proofs the word of God must of necessity grow and multiply. All that was necessary was to tell the story. This they did. They ran from one to another with the glad news, and "the voice of rejoicing and salvation was in the tabernacles of the righteous."

We of the Southern Baptist Convention have been telling this story for fifty years. During this time we have raised one million five hundred thousand dollars, and sent forth nearly four hundred missionaries to foreign lands, to say nothing of native assistants and work done among the people in our great country. Let us continue to tell it with unwonted zeal and interest till China shall become a celestial empire indeed, till "Ethiopia shall stretch forth her hands unto God"; till Japan shall go forth conquering in a holy war; till Mexico, Italy, and Brazil shall escape the fetters of superstition,

> And Cuba, fair Cuba, the queen of Antilles,
>   No longer by minions of popery awed,
> Comes sweet as her roses and pure as her lilies,
>   To be crowned by her Saviour, Redeemer, and Lord;
> Till from scarlet adornments as venal as bright,
>   She turns to be clothed with the garments of light.

Yea, let us tell this wondrous story "till the dwellers on the hills and in the vales shout to each other, and the mountain tops from distant mountains catch the flying joy—till nation after nation taught the strain, earth rolls the rapturous hosanna round."

XX

THE FIRST RESURRECTION[1]

BY REV. J. L. WHITE

"But the rest of the dead lived not again until the thousand years were finished. This is the first resurrection. Blessed and holy is he that hath part in the first resurrection: on such the second death hath no power, but they shall be priests of God and of Christ, and shall reign with him a thousand years." Rev. 20 : 5, 6.

THE doctrine of the resurrection is fundamental. Paul says, "But if there be no resurrection of the dead, then is Christ not risen; and if Christ be not risen, then is our preaching vain, and your faith is also vain. Yea, and we are found false witnesses of God; because we have testified of God that he raised up Christ; whom he raised not up, if so be that the dead rise not. . . . And if Christ be not raised, your faith is vain; ye are yet in your sins. Then they also which are fallen asleep in Christ are perished. . . . But now is Christ risen from the dead, and become the firstfruits of them that slept." Our preaching is not vain, our faith is not vain, our sins can be forgiven, our hope is steadfast.

This doctrine will never lose its sweetness as long as death follows life. It will be a consolation to the mother who watches her babe lowered into the grave, to the child who holds the hand of the precious mother till it is cold in death. That is a beautiful thought of the Israelites. As they enter the vault, taking a turf of grass, they wave it over their heads saying in

---

[1] Preached at Vermont Avenue Christian Church, Washington, D. C., during the Jubilee Session of the Southern Baptist Convention.

Rev. J. L. White

J. L. WHITE was born September 6, 1862, in Forsyth County, N. C. He was converted at sixteen years of age, and at seventeen was making a reputation in his State as "the boy preacher." Was graduated from Wake Forest College June, 1886, receiving the A. M. degree. While in college he was successively debater and orator, and at his graduation was valedictorian of his class. His first pastorate was the First Baptist Church, Raleigh, N. C. He has since served the church at Elizabeth City, First Church, Durham, First Church, Ashville, N. C ; and on February 1, became pastor of the First Church, Macon, Ga. In all of these charges he has been eminently successful, hundreds having been inducted into the membership, and the zeal and efficiency of the churches greatly promoted. He is in great demand for evangelistic service. To his own gifts is added those of his wife, to whom he was married in 1886. She is a woman of many excellencies of character and marked consecration to Christ.

chorus, "Thy bones shall flourish like the grass; oh, yes, my brother, thy bones shall flourish like the grass." Holding God's word in my hand, I proclaim, Resurrection! Resurrection!

There are to be two resurrections: one of the just, one of the unjust. These shall occur at different times with an interval of one thousand years. The first is the resurrection of the bodies of the just; the second is the raising of the wicked dead, or the resurrection unto judgment.

There is quite a difference of opinion as to what the first resurrection is. Some commentators, notably Albert Barnes, hold the opinion that the first resurrection is *the resurrection of principles*—of patience, courage, boldness, and constancy of the ancient martyrs. Mr. Barnes says that these principles have been buried. Surely this great man looked on the dark side. He is wide of the mark. There are as true men and women living to-day as the world has ever seen. Thousands would not count their lives dear were there occasions for testing their fidelity to Christ by trials. It is not then a resurrection of virtues.

Some few hold that the first resurrection means *regeneration*. There are many difficulties attending this rendering which are insurmountable. The language of the text forbids such a translation. Ἔζησαν, "they lived," is never applied in the New Testament to the soul disembodied, but to *man* in his complete condition of the body, soul, and spirit. Ἀνάστασις, "first resurrection," defines the living to be bodily reanimation, and the word always signifies in the New Testament, corporeal resurrection. The text teaches that there are to be two literal resurrections of the dead.

I. The just shall rise first. The text is sufficient proof. But the belief in the doctrine does not rest solely on this *one passage*. The interpretation of this

Scripture is in line with, and gives special and beautiful significance to many otherwise inexplicable declarations in the word of God.

1. The righteous shall be raised at Christ's second coming (1 Cor. 15 : 23). "But every man in his own order; Christ the firstfruits; afterward, they that are Christ's at his coming."

A different order in the resurrection is declared, and only those who are Christ's are to be raised at this time of his coming again. This is in perfect harmony with the blessed truth of the Lamb's marriage which shall occur at his second appearing (1 Thess. 4 : 14-17). In these verses there is no mention of but one class being raised, "those which sleep in Jesus will God bring with him." "For the Lord himself shall descend from heaven with a shout, with the voice of the archangel and with the trump of God: and the dead in Christ shall *rise first.* Then we which are alive and remain shall be caught up together with them in the clouds, to meet the Lord in the air; and so shall we ever be with the Lord." Blessed consummation of our hopes! Awakened out of sleep to behold our dear Lord and to enter into his joys! This is the peculiar honor of the redeemed. The rest of the dead, those who die without hope, live not for a thousand years.

2. Jesus made a sharp distinction between the general resurrection of the dead and the resurrection which some should be accounted worthy to attain to. In Luke 14 : 13, 14, Christ says, "But when thou makest a feast, call the poor, the maimed, the lame, the blind, and thou shalt be blessed; for they cannot recompense thee: for thou shalt be recompensed at the resurrection *of the just.*" Does our Lord teach *only* the resurrection of the just? No, verily. He explicitly teaches that all shall rise. Most certainly, however, he separates the dead, declaring a resurrection of the just at a time distinct from that of those

raised unto damnation. Jesus in his reply to the Sadducees makes the distinction (Luke 20 : 34, 35). The children of this age marry, but they who shall be accounted worthy to attain that world and the resurrection from the dead shall not marry. A resurrection of those worthy or of the just is referred to. In John 6 : 39, 40, 44, Christ lays emphasis upon the resurrection of just one class, namely, those who have become his own through redemption. The lost are not mentioned. They of course shall be raised, but evidently at a different time and in a different order.

3. The preposition used in the original confirms this rendering. The resurrection of the just is always spoken of as the resurrection *from* (ἐκ νεκρῶν) the dead, and whenever the general resurrection is mentioned, it is the resurrection *of* (without ἐκ) the dead. The first literally means *out from among the dead*, implying that all the dead were not raised at that time. Paul, when he spoke of the resurrection, to which he strove to attain and to which he was pressing forward with all his might, as a high prize for which he counted all else loss, uses two prepositions as if one was not enough to indicate his meaning, εἰς τὴν ἐξανάστασις τὴν ἐκ νεκρῶν, "attain *to the resurrection from among the dead.*" If Paul had been looking forward to the general resurrection, he need not have given himself any concern or made any sacrifice to attain to that, for the hour shall come when the dead, small and great, shall stand before his throne. The great apostle had in mind the first resurrection, the resurrection of the just. That was the prize before him, the high calling of God in Christ Jesus. To be accounted worthy to be found among the just at that day is enough to inspire any soul to righteous living. The sentiment expressed in Lady Huntington's immortal verse should thrill the heart of every saint :

> When thou, my righteous Judge, shalt come
> To take thy ransomed people home,
>   Shall I among them stand?
> Shall such a worthless worm as I,
> Who sometimes am afraid to die,
>   Be found at thy right hand?
>
> Among the saints let me be found,
> Whene'er the archangel's trump shall sound,
>   To see thy smiling face;
> Then loudest of the throng I'll sing,
> While heaven's resounding mansions ring
>   With shouts of sovereign grace.

I close this part of the discussion with the words of Alford: "I cannot consent to distort words from their plain sense and chronological place in the prophecy on account of any consideration of difficulty, or any risk of abuses which the doctrine of the millennium may bring. . . If in a passage where *two* resurrections are mentioned, where certain ψυχαὶ ἔζησαν (souls live) at the first, and the rest of the νεκροὶ ἔζησαν (dead live) only at the end of a specified period after the first, if in such a passage the *first resurrection* may be understood to mean a spiritual rising with Christ, while the second means *literal* rising from the grave; then there is an end of all significance in language, and the Scripture is wiped out as a definite testimony to anything. If the first resurrection is spiritual, then so is the second, which I suppose none will be hardy enough to maintain; but if the second is literal, then so is the first, which in common with the whole primitive church and many of the best modern expositors, I do maintain, and receive as an article of faith and hope."

II. "But some man will say, How are the dead raised up? and with what body do they come?"

To the first question there is but one answer: By the power of God. This is the promise of the Almighty. Why should it seem to be a thing incredible that God should raise the dead? Since God created man out of dust in his own image and breathed into him the breath of life and man became a living soul, cannot he also raise the body and give it back to the soul which has never died? It is interesting to run the analogy in nature, to see the similitudes all about us—in the flower springing up from the seed which has fallen into the earth and died; in the springtime the calling earth from its winter's tomb. Blessed parables of a glorious resurrection. But our hope rests on firmer prophecy, even the sure promise of our blessed Lord: "But if the Spirit of him that raised up Jesus from the dead dwell in you, he that raised up Christ from the dead shall also quicken your mortal bodies by his Spirit that dwelleth in you" (Rom. 8:11). "And God hath both raised up the Lord, and will also raise up us by his own power" (1 Cor. 6:14).

It will be an *actual* resurrection. What was buried shall rise again. What went into the tomb shall come out of the tomb. Personal identity shall be perfectly preserved in the resurrection process. The Bible asserts the sameness of the resurrection body. The wisest physicist cannot tell just where the principle of the organic life of the body is. The Scriptures do not explain wherein the sameness of the resurrection body consists, but they disclose the fact. Paul likens the resurrection to the sowing and sprouting of a grain of wheat. A grain of wheat always reproduces itself whenever it sprouts. There are imitations—the tare, but a tare is never wheat. We cannot tell just how a spear of golden grain will look next June, but we do know that it will be the *same* individual wheat plant. So we do know from the perfectness of the analogy, when we bury the body, that the same *individual man* shall rise on the resurrection morning. Identity shall be absolutely preserved. Dr. Owen said: "The translation of Enoch is divine testimony that the body itself is capable of eternal life."

The Apostle Paul describes the resurrection of the body in these simple and beautiful words: "It is sown in corruption, it is raised in incorruption: it is sown in dishonor, it is raised in glory; it is sown in weakness, it is raised in power; it is sown a natural body, it is raised a spiritual body." We shall be transformed and fashioned like "the body of his glory." We catch a glimpse of this glory in the transfiguration: "And as he prayed, the fashion of his countenance was altered, and his raiment was white and glistering." Dr. Gordon strikingly says: "The charcoal and the diamond are the same substance; only the one is carbon in its humiliation and the other carbon in its glory. So is this tabernacle in which we dwell, in comparison with our house, which is from heaven. The one is mortal flesh shadowed by the curse and doomed to be sown in dishonor; the other is that flesh made immortal and marvelously transformed."

III. Blessedness of having part in the first resurrection.

"Blessed and holy is he that hath part in the first resurrection; *on such the second death hath no power.*"

1. There is a second death. "And death and hell were cast into the lake of fire. This is the second death" (Rev. 20:14). About this death are all the horrors of hell. This is the death we are warned to escape. "The wages of sin is death"—the second death. Awful, terrific thought! Who would not escape it? Well may we shudder at the appearance of physical death. It is an enemy. It comes with the offer of a cold grave, dust, and ashes. Christ, however, robs it of its sting and shall raise us up unto a blessed immortality. But upon those who depart this life without hope, the second death has an eternal hold. Jesus said: "Marvel not at this, for

the hour is coming in the which all that are in the graves shall hear his voice and shall come forth; they that have done good, unto the resurrection of life; and they that have done evil, unto the resurrection of damnation" (John 5 : 28, 29). To the just it is *unto* the resurrection life; to the wicked it is the resurrection *unto death*. "Blessed and holy is he that hath part in the first resurrection; on such the *second death hath no power*." Behold the privilege and the pre-eminence and the glory of the believer's resurrection. Who would not strive to be accounted worthy to attain to this resurrection, for they shall be priests of God and of Christ and shall reign with him a thousand years.

2. This is the resurrection in which alone there is hope to sweeten life. In this lies our hope of being forever with the Lord; for only those who rise first together with those who shall be changed shall meet him in the air at his second coming. Having trusted him, having felt the power of regeneration by the Holy Spirit, we are assured that in the glorious day of his second advent we shall hear his voice and come forth to life. Then we shall see our blessed Lord and be with him forever. Glorious hope! Washington Irving was walking through Westminster Abbey, the city of the renowned dead. There gloom and silence and darkness and melancholy reigned. "Suddenly the notes of the deep-laboring organ burst upon the ear, falling with doubled and redoubled intensity, and rolling, as it were, huge billows of sound. How well do their volume and grandeur accord with this mighty building! With what pomp do they swell through its vast vaults, and breathe their awful harmony through those caves of death, and make the silent sepulchre vocal! And now they rise in triumphant acclamation, heaving higher and higher their accordant notes, and piling sound on sound. And now they pause, and the soft

voices of the choir break out into sweet gushes of melody; they soar aloft and warble along the roof, and seem to play about these lofty vaults like the pure air of heaven. Again the pealing organ heaves its thrilling thunders, compressing air into music, and rolling it forth upon the soul. What long-drawn cadences! What solemn-sweeping concords! It grows more and more dense and powerful—it fills the vast pile, and seems to jar the very walls—the ear is stunned, the senses are overwhelmed. And now it is winding up in full jubilee—it is rising from earth to heaven—the very soul seems rapt away, and floats upward on this swelling tide of harmony."

Like that, only grander, shall be the scene and sweeter the joy of the first resurrection. The trumpet shall peal forth, the graves shall open. Christ shall softly and sweetly speak to his own and his sheep shall hear his voice and shall awake from their sleep. Then with all the music of the heavenlies they shall be rapt away with their Lord. The transfigured Bride of Christ meets the Bridegroom. Hear the shout: "Alleluia, for the Lord God omnipotent reigneth. Let us be glad, and rejoice, and give honor to him; for the marriage of the Lamb is come, and his wife hath made herself ready." It is the hour of blissful fruition for the waiting Bride. She whose countenance was so often bedewed with tears, whose feet were pierced with thorns, has now the bridal veil upon her face and the nuptial joy in her heart.

The hope of the first resurrection breaks the seal of death which parts us from our loved ones who have fallen asleep in Jesus Christ.

During our memorial service held on the 26th of May, 1895, at Rose Hill Cemetery, Macon, Georgia, there was a most pathetic scene, which ought to be immortalized by some master artist. Little girls were strewing the graves of the heroic dead with flowers. There stood near one of those graves a man at least fifty years of age. His eyes were riveted upon the tomb. He stood as if transfixed and totally unconscious of all the rest of the world. By-and-by he knelt by its side as if in prayer, while the great tears fell fast upon the green grass with which the grave was overgrown. Why did he weep? That grave held the dust and ashes of father or brother, or substitute. He remembered the days of yore, boyhood's happy days. Dear son or brother, thy dead shall rise again. If he died in the Lord, if you are the Lord's, you shall meet nevermore to part. Blessed assurance, we shall meet our loved ones again. The grave shall give them back to us. Oh, yes, mother, I shall see you and walk the heavenly streets by your side. Yes; go to the home where the little chair is empty, where the sweet prattling voice of the baby has been hushed in death, and tell the living, thy dead shall rise in the last day. Comfort the brokenhearted and wipe away the tears of sorrow with these words. Walk out into the silent cemetery where the gloom of death has settled, and drive away the darkness with the light of this glorious hope.

Unsaved friends, let us talk very faithfully to each other just a minute. Dear boy, your mother lived and died in the triumphs of the Christian faith; you are far away from her Christ. Unless you come to him you shall never see her again. Mother, look upon that sweet babe in your arms. It is a precious jewel in God's sight. You have never let Jesus come into your heart. Jesus will take your babe in his arms, while you will be cast into outer darkness. Faith in Christ is the link that binds us eternally. Death can never break it. Hell has no power over it. Death may part us for a little while, but only for a short season. "Believe on the Lord Jesus Christ and thou shalt be saved." "Jesus said unto her [Martha], I am the resurrection and the life; he that believeth in me, though he were dead, yet shall he live. And whosoever liveth and believeth in me shall never die. Believest thou this?" God grant that this blessed truth may turn many to his dear Son and heal the homesickness of many in the thought of death.

WILLIAM LOWNDES PICKARD was born in Upson County, Ga., October 19, 1861. He took his degree at Mercer University, 1884. Full graduate of seminary in 1887. Ordained at Macon, Ga., 1883. Pastor at Thomaston, Ga., March to October, 1884; at Elk Creek and Fisherville, Ky., while in seminary. Called to First Church, Eufaula, Ala., September 1, 1887. After two years there, called to First Church, Birmingham, Ala. After nearly four years there, called to Broadway Baptist Church, Louisville, Ky., his present pastorate. June, 1889, received degree of D. D. from the University of Alabama. In 1886 he was married to Miss Florence May Willingham, of Albany, Ga., who is truly a pastor's helper.

W. L. Pickard, D. D.

XXI

THE EFFECTUAL CROSS[1]

BY W. L. PICKARD, D. D.

"For Christ sent me not to baptize, but to preach the gospel: not in wisdom of words, lest the cross of Christ should be made void." **1 Cor. 1 : 17.**

MANY places that were once filled with malaria have been transformed into beauty; but the transformation cost tremendous sacrifices.

The greatest change in all history is that which has taken place in the estimate of the cross. What could Paul have meant when he spoke of the cross as something to be guarded with conscientious scruple lest it should become void? Paul was once accused of being beside himself because of much learning; is he beside himself when he speaks to the Corinthians of the effectual cross? He speaks of preaching, and of preaching the gospel, and speaks of the cross as the central theme of this gospel. And he calls it the cross of Christ. He suggests that preaching must not be done in some ways lest the cross be made void. He implies the necessity of preaching so as to render this cross effectual. He speaks of the cross as something that can be used for the greatest of good to the world, or as something that can be made ineffectual. Our theme is, therefore

THE EFFECTUAL CROSS.

Let us look more closely at the cross—the thing

---

[1] Preached in Washington, D. C., during the Jubilee Session of the Southern Baptist Convention.

Paul wished to guard with such jealous care. It was an instrument of torture and of death. There were several kinds of crosses. On these were executed thieves, outlaws, highwaymen, conspirators, murderers. Crucifixion was punishment in comparison with which the head-block, the French guillotine, the gallows, and electrocution are as downy pillows; for death by all these last is instantaneous, almost painless. In case of the upright cross, the victim had a wooden or iron nail driven through his chest into the post, and was left to the lingering suffering. In case of the simple cross—the kind on which our Lord was crucified—the hands of the victim were sometimes tied to the transverse piece and the weight of the body left to distend every nerve until endurance was at an end—a death of hours, sometimes days. Again, sometimes the hands were nailed and the feet left unnailed that the full weight of the body might be left on the pierced hands. Again, the hands and feet were nailed. In addition to these things, in the cases of some victims, the legs were broken; in the case of our Lord his side was pierced. Death by the cross has been universally regarded as the most terrible suffering to which a human being could be subjected in the flesh.

The shame of the cross was deep and lasting. The bodies of the crucified were often left on it to decay, or thrown in the "potter's field" to dogs and vultures. The families of such were under the social stigma practically outlawed. In the light of these historical facts much is meant when it is said of our Lord: He "endured the cross, despising the shame." The burial of our Lord's body was an exception to the rule of the crucified. Blessed Joseph! Blessed Nicodemus! Nicodemus, we forgive thy timidity at the beginning of Christ's ministry since thou wast a hero at his death.

It was this instrument of torture that the apostle

desired to guard. Elsewhere he speaks of "glorying in the cross." By some means a great change has taken place. This transformation was due to one Jesus who had been crucified. He who knew no sin had suffered there as if he had been the deepest stained of all the sinful. He was greater than all law. He had sufficient virtue in him to outweigh all sin. When he endured the cross he did that for humanity which would through all coming ages uplift it. Since Christ was crucified, the cross has become the symbol of the power of God, through Christ, for lifting men from under the law of sin and death.

God's plan is perfect. Christ's blood is omnipotent. But God has elected to make his almighty plan efficient through means. The divinest ends of God are reached through means. And he has connected the gospel of Christ with our salvation from sin. And he has ordained the preaching of the gospel as one of the great means to the salvation of souls. Hence, all who are, in any sense, teachers of Christianity should be careful in their teaching, lest the cross of Christ should be made void.

First. The cross which symbolizes the wisdom and power of God, and the atonement made by Christ, may be made ineffectual by rhetoric—wisdom of words. Paul affirmed that he did not go to the Corinthians to preach "in wisdom of words." He said that such preaching would make the cross void.

God and Christ know the power of words. Words embody thought, and thought represents the heart. Hence by our words we are to be condemned or justified. The gospel of Christ has been written, by the inspiration of the Holy Spirit, in words. But words are to be used to reveal the cross and not to hide it. The Corinthians thought themselves very literary. They had been inclined to discount the teachings of Paul because he had not used fine rhetoric like some of the Grecian orators. They were thinking about *how* he said things, rather than about the *things* said. They desired to hear words that sounded wise, measured by a profane standard. Paul avoided any such display. He was afraid to present a rhetorical bouquet lest the people would look at the flowers and not at the cross. We have all heard discourses that were complete in analysis, dressed in silvery words, yes, finished to death. When they were ended, we felt no nearer to God, had not been stirred to deeper convictions of duty; they were flowers to be admired. A mirror is not to show itself, but to show other objects. Words are not to cover the cross, but to exhibit it. What the Corinthians needed was the water of life rather than golden dippers. Paul meant to use words that were like fish-hooks, words that would stick in the hearts of men and make lasting impressions. The Book says the time will come when people will have itching ears—they will wish the beautiful rather than the useful. Who doubts that Paul, under the guidance of the Holy Spirit, could have written a whole treatise on rhetoric and have used phrases that would have made the fastidious in Corinth applaud him. But he was showing the cross, and it needs no drapery.

2. The cross may be made void by efforts to display worldly wisdom.

Science has brought many blessings to man. It is usually defined as "that which is known; that which has been demonstrated to be fact." The definition ought to be enlarged a little. It ought to be, that which is demonstrated to be fact, and shall always stand demonstrated to be fact. This, because some men who were not eminently scientific and who were not eminent biblical scholars have often announced irreconcilable differences between science and the Bible; but investigation through twenty-five years more has shown that the supposed conflict was not a conflict between science and the Bible. In the world we observe law—law must have a law-maker; we see force—force must have an author and director; we see order—order must have an orderer; we see design—design must have a designer. The Bible was not intended to be a scientific book, except to give God's science of the salvation of men. It deals with the human race as lost in sin, and with Christ as man's Saviour from sin. Science tells that God is, that he exists; but it takes the Bible to tell what God is, and what our relations to him are and may be. The rocks tell us that God exists; but this knowledge leaves a veil between us and God. Revelation and the Christ of revelation rend the veil and show us God as the Father.

There is another way in which the cross may be rendered void by science, even in the hands of those who love it. Our context says: "For after that in the wisdom of God, the world by wisdom knew not God, it pleased God by the foolishness of preaching (by the preaching of a gospel that the worldly philosophy would call foolishness) to save them that believe." Worldly wisdom does not show the cross to dying souls. I do not doubt that Christ could have written a scientific book. In one discourse he could have told all the future triumphs of science. On the day when he stood on Olivet and wept over Jerusalem, he saw all that we know to-day, for he is "the same yesterday, to-day, and forever," but he did not write science, for if he had done that he would have been neglecting his "Father's business," and the needs of humanity. If the wisdom of the world could have saved souls from sin, there would have been no need of the cross. God neither wastes force nor time. Christ was not crucified for pastime.

The cross needs no defense, no apology. It is God's criticism of sin, and his apology of love. The cross was God's great battle-ground, through Christ, with sin. On it was sin's Conqueror. Behind it now stands the One who exclaimed: "All authority in heaven and earth is given to me." Can man by searching (unaided by revelation) find out God to perfection? The answer of the ages is, No. But the cross reveals God in his perfection, in his perfection as hating sin; in his perfect justice; in his perfect love. God, by the cross, has brought human wisdom to naught, that no flesh should glory in his presence.

3. The cross may be rendered void by forms and ceremonies. Paul said to the Corinthians: "I came not to baptize, but to preach the gospel." He did not belittle baptism. But he was hedging against the religion of mere form. He was emphasizing that which was first, viz., the gospel applied to the heart and conscience. The Jews desired signs and seasons. And signs and seasons go together as a rule. Set days, feasts, and fasts require forms, signs, and rituals. It is the tendency of human nature to exalt the sign above the thing signified. Many who have adopted the literal cross as an emblem of the suffering Christ, are ignorant of the Christ. Many who have adopted days of feasts and fasts, neglect Christ the balance of the time. Many through the centuries have seemed to think that they came especially to baptize, hence baptismal regeneration. God is a spirit and will have of his spiritual beings spiritual worship. When we begin to have seasons and signs the seen is substituted for the unseen, the visible for the invisible, and the bleeding Christ is veiled, the cross is rendered ineffectual. This tendency is dangerous. The eye must be more and more satisfied. The spiritual is subordinated, hence candles, crosses, saints' pictures, popes, priests, human dignitaries, human systems, signs, only signs. When Christ said on the cross, "It is finished," he meant the measure of his words. He meant that the atonement was

complete, and that nothing could add to the cross. When we try to add to the cross, we do cover it and belittle its power and grandeur.

4. The cross may be rendered ineffectual by a conception of it that is lower than God's.

Some use great "wisdom of words" in painting the cross as the exhibition of a beautiful moral sentiment. They paint Christ as the highest type of human devotion and unselfishness. This is only a half truth which vitiates the whole. It is one of those half truths which becomes more hurtful than a whole falsehood, for it deceives the worshiper and covers up the Christ who is to be worshiped.

Christ, as he walked among men and worked for humanity is an example for us; but Christ on the cross was not an example. An example is something to follow. Christ's death was not an example. It was not to be followed. It cannot be. It was an atonement. And none but Christ could make an atonement. Search earth, search heaven, search hell, none but Christ could meet Calvary and give the blood that had cleansing power in it.

> Not all the blood of beasts
>   On Jewish altars slain,
> Could give the guilty conscience peace,
>   Or wash away the stain.

> But Christ, the heavenly Lamb,
>   Takes all our sins away,—
> A sacrifice of nobler name,
>   And richer blood than they.

Second. How the cross may be made effectual.

1. By realizing what God means by the cross. God means one great fact to be burned into our minds and hearts by the cross. His own great thought of the cross is that the crucified Christ is the sinner's atonement. Atonement means "at-one-

ment." But mere definition in this case is inadequate to convey the meaning. When an atonement is needed there is enmity. Then there was enmity between the human race and God; and, as far as man was concerned, the difference between God and man was superlative in degree and everlasting in duration.

Let us look at God and man in their original relations. God creates man in his own image. God and man are happy together. They delight in each other's company. They walk and talk together in sweetest companionship. They are both holy. The continuance of this companionship is necessarily conditioned on man's holiness. The moment man becomes unholy, God and man become each repellent to the other. They can no more be companions than light and darkness can exist together. Man could sin. Man did sin. And sin made man a different being as to his whole nature. Sin separated man from God as widely as man is separated from the serpent. By sin, man's nature, his mind, his affections, his will, his blood, his body, all became changed. Man became subject to sin. Men's thoughts were sinful, he willed sinful things, his body executed sinful deeds, and with sin came death to spiritual life and fellowship which, before sinning, he had with God. With sin came bodily ills, aches, tears, and death. When all of this occurred there was complete separation between God and man. God delighted in the world of holiness and moral beauty; man in the world of untruthfulness, immorality, and deformity.

A great gulf was fixed between the two worlds, and no human bridge could span it. It was not a gulf arbitrarily fixed by the wish of God, but one that sin had fixed, a gulf that must necessarily exist between the sinner and the sinless God.

Sin made man an enemy to God. But man could not change his nature back into holiness. Some higher power must change man from a sinful being to a holy being. Could Adam and Eve have lived a million years in the flesh, and made a billion efforts to change their nature, all would have been in vain. They could no more have changed their nature than could the lily become an oak, or the serpent a lordly eagle. And what is emphatically true, they did not change. And what is emphatically true again, their race, of itself, has not changed. Sin brought ruin and death to Adam and Eve, and the trail of the serpent has been over all till now. Could they have lived upright beings after sinning, still they stood as traitors, and their traitorous nature would have been transmitted to their children. For when their first child was born after they had sinned, he was in Adam's image and not in God's. So far as the human race was concerned, then and now, it could not, and cannot atone for sin. Unless God comes to the rescue, it was helpless, doomed, and of itself it is still helpless, doomed. Can you make an atonement? Can I? Guilty, helpless, doomed!

Furthermore. As a mere act of making sinful man holy, as a matter of forgiving sin, simply speaking man's sins forgiven, God himself could not do this. The guilt was still fixed.

God's nature is holy. The thought of a compromise between sin and God is an intellectual impossibility. You can't conceive of such a thing without dethroning God. God never forgave a sin. Nor will he ever forgive a sin. To forgive a sin would be to wink at it, to excuse it, to compromise with it. But God has arranged a righteous plan by which he can justify one who has sinned, and all who have sinned, but it is only by blotting the sins out in blood. The existence of hell is that there may be a place to itself where unforgiven sin may hold its willing subjects forever separated from those whose sins have been blotted out. God's justice and nature require that no sinful being can become his companion, that the being's **sin must be** blotted out, and **the man must** become a new creature in Christ Jesus.

It was **not a piece of momentary arbitration** that **connected the cross with** man's **salvation from sin. The mind of** God comprehends the **universe on this question.** If blazing stars **and** burning **suns could have** bridged **this** chasm, the canopied vaults **and sunlit domes of** countless worlds would have **been** consecrated **to** the work. If fallen angels could **have** been used for this work, **they** would have been consecrated to it. If sinless angels could have done this work, they filling the courts of heaven would have been consecrated to it. If **God** the Father, in his plans, could have done this without the cross, there would have been **no** Calvary. In the plans of **the** triune God, none but Christ could do this mightiest **work** of works. And he could **not** accomplish it while on the **throne** with the Father. Nor yet could he do this **as a sinless** being in Bethlehem, Nazareth, and Gethsemane. **To** grasp the scope of **his** work and to exclaim: "**It** is finished," he must, **as** the Lamb **of** God, appointed from before the foundation of the world, be lifted up. To Calvary he must go.

This was not, and is **not** primarily, **a** matter **of love.** God loves us with matchless passion, and so loved us as **to** send his Son **to** us, but he would not have sent his Son if it had not been necessary. It was a question, and is a question, of justice in paying the sinner's debts. The sinner was in debt to God and righteousness, and had naught with which to pay. If Christ pays not this debt, we must be forever banished from the presence of God. He who pays the debt must be able to satisfy **justice, all** its righteous demands. Some one **whose holy** nature was infinite **must** suffer under this broken law **as** man's substitute, **and for man,** and **in man's stead** suffer the penalty of the law. Hence **Christ took on** him the seed of Abraham. **He** who knew no sin **was made** sin for us. When this was done justice was met. God had the fountain of blood with which to wash away sin. He could be approached by man, and man could lovingly come to him and pillow his head on the divine bosom. When we place the cross in this position, we place it where Paul placed it, as the way, the only way, the all-sufficient way, of a sinner's salvation.

This exhibits the cross as God's criticism on sin. There never was a little sin. The smallest sin will damn the greatest soul, unless that sin shall be blotted out. If from the fall of man until this hour God had never come to man's rescue, leaving sin to run its awful course, what would be the condition of the world? If God had not raised up an Enoch, a Noah, an Abraham, an Isaac; if he had not raised up Moses and given him the law; if there had been no judges, no prophets, and no Christ, no words nor works of divine intervention for man, how would human history now read? We shudder at the thought. Honesty, uprightness, honor, purity, law, marriage, civilization, virtue, have all been projected into the race by the mercy of God. If sin has so blackened the world and ruined so many souls, despite the work of God and Christ, what would have been the picture if God had forever withdrawn from the human race? By the cross God says sin is the most terrible enemy to God and man that there is in the universe. Hence, the flowing blood is the philippic of God's wrath against all sin. What shall we say then? "Shall we continue in sin that grace may abound?" Let us exclaim with Paul: "God forbid."

2. The cross may be effectual, not only by presenting it as the atonement for sin and God's criticism on sin, but as God's consuming passion for the salvation of the lost. The atonement shows God's love of justice, shows justice; the spirit of the atonement exhibited the love of God and Christ for man. "For

God so loved the world that he gave his only begotten Son, that whosoever believeth in him should not perish, but have everlasting life." Again, "Christ loved us and gave himself for us." The spirit of atonement was one of such matchless love that it willingly gave the only begotten Son of God to be man's substitute. God and Christ did this of their own loving accord.

Let us try to measure this love by what Christ endured for us. The Jewish Sanhedrin, in a mock trial, condemned him to the cross on the false charge of blasphemy. The popular cry of the Jews was that Christ was an enemy to Cæsar. This was false. The scarlet robe that was in mockery placed on Jesus and the crowning of him with thorns was not a part of the law of crucifixion. The buffeting and other insults to which he was subjected was not a part of the law of crucifixion. He could have thwarted all of this, but he endured. He was willing to bear all that sin could place on him, that he might conquer sin, all because he loved us.

The legal steps in punishment by crucifixion were: Stripping the victim, scourging him with a scourge into which nails and pieces of steel were often put; hence, the victim suffered agony even before reaching the cross. The victim had to bear his own cross to the place of execution. It is likely that Christ's scourging rendered him unable to bear the cross to the place of crucifixion, hence, Simon the Cyrenian helped him to bear it. The victim was tied or nailed to the cross. Our Lord was nailed to it. To the one being crucified was usually given a medicated drink to drown the senses. Jesus refused this that his senses might be clear to the end. He was "drinking sorrow's cup." He was insulted by being offered vinegar and hyssop. All of this he endured without one murmur. This all exhibited God's love for us. See now the suffering. The distended position of the body on the cross put the nerves to their greatest tension, causing indescribable pain. The hands and feet are especially nerve-centers, and the nails through these caused excruciating pain. Because of the distended position of the body, more blood flowed through the arteries than could flow back through the veins, hence an overflow of blood to the head, causing suffering beyond the power of language to describe. All of this caused burning thirst. Added to all this, in our Lord's case, there was a moment when the Father forsook him. All this Christ endured. What a criticism on sin! what a commentary on love! Did he ask the Father why he had forsaken him? It was justice driving the last nail. This must be before life, death, and hell could realize the meaning of the expression: "It is finished." Do you wonder that the sun veiled his face from twelve to three o'clock? He was being crucified who made the sun and kept it rolling in its orbit. No wonder it drew aside to mourn. Do you wonder that the veil of the temple was rent? The last great sacrifice in the plan of redemption was being offered. The veil of the "Holy of Holies" would no more be needed. No wonder the rocks were rent, for the rock of ages was being cleft, and from it was flowing a stream for the washing of the nations. No wonder the graves gave up their dead, for he was dying who was to conquer death. No wonder the earth quaked, for the time is coming when he who was enduring then shall speak, and the quaking earth and seas and hell shall give up their dead and to his presence they shall come! Consuming passion, did I say? Yes, consuming love for the lost! Oh, passion of God's passions, the love that Christ exhibited on Calvary! The cross, the cross, let it ever stand clearly before a needy world as the symbol of God's power to save.

3. The cross may be made effectual by our crowning it with glory.

Paul gloried in the cross, preached it, and suffered for it. The blood-stained cross stands in the center of human history and human progress. To it, all history converges. From it, all real progress proceeds. It has freed the hearts of men from sin. It has broken the shackles of the consciences of men; it has introduced to the world the true conception of the dignity of man; it has changed those who were in prison cells of sin so that they dwell in palaces of joy and hope. It has given men that truth that has made them free indeed. It has changed tyrants and autocrats into men of fraternal spirits. It has changed savage nations into the highest types of Christian civilization. It has exalted the sense of honor, justice, and righteousness in the minds and hearts of men everywhere. It stands behind earth's greatest discoveries. It is the key given of God to man to unlock the vaults of the great hidden treasures in all spheres. It is exalting love and reason above hatred and the sword. It is making the world a brotherhood. It is blessing and protecting even the infidel and scoffer. It is making glorious conquests everywhere. It has multiplied the Twelve who loved one another into countless millions who love each other. It has changed the love-chamber in the upper room in Jerusalem, to a palace as wide as the world, frescoed with love as pure as the crimson blood that flowed on Calvary. It has made labor sweeter. It has not taken all the thorns from the earth, but it has made the flowers more numerous and more fragrant. It touches the whole creation and the whole creation does not "groan and travail" in such pain as it did before the cross and the Christ met. The world is crowning the cross with glory. All science, all progress, all knowledge, all governments, are placing flowers at its base and glory on its head, and Christians in larger numbers and in sweeter anthems are singing its glory day by day.

THE EFFECTUAL CROSS

But this is not all. Paul viewed the cross in greater glory and splendor than we have yet mentioned. All truth that touches moral beings centers in Christ. That for which he died on Calvary must be acknowledged supreme in the universe. The day of reckoning is coming, and when that day comes, the great day of Calvary's triumph will have come. The angels who never sinned will then see the cross as Christ saw it. All of the redeemed will understand the necessity of the cross as never before. And all of the damned will acknowledge then the love and justice of Jehovah, and their wrath will give him praise. The intelligent universe will have but one opinion of the cross and the Lamb. The kingdoms of the universe will then be redeemed back to God and the universe shall sing:

> All hail the power of Jesus' name.

Brethren, every being in the universe shall confess that Christ's blood was not shed in vain. But oh! what is your relation and mine to the cross? Have we been washed in the blood? Is the bleeding sacrifice our personal Saviour? Is he reigning in our hearts? Is the sweet song of redemption our song? Will the final hallelujah for the cross be our blissful shout? Shall we be with him in his final triumph? When spiritual death is cast into hell, and when all tears are wiped from the eyes of the redeemed, shall you and I be among the tearless ones? God grant it.

> Dear dying Lamb, thy precious blood
>   Shall never lose its power,
> Till all the ransomed church of God
>   Be saved to sin no more.

XXII

A KINGDOM BUILT ON A CROSS[1]

BY REV. E. Y. MULLINS

"Except a corn of wheat fall into the ground and die, it abideth alone; **but** if it die, it bringeth forth much fruit." John 12 : 24.

JESUS came into the world to set up a kingdom. In the synoptic Gospels the subject-matter of all his preaching is the kingdom of God. He announces its approach. He describes the character of its subjects. He predicts its progress and enlargement. He does not omit **to** declare its final consummation. But in the earlier stages of his ministry **there** is a strange reserve in his statements about the extent of his kingdom. "I am not sent **save to the** lost sheep of the house of Israel." Yet ever **and anon**, there comes up from the great deep of his mind **and heart**, like an upspringing from the depths of **the** sea, a phrase or sentence or brief parable which tells of a kingdom whose spreading branches shall shelter the storm-tossed sons of men from the face of the whole earth, or which shows **us** that as he gazed out into the distant future he beheld vast streams of humanity pouring **into his** kingdom from the north, and south, and east, and west, and sitting down with Abraham and Isaac and Jacob at its festal board. The heart of Jesus was never out of touch with the great suffering heart of the world. And now as he stands face to face with the cross, oppressed and straitened in spirit, how it **must** have thrilled and satisfied **him to**

---

[1] Preached in Twelfth Street Methodist Church, Washington, D. C., during the Jubilee Session of the Southern Baptist Convention.

Rev. E. Y. Mullins.

E. Y. MULLINS, son of Eld. S. G. Mullins and Mrs. C. B. Mullins, was born in Copiah Co., Miss., January 5, 1860. His paternal grandfather was a minister. Mr. Mullins was converted in Dallas, Tex., at a great revival held by Maj. W. E. Penn in October, 1880. Was educated at the A. and M. College, of Texas, and after conversion took the full course at the Southern Baptist Theological Seminary. He was pastor in Harrodsburg, Ky., 1885 to 1888, and of Lee Street Church, Baltimore, from 1888 to 1895. He has, at this writing, just been elected associate corresponding secretary of the Foreign Mission Board of the Southern Baptist Convention. Both he and his wife have for several years exerted a wide influence for the cause of missions.

hear the announcement that Gentiles desired to see him. The coming of the Greeks at the time was a providential coming, and the mission was the same as that of the angel in the garden which came to strengthen him. It was as if the Father pressed a draught of strengthening cordial to his lips before the trial; as if the first-fruits of the cross were bestowed to prepare him for its agony. The text constitutes the deepest answer to the inquiring Greeks. Observe that it amounts to a confession on the part of Jesus that his holy and spotless life, taken as a means of drawing men and consolidating a kingdom, was a failure. The grain of wheat abideth alone except it die. His approach to the Jewish nation had turned out a failure; they were about to crucify him. His attempt to attach a little circle of fishermen to him had turned out a failure; they were about to flee like frightened sheep at the bark of a wolf. Perhaps the bond that bound them to him may be dignified by the name of love; but it was a feeble thing compared with the love which followed the cross. It then became martyr-love, and compared with it the former love was as "moonlight unto sunlight and as water unto wine." So the coming of much fruit could not antedate the cross. There was in this no disappointment, and nothing unexpected to Jesus. The cross was his goal when he forsook his throne for this earth. He knew the loneliness of his high and holy purpose, a loneliness which bereft him of human sympathy and companionship and love which his heart craved. Now in his death the loneliness is to be intensified. Are not the words of the poetess true?—

Yea, once Immanuel's orphaned cry this universe hath shaken:
It went up single, echoless, My God, I am forsaken.

But blessed be God

It went up from the Holy's lips amid his lost creation,
That of the lost no son should use those words of desolation.

I. *The saving significance of the cross.* **Standing** in a grain field you observe the tender shoot appear above the soil. Below the visible manifestation there is at work a mystic and wonderful power, a power capable of projecting straight into the air by slow degrees a graceful and majestic stalk; a power capable of crowning the top of the stalk with a rich fruitage of grain, and that grain so sweet and nutritious as to be the bread of the human race, the universal food. And what is the cost of the head of wheat? Death in the dark earth below. So Jesus came to project a kingdom above the surface of the sin-cursed and sorrow-stricken and God-hungry world, that should shelter it, and feed it, and satisfy it, and redeem it. The cost of that was death. The surging tides of life were in him, but they could be released only as he gave himself up in voluntary self-surrender. But in pointing to the process of increase required by the wheat grain, Jesus does not assert that it is identical in all respects with the process of increase required in his life. It is not the continuation of a law of nature upward into the realm of grace that is here pointed out. The tiny grain of wheat must fall into the earth and be dissolved by death before it will relax its grasp of the life potencies which slumber in its bosom; and so the life of Jesus must be dissolved ere the waving grain fields of the spiritual harvest can gladden the eyes of the angels and of God. Yet in the one case death is a physical necessity and in the other a moral and spiritual one. The necessity was this: As Jesus looked down from heaven upon earth he beheld a doomed race, doomed because of transgression and because the righteous Father had enacted pain and suffering and death as the penalty of transgression. And so, unlike the unconscious and passive grain of wheat which falls into the earth and dies, Jesus chose to be born and chose to die, inviting the full force and penalty into his own bosom; and bowing his head beneath the black flood of death, he abode there until it spent its force, and then choosing to rise from the dead, he came forth the Lord of life. And shall the world stumble at this law of sacrifice so sublimely exemplified in the offering of the Son of God? If the law of substitution be recognized elsewhere should it be repudiated here? If the world applaud the nobility of the mother who quenches the flame of her own life at the bedside of her sick child; if the world enshrine the story of Damon and Pythias in its memory as the glorification of human friendship; if it be confessed that one generation suffers that the next may profit by its experience; if the mighty forest grows up out of the soil enriched by the forest of a former age, if one order of the lower animals is in the plan of nature made as food for another; if all human progress be the result of sacrifice; if our free institutions were bought with the blood of the fathers of the Revolution; if the peace of fellowship which cements the two sections of our land to-day be recognized as the purchase of the men who sleep in one thousand cemeteries North and South—I ask if the law of sacrifice be so universally admitted, shall it be that Calvary is the only spot in all God's universe where it shall be excluded? God forbid.

But the saving significance of the cross relates in part to the effect on Satan. Christ came to cast out the prince of this world. Marvelous is the method employed to accomplish it. He does it not with thunderbolts of wrath, not with fiery chariots and an army of angelic cohorts. He conquers Satan by surrendering to his power. "Come," says Jesus to the arch enemy, "bind these hands and these feet with your strongest chain, transfix me with your most deadly arrow, death; close these eyes, blanch these lips, still this throbbing heart, entomb me in rock and seal it and guard it well." And the sepulchre smacks its satisfied lips over the cold clay of the dead Christ. Laugh demons! Exult Satan! Weep angels! Gather in little groups, ye broken-hearted disciples, and pour out your grief to one another. But hark! That was the rumbling of an earthquake. Look! That flash of light before the dawn is an angel dropping through space to the door of the tomb, and behold, within the sepulchre the blush of life mantles the face of the sleeper; he sits up and calmly disrobes himself of the grave-clothes and steps forth the victor over death forevermore. Satan has no other weapon of attack. He has done his worst and failed. He is conquered. The pent-up tides of life which have been surging in the bosom of Jesus have at last broken through their bounds, and the wilderness and the solitary place can rejoice and the desert can blossom as the rose, and all the choirs of creation can catch up the song of redemption and pour forth their floods of praise to God who loveth and redeemeth the world. The wrath of God was now spent, and henceforth there is a way of escape for man. And like the lonely traveler on the Western prairie, who, when he descries in the distance the lurid black line of a great prairie fire rapidly approaching him, takes a match and burns away a spot and in this spot takes his stand until the raging sea of fire has swept past him, leaving him standing unscathed in the spot where the devouring element has already accomplished its work—so poor lost humanity can take its stand in the one spot where the wrath of God has spent its force, at the cross of Chris', and gaze with unblanched face upon the fiery waves of judgment that shall roll over the earth at the appointed hour.

II. *The law of the cross the law of discipleship.* What was the change which Jesus proposed to himself in turning ordinary men into disciples? The requirements of a genuine disciple are tremendous. The general characteristics of the disciple are clearly revealed throughout the New Testament. He must be one who lives in two worlds at the same time. While his life is spent on earth his affections must be in heaven. In the midst of the seen he must keep a firm grip upon the unseen. With ten thousand enemies within and ten thousand other enemies around him, he must walk a victor through the world. In the midst of hate and persecution he must love. The body of disciples must become an organization or a kingdom diverse from all other kingdoms and yet must flourish side by side with them all; it must have such coherency and endurance that its dissolution shall be beyond the reach of any earthly power of any age; with a wide gulf of separation rolling between its members and other men, they must yet be able and willing to reach across the gulf and save their haters and persecutors. How shall such a disciple be produced, such a kingdom be built up? Certainly not by the unaided power of moral truth. Philosophers had announced truth enough to establish even a kingdom of love before Jesus. Each had succeeded in gathering around him a little handful of adherents. But whenever the leader died the movement died. Not so with Jesus; when he died his movement began. And it was in this Jesus differed from all other teachers. He applied the law of the cross to the heart of the disciple. Regeneration, increase, life, power through death. Discipleship means crucifixion. Consecration means a cross, a sepulchre, a resurrection. "He that loveth his life shall lose it, and he that hateth his life in this world shall keep it unto life eternal." It is related that when the Roman Colosseum was being dismantled by the inhabitants of the city no way could be found to check the work of destruction until one of the popes, fearing lest the splendid structure should be utterly demolished, hit upon the expedient of erecting a cross in the center of the massive pile, thus rendering it a sacred edifice. The effect was magical in arresting the ruthless hand of destruction. So the cross in the center of man's being alone can save him. To attempt to build up Christian character by preaching that leaves out the cross as the basis of it is to adopt the very process that Christ pronounced a failure, the process he came to displace. Thus by applying the law of the cross to his disciples Jesus produced the most beautiful, most noble, most magnificent type of character this world ever beheld. Socrates, the noble old Greek philosopher, chose death rather than to surrender truth. But he died for something of his own, a system of teaching which was the offspring of his own brain. The Christian on the other hand, is crucified unto another, is a martyr, if necessary, for the sake of another. He is crucified unto Christ when he makes over himself, the priceless core and center of his being, unto Christ, and for Christ's sake he makes himself over to a perishing race. This new bond established by the law of the cross easily snaps all others, easily takes the supreme place. It breaks the love of money for its own sake and brings all and lays it at the feet of Jesus; it is stronger than brother-love, or sister-love, or father-love or mother-love, yea than all of them combined. It is mightier than the love of home and of country, and even of life itself, and than the fear of death. To prove these statements I have but to remind you that it produced a Paul, a Luther, a Carey, a Judson, and ten thousand others whose names glow on the pages of sacred history and who themselves blaze like seraphs around the throne tonight.

III. *The law of the cross the condition of the world's evangelization.* The weakness of modern Christianity is its defective views as to the cost of spiritual power. To effect spiritual results in the hearts of men and women, spiritual agencies alone can avail. The cross is the measure of the cost of life for the world. The law of the cross in the lives of the followers of the Crucified is the only means of making that cross effective. Crucifixion is the cost of all spiritual power; consecration is only another name for death. Any cheaper process of attaining the result is doomed to failure. Every genuine spiritual result in heathen lands or our own land is the only and true measure of the forthputting of spiritual energy before. Given an exact measure of the spiritual power in the life of any man, and it requires no inspiration to predict the exact result. A great deal is said about the obstacles to the spread of the gospel. The founder of Christianity counted and measured all the obstacles before he came to supply a means of surmounting them. The gospel presupposes obstacles, and where this deepest law of spiritual power finds play in the people of Christ there are no obstacles. Impediments to the gospel are such only when Christ's people attempt to match them with the wrong thing. Let the law of the cross be wanting and there will always be obstacles. Straws mark the direction of the current. Some one appealed through the paper the other day to the wealthiest Christian man to give all his money and that would convert the world. Much as the cause needs money, much as we should strive to increase our gifts all along the line, it is my deliberate conviction from my text, that if all the millionaires in America should put their aggregate wealth at the disposition of our Boards, the world would not necessarily be any nearer conversion than it is. If indeed such an outpouring of wealth were the index of a growth in spiritual power, then there would be hope.

Brethren, if God is in human history at all, the center of his providence is the cross. If God spares the sin-stained and atheistic world, it is solely that

w

the cross may make its way over it. If God permits you to live and to accumulate wealth, it is that you and it may be assimilated with the Christ of Calvary in the world's evangelization. It were better never to have been born than to abuse this obligation and this supreme privilege. If the great material advances of the world and the discoveries which have marked the past century have any significance at all, they relate to the work of the cross on earth. Yes, I believe it is the "crisis of missions." Because God has shut his people up to circumstances which leave them only one plea in case of failure. In times past Christians could explain the failure to send the gospel over the earth on the ground of persecution, or of poverty, or of want of an educated ministry, or the hostility of the nations to missionaries, or of their own obscurity and feebleness as a people, or lack of means of transportation. But to-day there is only one explanation available, viz.: "We do not want to give the world the gospel; we do not love the Christ enough to care whether the world is saved or lost." The world looks on as the churches confront their task, devils look on, angels look on, God looks on, Christ looks on. The question of missions is to-day the test question of Christianity. The world is going to view Christianity as a success or a failure according as the churches solve the problem of missions. Infidelity, in whatever form it makes the attack, cannot damage the Bible or the cause of religion as it will be damaged by failure in the mission work. Heresy here is the most fatal of all heresies. God make us true and loyal in this supreme test of our age.

D. I. PURSER was born in Copiah County, Miss. When scarcely sixteen years of age, he joined the Confederate army, and throughout the civil war was a gallant soldier. He began to preach when about twenty-four years old, and has served as pastor at Port Gibson and Crystal Springs, Miss., Birmingham, Ala., and is now pastor in New Orleans, La. Dr. Purser has made a fine record. Churches under his care have, without exception, grown in numbers and influence, and he has often sent out new churches. As State evangelist, at different times, for Mississippi and Alabama, he has been successful without being sensational. Believing strongly in the Bible, he studies it carefully and preaches it faithfully. In self control, unselfishness, common sense, and energy of thought and action, may be found the secret of his success and popularity.

XXIII

HONOR FOR SERVICE[1]

BY D. I. PURSER, D. D.

"If any man serve me, him will my Father honour." **John 12 : 26.**

THIS is an age of honor seeking. **We urge our** children to strive for the honors **in school ; we** rejoice with **them** when they obtain these honors. We are glad when we or our countrymen are honored ; and from our hearts we say, God speed the day when all our men may be worthy of honor, whether they **are** awarded the meed of praise by being entrusted with responsibilities **or** not. It is in no wise wrong to seek honor, if only it be sought in **an** honorable **way** in "well-doing." The Apostle Paul urges us to "**seek** for glory and honour and immortality, eternal life" (Rom. 2 : 7). Avowing then, the wisdom of **a** Christian's seeking honor, we ask : How shall he obtain it ? **Our** text gives **us** a simple, concise answer, "If **any** man serve me, him will my Father honor." **This** text naturally divides itself **into** two parts :

I. The service required or rendered.
II. The honor conferred or received.

There is one question which confronts **us at almost** every step in life, certainly **at** every important turning point, viz.: "Will it pay?" If any business proposition is made to us, any proposition relating **to** social **or** domestic life, the first question that thrusts itself **upon us is,** "Will it **pay?**" In this intensely

---

[1] Preached in the Foundry Methodist Church, Washington, D C., during the Jubilee Session **of** the Southern Baptist Convention.

255

practical age, when men and women are seeking the prosaic, business side of every pursuit in life, it is natural for us to consider, for ourselves and for those we love, this question concerning the proposition of the text. We may settle it here, just as we do in other matters, viz., by estimating, as far as possible, the outlay and the income. If a man invests five thousand dollars and receives ten thousand dollars, he knows he has made a good investment. *It pays and the man is pleased.* But if he receives only four, or three, or two thousand dollars in return for an investment of five thousand dollars, he knows he has made a bad investment. It *does not pay*, and the man is disappointed. When we seek to know whether it pays to be a Christian, we inquire, Does the honor promised compensate for the service rendered?

I. Let us examine and see what are the leading characteristics of this service.

(*a*) It is sincere, honest, heartfelt. We may deceive others and even ourselves, but we cannot deceive God, whose eye peers down into the deepest recesses of our souls. (*b*) The service is to be rendered *to Christ*, "If any man serve *me*." Many men serve themselves, or their local churches, or their denominations, and serve them alone; whereas, the local church, the denomination, and every other enterprise, should be served only so far as we can glorify God and serve Christ thereby. It is possible, yea, even probable, that many who claim and even seem to serve Christ are never honored here or hereafter, because they are only serving self. The motive which actuates us must be a desire to glorify God. Selfishness, therefore, must be eliminated from our hearts, and self-interest from our plans and calculations in order that we may render acceptable service to Christ. This service must not only be the result of proper motives, but must be (*c*) exact, according to the letter of the law as far as we can understand its teachings. We are not to be our own judges of what we are to do, but must from our hearts say, "Lord, what wilt *thou* have me to do?" Willing, faithful, obedient service is the only scriptural evidence of our conversion, of our faith in Christ, and our oneness with him, and of the acceptableness of our service to him. This service is the most difficult undertaking of man.

First, because it requires perfect submission to God's will.

Second, it requires us to acknowledge our nothingness and forces us, by God's grace, to strive to root out all pride from our hearts. After we have fully surrendered ourselves to Christ and become Christians, on the heart's unseen battlefield the fierce war continues all along life's journey. All intelligent Christians admit that all our time and energies must be devoted to him who died for us; that whatsoever we do, whether in word or deed, we must do all to the glory of God. But, by reason of the value and greatness of the honor conferred on those who serve Christ, were the difficulties of such a consecration tenfold greater than they are, I would still insist that serving God is the *best investment* ever made by mortal man. The world says, "Where is the honor? The wicked spread themselves as green bay trees, while the good and pure go on in poverty; the unjust gather to themselves great wealth, while the righteous have a hard struggle for bread. But who thinks of honoring the Christian? and with what is he honored?" I answer, The honors are conferred not by the puny hands of weak men, but by the King of kings.

II. The Christian is honored:

First, *with the gift of eternal life.*

What is eternal life? I cannot tell you; your pastor cannot tell you; no man among all these pulpit orators and educators who compose this great convention can tell *all* that is comprehended in the term eternal life. We can make some suggestions by way of aiding you to estimate its value.

The immense travel from North to South in the autumn and from South to North in the spring, is not confined to the wealthy, but is largely made up of poor people in search of health. Many fathers and mothers practise the most rigid economy while at home and away in order to spend much of their time at watering places, striving by every possible means to prolong their lives. Visit our almshouses and our charity hospitals. See those poor unfortunates! those deformed, helpless, physical wrecks, without homes, money, friends, relatives, or loved ones. Some one has called them, "Repulsive objects of charity." Did I hear you say, "These would be glad to die"? Not so. Even here you fail to find a willingness to give up life unless calmed by the Spirit of God, or made reckless by a spirit of desperation. You turn away from such scenes and whisper to yourself, "Yes, all that a man hath will he give for his life." Yes, the natural man holds on to the thread of life with wonderful tenacity, and will suffer on and on, year after year, rather than part with that mysterious thing we call life. Now, if this life of weakness and doubt, of fear and trembling, be so desirable and valuable, what will that life be where weakness is turned into strength, and doubts shall fly away? If this life, where the flowers fade so soon is worth clinging to, *what* will be the joy of dwelling in that land where "eternal spring abides and never-fading flowers"? If this life, where sorrow, pain, and bereavements are constantly sweeping over us, is worth such sacrifices as are made to hold it, what will that life be where there shall be no more pain, nor death, nor loss of loved ones? If this life so charms us, where the night of trouble and disappointment comes with its long, lonely hours, and the night of death constantly confronts us, *what* will that life be where the gates stand open *by day?* For there is no night there. No night of sorrow, no night of disappointment, no night of sin, no night of bereavement, no night of death is there. All, all is one eternal day! The **souls of** the redeemed shall live **on while God lives and** eternity lasts; for if **any** man serve **Christ,** he shall "survive the wreck **of** worlds," and shall bask forever in the sunshine of God's glory.

> We know not, **we** know not,
> All **human** words show not,
>   The joys we may reach;
> The mansions preparing,
> The joys for our sharing,
>   The welcome for each.
>
> Here deep is the sighing,
> And strong is the crying;
>   Here brief is the life!
> The life there is endless,
> The joy there is endless,
>   And ended the strife.

If it be an honor to pass out of the high school into the university; an honor **to** climb from the county court-room to the chief-justiceship **of** the United States, who shall undertake **to** measure the honor to be accorded to him who may dwell *forever* with God, spending **eternal** years

> Progressing in the love
> That's **only** learned in heaven! His **mind,**
> Unclogged of clay and **free to soar,**
> Hath left the realms of doubt behind;
> And wondrous things, which finite thought
> In vain essayed to solve, appear
> To his untasked inquiries, fraught
> With explanation strangely clear!
> His reason owns no forced control
> **As** held it here in needless thrall;
> God's mysteries court his questioning **soul,**
> And he may search and *know them all.*

Adoption into God's family is the second honor conferred upon the faithful servant of Christ. We hear much about families and their relative standing. Our newspapers devote whole columns to the "four hundred" of New York, to "the F. F. V's.," to "the first families of Kentucky," to "the first families of Charleston," etc. It is regarded as a great honor to be connected with one of these honorable families.

What are regarded as the elements of an honorable family?

First, ancient historic recognition. Some years ago Henry Ward Beecher and his sister, with a number of others, met at Martha's Vineyard, to ascertain if possible their family genealogy. Many others in all parts of our country can speak with commendable pride of their forefathers who marched under the command of our American chieftain during the Revolutionary War. Many can go back and trace their line of descent through the Huguenots and Puritans to worthy ancestors beyond the sea. Queen Victoria boasts of having descended from the house of David. But let us turn to the third chapter of Luke and read of Jesus, who was supposed to have been the son of Joseph, and then follow his line of descent back beyond David to Noah, Enoch, Seth, and Adam, who was the son of God. So by faith in Christ Jesus *we* are "born, not of blood, nor of the will of the flesh, nor of the will of man, but *of God*." By the operation of the Holy Spirit we become partakers of the divine nature. The Holy Spirit applies to our souls the efficacy of the blood of Christ, so that we become blood-kin to God through his son Jesus, who claims us as his brethren. So then we are the children of God, and are members of that family which antedates all other families.

Second, another element of honorable family descent is *wisdom*. We speak of our great Washington, of our Lee, Clay, Calhoun, Webster, Madison, and Jefferson; we cross over to Europe, where they are now struggling for liberty of soul and body, and longing for the day to dawn when the freedom of soul and liberty of conscience enjoyed by our American people shall be enjoyed by them. But there seems to be no man wise enough to lead them out of bondage. I ask, why is this? and the answer comes from the word of God, "The world by wisdom knew not God." But our Father is infinite in wisdom, good in greatness, and great in goodness. Then as people come to realize their need of wisdom, let them heed the admonition of God's word, "If any man lack wisdom let him ask of God, who giveth to all men liberally and upbraideth not" (James 1 : 5); for the head of our family is "great in counsel and mighty in work" (Jer. 32 : 19); and "among all the wise men of the nations, and in all their kingdoms there is none like unto him" (Jer. 10 : 7).

Third, *wealth* is regarded as a third mark of family pride. Job was the greatest man in the East. The Lord blessed Abraham with herds and cattle and gold and silver. Solomon's riches and influence were a wonder in the world, and called forth from the Queen of the South the expression, "The half has not been told me." In our day we have the Rothschilds, Goulds, Vanderbilts, Rockefellers, and many other millionaires. But what are such families! Even if they should all pool their interests and call it one fortune, it would be only as a drop in the ocean compared with the wealth of our Heavenly Father. All the merchandise and banks, railroads, factories, stocks and bonds, mining and naval interests, are as nothing to him. He can dispose of crowns and sceptres as easily as a child breaks a toy. He can set up and as easily tear down. We who are born of God are the children of a glorious king. Our Father is the owner of all the silver and gold of the world, and the cattle on a thousand hills is his also. We have not yet come in possession of our patrimony, but

> We can read our titles clear
> To mansions in the skies.

Twenty years ago in New Orleans, an influential, intelligent, wealthy man picked up a little newsboy, and adopted him as his own child. The elegant family mansion, with all its costly furniture, its superb paintings by the old masters, its musical instruments, the costly equipages, sugar plantation, the *honored family name*, with all the man owned, became the property, through legal heirship, of that little boy, who, until that adoption was a barefooted waif. He was sent to the best schools and colleges. Found without parents, without home, without reputation, nameless, *all* became his. Was he honored? How incalculably greater the honor bestowed upon spiritual orphans who, though strangers and foreigners to the commonwealth of Israel, have been adopted into God's most glorious family, where angels are the servants, the Son of God the Elder Brother, and God himself their own Father!

Finally, we mention *the home he gives us*, for truly, "there's no place like home." The question of past ages has been, "If a man die, shall he live again?" and not only *shall he live* but *where? Now*, these great questions are answered; for Christ brought life and immortality to light, and he said, "In my Father's house are many mansions, I go to prepare a place for you." For us, then, he has prepared a home, where the family shall all be gathered when time shall end and our labors are finished.

"Home! sweet, sweet home!" So many have no home here in this world. There are persons whose ancestors for many generations have been tenants in other people's houses. Many families in this our favored land of liberty have no homes, and perhaps never will have any. The great corporations not only own the factories, but the houses in which the laborers live; they almost own the laborers. How different when we think of "our Father's house"! If we never own a home here, by the grace of God we may own one in heaven. There are many thousands whose homes to-day are mortgaged, and thousands of homes have been sold by foreclosure of the mortgages and the families turned out in the cold, heartless world. But not so is it with our home above. No power on earth or in hell can mortgage our home which our dear Lord has gone to prepare.

Oh! how our thoughts run back to our childhood's home, and we seem to enter into a different atmosphere, or, our minds may dwell on our present homes where wife and children are! We may be entertained by some friend, and in his home, a palatial residence, with all the garniture of art, the finest furniture, exquisite bronzes and paintings, with musical instruments, rich in construction and tone. Whole libraries of costly books may be there. We may wander in the terraced lawns, amid rare flowers and shrubbery. Our friend may anticipate our every wish. But as the day grows old, and the stars peep from behind the heavenly dome, our hearts fly over vale and hill, over mountain and ocean, and we say,

> Be it ever so humble
> There's no place like home.

The sacred memories, the loving hearts, the familiar faces, and the musical voices of a *real* home, can never be forgotten, nor reproduced when gone. The heart feels lighter, the sun shines brighter, the birds sing sweeter, the stars seem nearer, the days fly fleeter, and heaven seems dearer to us when we are in the midst of those influences which produce what we call home. But here "the eagle stirreth up her nest" and the sweetest homes are broken up. Sons and daughters marry and scatter. For a long time there were feast-days, bright Christmas times, father's and mother's birthdays, Thanksgiving days, when we all went home to a "family reunion." Father and mother would meet us and call us boys and girls; and with neighbors and friends we would spend a few happy days together. The old hearthstone was there, the bright fire, the old armed-chairs occupied by father and mother, the old clock was on the mantel, saying "Ever forever; forever, never." But it *did* stop, and the old home is broken up. Perhaps the house is standing yet, but it is occupied by strangers; or, even though some member of the family may still own the premises, these home reunions are now no longer possible to most of us; for some of the dwellers there, have passed

>Beyond the parting and the meeting,
>Beyond the farewell and the greeting.

But by-and-by God shall honor us with a great family reunion which will never break up.

>Beyond the frost-chain and the fever,
>Beyond the ever and the never,
>We shall be soon.

We have had some great expositions and world's fairs. The works of art, the inventions and discoveries of men, and the productions of nature have been brought together, and the children of the civilized nations of the earth have met and clasped hands with the semi-civilized and the real heathen. All have come together in a reunion of the families of the earth. But how short has been their stay, and how unsatisfactory has been their meeting with each other! But, the mighty God, even the Lord, hath spoken, and called the earth from the rising of the sun unto the going down thereof. **Out of Zion, the perfection of beauty, God hath shined. There is to be a great national and international family reunion, for** "they shall **come** from the east and **from** the west, from the **north** and from the south, and shall sit down in the kingdom of God." Jesus Christ himself will welcome us; from the King's son will we hear the "Come, ye blessed **of** my Father, inherit the kingdom prepared for you from before the foundation of the world." We will stay there days, weeks, months, and years, and

> When we've been there ten thousand years,
> Bright shining as the sun,
> We've no less days to sing God's praise,
> Than when **we** first **begun**.

Keep silence, and hear the rustling of the great throng as they go sweeping through the gates! Look and see the righteous marching in, angels harping the "Harvest Home," **and** Jesus receiving them with outstretched arms!

> Love, rest, and home!

Come, Holy Spirit, and teach us all to render acceptable service to him who loved us and gave himself for us. Amen and amen.

x

XXIV

INFIDELITY AND CHRISTIANITY CONTRASTED[1]

BY T. H. PRITCHARD, D. D.

"Their rock is not as our Rock, even our enemies themselves being judges." Deut. 32 : 31.

THE text was uttered by Moses under peculiar circumstances. The leader of Israel was now a hundred and twenty years old, and the Lord had said unto him, "Behold, thou shalt sleep with thy fathers, for thou shalt not go over this Jordan into the land that floweth with milk and honey." But before he should ascend Mount Nebo and surrender his pious soul to the God who gave it, the Almighty commanded him to deliver a dying charge to the sorrowing multitudes that had assembled to witness his departure. The chapter I have just read, opening with so much sublimity, was the valedictory sermon of Moses, and critics assure us that within this short discourse may be found the varied excellencies of every species of composition. Here are the terse and pithy expressions of vigorous prose, the sparkling beauties of poetic imagery, with the loftiest strains of sublime and grateful praise.

Such being the literary excellencies of this sacred production, we are not surprised to find the God of Moses so frequently represented by the simile of a rock. Indeed, to express that which is sure in its foundation and enduring in character, the figure of a rock has always been a favorite one with the poets.

---

[1] A baccalaureate sermon.

THOMAS HENDERSON PRITCHARD was born in Charlotte, N. C., on **the 8th of** February, 1832. His father, Joseph Price Pritchard, was a native of Charleston, S. C.; was reared an Episcopalian, but became a Baptist from principle, and preached the gospel for fifty years. He died in Texas, in 1890, at the advanced age of eighty-four. His mother, Eliza Hunter Henderson, was the daughter of a family that traces its history from Thomas Henderson, who emigrated from Scotland and landed at Jamestown, Va., in 1607. His descendant, Samuel Henderson, was the progenitor of the North Carolina branch **of** that distinguished family, being the father of Judge Richard Henderson, **and** the grandfather of Chief Justice Leonard Henderson. Dr. Pritchard was graduated from Wake Forest College in 1854, delivering the valedictory. In 1858 he read theology with Dr. John A. Broadus, at Charlottesville, taking a course in the University of Virginia at the same time. He has been pastor of the Franklin Square Church, in Baltimore, the First Church, Raleigh, N. C., First Church, Petersburg, Va., Broadway, Louisville, Ky., Wilmington, N. C., and is now serving the Tryon Street Church, Charlotte, N. C. Dr. Pritchard **was** president of Wake Forest College for three years. He preached the Convention sermon when that body met in Charleston, in May, 1875. He received his doctorate from the University of North Carolina, **in** 1868.

Virgil, in describing the decision of character of old Latinus, represents him—

> As a rock unmoved, a rock that braves
> The raging tempest and the rising waves,
> Propped in himself he stands,

and proudly dashes back the impotent billows of his enemies' wrath. Isaiah speaks of the protecting power of God as resembling the shadow of a great rock in a weary land, to screen the way-worn traveler from the bitter winds which prevail at night and the scorching rays of an Oriental sun. And David breaks forth in his rapturous faith, "He is my rock and my fortress, the rock of my salvation and my refuge forever." It is most comforting to the pious soul to express its confidence in "the sure mercies of David" by that which is thus stable and enduring.

The word "rock," you observe, occurs twice in the text, and has a different meaning according to its application. Its sense is determined by the pronouns which precede it. In the one case it represents the eternal God; in the other various theories and speculations which the enemies of religion entertain.

The kind of evidence to be adduced demands a moment's consideration before we proceed farther. Our enemies themselves are to furnish the proof of their own convictions. Now in all our courts of justice, evidence submitted by a person in his friend's favor is regarded as valid, even though it may be known that he is anxious for that friend's acquittal. Testimony by parties entirely disinterested is, from moral considerations, entitled to more weight; but when the force of truth is such as to make men swear in favor of their enemies, the conviction that they speak the truth is always most satisfactory and conclusive. But still more when it is known to be an implacable enemy of the accused, and for his conviction he suppresses or garbles the truth, and is detected in his infamous design, the innocence of the accused is but revealed in the more beautiful and transparent colors. Let us remember this in the discussion to which we are about to address ourselves.

1. (*a*) Among the enemies of Christianity we notice, first, the atheist, who denies the existence of God, and declares that the physical organization which we call the world is the result of chance; that notwithstanding the wonderful beauty, the perfect regularity and evident design everywhere exhibited in the material universe, it is all the result of a fortuitous arrangement of the particles of matter. We might ask, whence originated these particles of matter? Were they too the result of chance, and of that undefined something which he calls fate? Did man, the very paragon of animals, spring up from the earth as do the fruits of the field? Did chance mold the symmetry of his form and bestow the lofty capacities of his intellect? Why do we not now behold human beings in the transition state being converted by chance from inanimate particles of matter into sentient, intelligent creatures? The whole theory is an absurdity. What is chance? We take the paring of an apple, as children often do, and throwing it on the floor say, if in falling it forms a letter, it is by chance. We see, from the nature of the experiment, that the more complicated its character, the less probability is there of an intelligible result. If, instead of the apple peel, we take a hatful of letters and scatter them at random over the floor, how long might one be thus engaged before a single sentence or even a word would be formed? Would it not be absurd to hope thus to create a book of poems? But the great book of creation is far more complicate and exhibits far more of design than the "Iliad" of Homer, or the "Paradise" of Milton. But why waste time on such folly? Verily, the Scriptures have declared, "The fool hath said in his heart, there is no God." The

INFIDELITY AND CHRISTIANITY CONTRASTED 269

rock of the atheist is a fool's position, **the Scriptures being judge.**

This, beloved, is speculative atheism, and though treatises have been written in its support, I very much question whether any sane man ever held such opinions. Would to God there were none other than speculative atheism in the world. But, alas for poor sinful nature, alas for the cause of Christ and the conversion of the world, we are all more or less practical atheists. We profess to believe that there is a God, and that he will reward those who diligently seek him. We believe that God will judge us in that great day for which all others were made, and yet in the very presence of the living God we commit sin and deport ourselves as if there were no God. When the celebrated Luther Rice heard of the sufferings of the missionary Ward in India; when he read that the East India Company, determining to expel all ministers of the gospel from their territory, had driven him forth from the face of man to dwell in the jungles among wild beasts and poisonous serpents, and that he still persisted in remaining there that he might tell the poor heathen of a Saviour, Dr. Rice was moved to tears, and exclaimed to those around him: "Ah! brethren, Brother Ward believes there is a God."

(*b*) The deist is also an enemy to the Christian religion, inasmuch as he rejects the Bible and Jesus Christ, though he does admit the existence of a God. The name deist was first assumed by some persons in France and Italy, who wished to disguise their hatred of Christianity under some less opprobrious name than that of atheist. Deists have no particular system of religion, but profess to be guided alone by reason and nature. They affirm that there is no necessity for a direct revelation, and therefore discard the teachings of the apostles and evangelists as so many dreams and fables. They hold, indeed, that God created the heavens and the earth, and that his character is revealed in his works—that we may "look through nature up to nature's God." In support of his position, the deist appeals to history, and from the fact that a few individuals among the heathen have believed in but one God, and because all people of every age have had an idea of some existence superior to themselves, they therefore argue the sufficiency of the light of nature. Now just at this point we take issue with the deist, and will introduce his own witness to testify in our favor. And in taking this position I do not mean to disparage the light of nature. When properly interpreted, it does develop in a most beautiful and striking manner the character of the Creator. But I maintain that without the Bible we could never accurately comprehend the utterances of nature. It is true that David could say, "The heavens declare the glory of God, and the firmament showeth his handiwork," but David was an inspired man, and held the true doctrine of theism; but I repeat it, that I do not believe that any man ever has or ever will learn from nature alone so much of his duty to God as to secure his salvation. The priests of Egypt, it is said, taught that there was but one God, and so held a few of the philosophers of Greece and Rome; but the Egyptians, doubtless, derived their theology from the captive Israelites, while the ancient philosophers received their notions from these same Egyptian priests, or directly from the prophecies of the Old Testament. Aristobulus, an ancient historian, tells us, and his testimony is corroborated by a statement in Second Maccabees, that there was a Greek translation of some of the books of the Old Testament four hundred years before Christ, and that Socrates, Plato, and Aristotle consulted it in the composition of their philosophic works.

In the Alcibiades of Plato there is a description of a lawgiver that was to come, which is almost an exact copy of the graphic account of the Messiah in the fifty-third chapter of Isaiah. Indeed, Plato tells us himself that he derived his notions of God from the Syrian Fraternity; which Syrian Fraternity was none other than the Jews themselves, unto whom were committed the oracles of God.

But to bring the subject home to the deist. Would he be willing to exchange his existence in the nineteenth century with the wisest of the sages of antiquity? Would he be willing to entertain their notions of morality and worship their gods, even in the most cultivated and enlightened times of the past?

Take Greece, for instance, in her palmiest days—when Athens was the intellectual eye of the universe, when Demosthenes thundered from the Bema, when Plato wrote and Pindar sang and Praxiteles used the chisel, when, in fine, painting, poetry, sculpture, and eloquence existed in a perfection never since attained—ask the deist if there have been greater natural men than the giants of that age who sought to solve the problem of man's being and destiny, and then let him give his testimony for Christianity. Would he be willing to worship such creatures as were Jupiter, Bacchus, Venus, and Mercury, with all the enormities ascribed to them, crimes and vices which, if committed in this age, would bring down upon the perpetrators the vengeance of an infuriated mob? Question him as to the state of morals then existing—the condition of woman, the treatment of slaves, prisoners, and deformed infants. Did nature inspire Plato to teach the doctrine of a community of wives, Lycurgus to commend dexterous thieving, Solon to allow sodomy, and Seneca to encourage drunkenness and suicide? Would the deist dare commend these dark and impure precepts as worthy of general acceptance? No! no! The intelligent deist would not be willing to live in an age of reason, even though that reason might be developed to the highest degree.

But we have listened to the testimony of the strongest witness the deist can produce, as drawn from the experience of the most cultivated nations of the past, and we find that the world by wisdom knew not God *then*, nor does the world by wisdom know God *now*. Let us bring to the stand the most intelligent and refined heathen nations of the present age. Take the Chinese for instance. They are a cultivated people. It is said they discovered many of the mysteries of astronomy before Copernicus or Galileo lived. They had invented glass and gunpowder and the art of printing, before other nations. One has to think in but the most cursory way to read the answer.

The fact is, that the deist who may have correct notions of morality has not derived those ideas from nature, but has stolen them from the Bible; and while he writes books to dishonor the oracles of God, he plagiarizes from that sacred volume the very best and purest thoughts of his own works.

The declaration of the Scriptures is explicit. There is no other name under heaven, given among men whereby we must be saved, but that of Jesus, and we may question whether any individual of all the nations that have successively disappeared from this earth's arena has been saved by reason and nature. The history of reason guided by the light of nature, in all ages, has been one of darkness and doubt; far, very far, from the clear and steady light which streams upon the Christian's path from the Sun of Righteousness. Verily the rock of the deist is not as our Rock.

(*c*) The subject of infidelity and skepticism next claims our attention. Infidelity is a perfect Proteus in character—it assumes so many and such varied forms that it is difficult to define it accurately.

Suffice it to say, that as the term imports, infidelity is unbelief—a want of faith in God, and a rejection of all, or some of the principles of the Christian religion. It has presented in different ages and countries various phases. In France it led to an abolition of the Christian Sabbath, and an utter refusal to recognize an overruling Providence. The weapons of attack resorted to by French infidels have been the coarsest ribaldry and the boldest blasphemy. In England, infidelity has been more philosophic, and affects to exhibit the discrepancy between the revelations of science and those of the Bible.

The infidelity of Scotland has differed but little from that of England, though, perhaps, it is somewhat more respectful toward religion, probably because of the piety of public sentiment in that most moral of all countries. In Germany, infidelity is pantheism, the prime article of which faith is, that the universe is God. By some a system is held called neology, which has its basis in the science of metaphysics, and abounds in conjectures and speculations of a rationalistic character, leading men to rely upon reason and nature, rather than revelation, for spiritual light.

In the United States we have infidelity diversified. Scientific infidelity, spiritualism, transcendentalism, as held by Theodore Parker and Waldo Emerson; free-loveism, communism, Universalism, Mormonism, and many others not less pernicious, though more restricted in their influence.

2. When we observe such phenomena in the history of the moral world, we are constrained to ask, Why do men reject the wisdom of God and embrace such follies? The reasons are manifold:

(a) With some, such notions arise from an affectation of singularity. They are ambitious of the character of original thinkers, and from a morbid sense of independence, wish never to tread in a beaten path. Satisfy them that all the world holds a system as true, and for that very reason they discard it. The notions of morality which have come down to us, venerable for their antiquity and revered for their purity, they regard as exploded follies, fit only to be held by the old fogies of this progressive age.

As for themselves, they must have something new, and no matter whence its origin, or how absurd its essence, if it is something unusual, they at once embrace it; and not unfrequently may these sapient philosophers be heard delivering, with all the zest of original discovery, objections against Christianity as old as Porphyry and Celsus, and which, perhaps, they think they may gain the credit of inventing.

(*b*) Infidelity often springs up in the heart from another kind of pride—pride of learning. The arrogant self-sufficiency generated by human learning has doubtless been a fruitful source of infidelity in all ages. How different this spirit from that which always distinguishes the truly erudite and wise! "A little learning is a dangerous thing," but sound and extensive knowledge serves to correct this unseemly pride and induce a solid frame of mind. Socrates, the wisest of the ancient philosophers, professed only to know that he knew nothing, and Sir Isaac Newton, the greatest philosopher of all time, when complimented on his great attainments in science, replied with beautiful modesty, "that he had accomplished but little; he had been but as a child gathering a few pebbles on the beach, while the great ocean of truth lay unexplored before him."

(*c*) Again, it is a lamentable fact that the conduct of professing Christians furnishes one of the strongest pleas for infidelity. They have the form of godliness, but deny the power thereof in their daily deportment, and thus the world is taught to doubt the vitality of religion, and lapses into infidelity. It is in the house of her friends and by the unfaithfulness of her own adherents that the heaviest blows are dealt against Christianity. Were they but true to their high vocation, infidelity would be deprived of the food upon which it fattens, and would hide its diminished head in shame and dishonor. Let us never forget that "Conduct hath the loudest tongue."

(*d*) But not to be tedious in assigning the causes of infidelity, the great and prime reason why men are infidels is because they wish to be; because of the wickedness of their own hearts; because the gospel has upon its very frontlet the command of Christ, Deny thyself, and take up thy cross and follow me. The truth is, "infidelity is rather a disease of the heart than of the head." Men believe Moses false and the Bible a bundle of fables, because by that Bible their own evil deeds are condemned; because they love darkness rather that light. The Earl of Rochester, once an arrant infidel, used to say in his old age, laying his hand upon the Bible, "Here is true philosophy. This is the wisdom that speaks to the heart. A bad life is the only grand objection to this book." This last declaration is intensely true. The history of infidelity shows scarcely a single exception to this sweeping declaration. No man who has any self-respect would care to read aloud in company some expressions in Voltaire's works, even when treating of the most sacred subjects. J. J. Rousseau has acknowledged in his "Confession," that on one occasion he had the baseness to steal an article, and rather than confess the theft, he suffered an honest servant girl to lose her place and her character. His book of confessions closes with these remarkable words: "Whenever the last trump shall sound, I will present myself before the Sovereign Judge with this book in my hand, and loudly proclaim, 'Thus have I acted—these were my thoughts—such was I, Power Eternal! Assemble around thy throne the innumerable throng of my fellow-mortals. Let them listen to my confessions; **let them** blush at my depravity; let them tremble at my sufferings. Let each in turn **expose** the failings and wanderings of his own heart **with** equal sincerity, and, if he *dare*, say, "**I was** better than that man." ' "

How utterly abandoned must **have been the man** who could affect to make **a** merit **of** such confessions before the throne of the Most High, and who could **thus** charge all mankind with guilt equal to his own! "**No** books are so plain as the lives of men, no characters so legible as their moral conduct." The great offense of the cross is its purity. 'Twas the ineffable innocence of the Saviour that filled the heart of Voltaire with such malignant rancor and made him close his letters to his familiar friends with the expression, "Crush the wretch!" meaning thereby the blessed Jesus. Fit language of the great apostle of infidelity, the high priest of Satan on earth. Nor has infidelity changed in its spirit and essence since the more able **and** vehement of **its** advocates have passed from the scene of action.

3. (*a*) Another feature of infidelity closely allied **to** the last, is the ignorance of its adherents in respect **to** that very religion they so vauntingly disclaim. I am free to admit that many of them have been men of great attainments in science and literature; nevertheless, these very men have, through sinful ignorance, rejected the Christian religion. Their own confessions prove this. Tom Paine confines himself to the **Old** Testament **in** assailing the Scriptures, and Hume confesses that he never read the New Testament through in his life, while Voltaire betrays his egregious ignorance by speaking of "the book of Moses, the book of Genesis, and the book of Pentateuch."

(*b*) And yet again; **the manner** in which infidels have attacked Christianity—the unfair and dishonest means to which they have resorted, prove that their rock is not as our Rock, and that their cause is not only a weak but a wicked one. Infidels harp upon the mysteries of the Bible, as if there were not mystery in everything God has made, and as if we might expect with our finite powers to comprehend everything in a book which reveals the character of the Infinite. They detect trifling errors in chronology and history, which have been time and again explained and reconciled, and though they are fully apprised of this, each successive school, in the most disingenuous manner, iterates and reiterates those charges as if they were vital to the cardinal doctrines of Christianity.

(c) A very frequent and plausible objection **preferred** against Christianity by its enemies is the **want** of unity among its own adherents. There are so many different sects, holding such diverse systems of doctrine, that it is affirmed that nothing may be relied on as true, and therefore it is the part of wisdom to reject the whole. Now, it is a lamentable fact that there are many sects; it is true, moreover, that we do sometimes contend among ourselves with a degree of acrimony which the spirit of the gospel does not justify.

But is this a legitimate objection to Christianity? Is there not a union of sympathy in the experience of all true Christians? You may gather Christians from all parts of the globe—bring a Hottentot, a Greenlander, a South Sea Islander, a stupid African or a cultured Caucasian—I care not where they may have been born or what dialect they speak, if genuine Christians they will all have substantially the same experience, the same repentance, the same faith, and will hope to reach the same heaven at last.

But does not this objection recoil with **fatal** force against all the systems of infidelity? Some systems declare there is a God, others **deny it.** Some affirm that the soul is immortal, others **do** not admit that man has **a** soul. One **system** contends that man should be under some kind of moral law; another that he is a law unto himself, and should follow his own inclinations. Their confusion is like that of the tower of Babel, and yet they denounce the believers in Christianity as superstitious and credulous dupes, because we will not trample under foot the "sure mercies of David," and embrace their false and baseless systems of sin and iniquity.

But finally it is in death that the true merits of infidelity and Christianity appear. The dying beds of infidels, in utterance distinct and awful, declare that their rock is not as our Rock.

The well-known story of Col. Ethan Allen is a striking illustration of the utter insufficiency of infidelity in the hour of death. Col. Allen was a gallant patriot, but an avowed infidel. He had an only child, a beautiful daughter on whom he lavished every care. When in the flush of early womanhood, this daughter sickened and died. As she lay, awaiting the approach of death, she took her father's hand and said: "Father, mother has told me to take Jesus as my Saviour, while you have told me that Jesus is no Saviour. Which must I believe now?" The heart of the strong man was moved to its profoundest depths. He had faced the cannon's mouth unblanched, but he trembled like an aspen before his dying child, as with choked utterance he replied, "My daughter, believe your mother."

Some years since, one of two young Americans, who were in Paris, was taken ill. In seeking a nurse to care for his sick friend, the other encountered an old woman who had nursed Voltaire in his last illness. The first question she asked when applied to was, "Is your friend a Christian?" "He is," replied he, "but why do you ask such a question?" "I nursed Voltaire," rejoined the old woman, "and I wouldn't see another infidel die for all the gold there is in France."

INFIDELITY AND CHRISTIANITY CONTRASTED 279

How different the condition of the great apostle to the Gentiles, when about to be put to death: "I am now ready to be offered, and the time of my departure is at hand. I have fought a good fight, I have finished my course, I have kept the faith. Henceforth there is laid up for me a crown of righteousness which the Lord, the righteous judge, shall give me at that day, and not to me only, but unto all them also that love his appearing."

Byron wrote thus sadly the year he died:

> My days are in the yellow leaf,
>   The fruits and flowers of love are gone;
> The worm, the canker, and the grief,
>   Are mine alone.
>
> The fire that on my bosom preys
>   Is lone as some volcanic isle,
> No torch is kindled at its blaze;
>   A funeral pile.

Permit me, in conclusion, to present this contrast as drawn by the poet Montgomery in a few masterly strokes:

> Lo yonder, in that fancy-haunted room
> What muttered curses tremble thro' the gloom,
> Where pale and shining, and bedewed with fear,
> The dying skeptic feels his hour draw near.
> From his parched lips no meek hosannas fall,
> No bright hope kindles at his last farewell.
> He gnashes, scowls, and raises hideous shrieks,
> As the last throes of death convulse his cheeks;
> He rounds his eyes into a ghastly glare,
> Locks his white lips, and all is mute despair.

To the infidel he says:

> Go, child of darkness, see a Christian die,
> No horror pales his lips or dims his eye;
> No fiend-shaped phantoms of destruction start
> The hope religion pillows in his heart;

When, with a faltering hand, he waves adieu
To all who love so well and weep so true;
Meek as an infant to the mother's breast
Turns fondly longing for its wonted rest,
He pants for where congenial spirits stray,
Looks to his God and sighs his soul away.

Verily "their rock is not as our Rock, even our enemies themselves being judges."

J. B. CRANFILL was born in Parker County, Tex., September 12, 1858, of Baptist parents. His father, Rev. E. A. Cranfill, is still living. His early life was spent on a farm and as a cowboy, and his education was procured from the Texas country schools of that period. He was converted at the age of eighteen and joined the Baptist church. In 1878 he married Miss Ollie Allen, at Crawford, Tex. After his marriage he practised medicine for about three years, and then began the publication of the "Gatesville Advance," a weekly paper which became distinguished for its advocacy of temperance and prohibition. In 1886 he was licensed to preach and was ordained by the First Baptist Church, Waco, in 1890. From 1889 to 1892 he was superintendent of Texas Baptist mission work. He is editor and sole proprietor of the "Texas Baptist Standard," and proprietor of the "Kentucky Baptist Standard," and the "Indian Baptist Standard." He is the compiler of a book of sermons by Dr. B. H. Carroll. In addition to his editorial labors and literary work, he has been prominently identified for many years with the prohibition movement, having been the candidate for vice-president of the United States on that ticket in 1892. He is also in great demand as a lecturer.

Rev. T. B. Crandell

XXV

A MAN IN HELL

BY REV. J. B. CRANFILL.

"The rich man also died, and was buried; **and in hell** he lifted up his eyes, being in torments." Luke 16 : 22, 23.

IT is well from time to time in this short journey of our lives to stop and take our bearings, not only as regards this world, but as regards eternity. This is a very busy life we are living; there is a great rush, great excitement, great and powerful movements, with a broad sweep of power; and in the whirl and excitement we sometimes **are** prone to forget that after a while this fitful fever shall end; that after a little these that abide with us now shall have gone, and after a little while we shall have taken up our abode eternally in heaven or in hell. There are but two places of abode for the spirits of men after death. One of these places is heaven. God, Jesus on the throne, the angels and spirits of just men made perfect are there. That is heaven. In hell are the devil, the devil's angels, and the spirits of evil men who have passed into that nether world.

The text before us, or rather the entire lesson—for I wish to speak about the entire lesson rather than the few words announced **as a** text—begins by saying that there was a certain rich man. It does not give his name. It does not matter what his name was—a certain rich man. It is not a crime to be a rich man. There is many a poor man that is rich in a certain sense. He is rich in evil; rich in bad deeds; **rich in** evil associations; **rich** in his scorn of God.

Riches in themselves are not criminal. There is many a rich man, as we count riches, whose heart is tender, and who is really rich toward God, and who is touched with a feeling of the infirmities of every poor beggar under the shining stars. It is not a crime then to be rich; and I have never had any sympathy with the great cry of people against the rich. It is a great temptation to be rich. I never shall forget the prayer recorded in the Old Testament, "Give me neither poverty nor riches." I have thought sometimes I would like to be rich. I fear it comes to us all in some time of special temptation, of special allurement by the world. We wish we could be rich; but when we come to think about it soberly, we had better not be really rich in this world's goods, because there come great temptations with riches. But as I said before, I have no sympathy with the idea that is getting deeper and broader in our country, that to be rich is evil in itself, and that riches must be pounced upon and destroyed and divided out among tramps and anarchists. All such doctrine comes from the devil. Neither is it a crime to be poor. The really poor can be rich toward God. Look at this man's name now. The poor man has a name. There was a certain rich man, and then there was a certain beggar named Lazarus. You know Lazarus' name meant "helped of God." That is the interpretation of his name.

And now let us go and see the picture. See the mansion with its broad spacious grounds, the blooming flowers, and the fruits in the fields; and then see down at the gate a poor man with a crutch. There he was, laid at the gate, full of sores. Lazarus had very likely been a very prosperous workingman. It is quite likely that at one time he had wrought mightily with his hands and made his daily bread and looked up to nobody except to God. But oh, the great misfortune of a poor man when he is sick. I tell you it is an awful thing to be sick at all, but it is transcendently awful to be sick when you are poor, when you cannot make the daily two dollars. Not long ago it came very close to me. A man in my employ, and as kingly a man as ever wore the crown of honest labor, got sick, and I could see the pain written all over his face when he failed to earn his two dollars a day. It was dreadful. And the fact that Lazarus was a beggar was no disgrace to him, because he was sick. He was not a beggar by choice. He was not a tramp. He did not go around, a healthy and stalwart man, and go to the back kitchen door and say, "I wish you would give me some bread." I have no respect for a tramp—I mean a well tramp. A man in this country who would go out begging for a cup of coffee, who has two good strong arms on him and health flushing his face; shame on him! Lazarus was a beggar because he was sick, and here he was at the rich man's gate. You look at these plain statements of fact. Most of the commentaries say that this was a parable. It may have been a parable, but I don't believe it was a parable. In another place where Jesus mentions a rich man the Scripture says, "He spoke a parable unto them." In this case there is no parable in it, but a plain statement of plain, everyday facts. This plain statement was not a parable, as I understand it, but Jesus Christ rent the veil and made that recital of an everyday occurrence in every age. He simply raised the curtain and said, "And Lazarus died."

Let us now think about the rich man a moment. He was having a good time; he fared sumptuously every day. He went and took a box at the theatre and saw the play with opera glasses. He played his game of social cards, and bet a little. He was not really a bad gambler, or else he would not have been rich. And he attended the "german," went down to the saloon on Sunday and drank his wines and whiskies. He was probably a member of the local political executive committee and had influence in the community; a man who thought about everything except God and heaven and eternity; grasping his money, despising God's homeless poor that came to his gate and begged: "Oh, mister, just let me come after dinner is over and eat the crumbs that fall from the table!" He took a stick and drove him away from the gate.

"There was a certain beggar." I have thought about that beggar many a time. I do not think I will ever again let any beggar pass me by without giving him something. I do not mean tramps. As I before stated, I have no respect for tramps; and I wish you would never have any respect for tramps. But I talk about beggars, people who are really in distress, who have sadness written on their faces and poverty marked all over them. It was only the other day in the city of New York, a poor beggar on Broadway came up to me and said, "Oh, give me money; help me." You could see poverty all over him; see that hope had left his heart and despair had come to live with him. I make a plea here to-day, whether you have much or little, that you remember the homeless poor, and help them. The day will come when it will have been more to you to have invested money in a really deserving poor man than to have had a million dollars stock in the Bank of England.

But see the change of scene. Look how sublimely our Saviour goes right on with the story. He does not stop to explain anything about the difference between time and eternity. That is not his purpose just now; but he is depicting the lives of these two men. And he says: "The rich man also died and was buried." See the contrast between the statement made just before about Lazarus: "And . . . the beggar died and was carried by the angels." He did not stop to say whether he was buried or not. The chances are that he was not buried. Probably he dragged himself into some lonely, sequestered spot, and there died. Jesus did not say that he was buried, but the rich man died and was buried. See the funeral procession. Maybe no real mourners even then. He had five brothers, but they were probably glad he was dead. They will get his money now and have a good time over it. But here is the long funeral procession following the man out to the grave, with all the trappings of funerals. On this point I wish to say a word in passing. The saddest thing to me, sadder than the funeral itself, is to see the great pomp and circumstance of some funerals. Oh, the money that is wasted, literally wasted, burying men. Some of the rich pay out thousands of dollars for funerals, and on every side God's cause lifts up its empty hands and the hungry and poor and thinly clad are dying for the very bread of life. Lazarus died and was carried by the angels. The rich man died and, in hell he lifted up his eyes—in hell.

Now this brings us to the subject of our sermon, "A Man in Hell." Stop a moment. Is this an idle picture? The worst and most malignant enemies that Jesus Christ ever had never accused him of telling a lie. You take all the literature written against him to prove that he was not divine, and with one consensus of opinion, one acclaim, one voice, all literature says, "Jesus Christ was a good man." And here he says that this man lifted up his eyes in hell. The curtain is raised. There is the man in hell. Time to him is dead. Opportunity to him is gone forever. He has passed from life's arena. There was sunshine yesterday; the funeral to-day; hell to-day. Eternity, eternity, eternity, has come and the man is in hell. See him. He prays—the first time perhaps in all his life that he had ever prayed, and he says, "Oh, Father Abraham!" Repentance has come.

Did you ever visit a jail? The most humble lot of

repentant sinners on earth are in jail. I have talked to men, I have preached to men in jail. They will all give their hand; they all want to be saved. Why? Because they are caught. Not because they committed a crime, but because the sleuth-hound of the law has tracked them down, and now they find themselves incarcerated and the bolts and bars shut them in and there is no hope of escape. They are all humble, all penitent. All of them say, "I wish I was out again. If I were I would be a better man." Turn one out and he would steal a horse to-morrow night.

A man in hell! There was a quaint, strange book anonymously written in England entitled, "Letters from Hell." I wish all sinners might read those letters, though they are imaginary. But, oh, hear the cold, solemn words of Jesus. They are not imaginary. Don't they cause the cold chills to run over you to-day as you hear the words of our Saviour, awful in their terror and truthfulness? "In hell he lifted up his eyes." I don't suppose he believed in hell at all while he lived. I suppose he had argued many a time to prove that there was no hereafter at all, and he had said, "Oh, this nonsense that these people talk about. There is no such place. Get the thing out of my mind, I don't want to hear about it." But hear me to-day, fellow-traveler to the grave: shutting one's eyes does not put out the fire. You may hear the crackling of the flames and the jingle of the firemen's bell, and the shout of the firemen's captain. You may hear the word, "Fire!" And yet you shut your eyes and say, "I don't see any fire; I don't believe there is any fire." But the fire rages still, and block after block of buildings is consumed and crashes in. Oh, vain man, to-day I thunder in your ears, warranted by the word of God and by the burning sentences of Jesus of Nazareth—there is a hell! And every unrepentant man, when the gate of death confronts him and opens wide its portals for him to pass in, will go down into that darkness—into that darkness from which no traveler has ever returned, and in the gloom of whose surroundings no prayer has ever been answered. Hear him pray, "Oh, father Abraham." Here is prayer to-day. I talked to a man once who said he never had prayed in his life, and didn't believe in prayer. But hear me to-day: The man that dies without believing and praying, wakes up in hell with prayer on his tongue and says, "Oh, father Abraham." Here is realization at last.

We have often seen men building sidewalks of cement. When the cement was first put down they put planks over it. Why? It was soft. They are to protect it. Once in a while a dog will get on anyhow, and there is his track on the cement sidewalk. Now the cement is as hard as adamant. Nothing could make a track on it now. Its days of softness are gone. It has become fixed, and no imprint can be made on it now. Once a little, tiny bird, singing in the trees beside it, could have lighted on it and left its little footprints there. It was soft. Once upon a time the man who is in hell to-day was a little boy playing at his mother's knee, and he had a tender heart in those childhood days, and oftentimes he wept. There were times when he looked up into his mother's face and asked her about God, and there were other times when he knelt down beside his little baby bed and said his childish prayer. That was a time of innocence, a time when there was a heart to feel and an ear to hear, but those times are gone forever. A hell, a real, eternal, irrevocable hell, awaits the impenitent man or the impenitent woman.

And look at what Abraham said to him, "Son." And the very next word he said was, remember—"Son, remember." Oh, memory, art thou living yet? Quickened indeed by the very impulse of the burning flame, memory revives and takes the back track of the man's life and goes back into those days of innocence and love, goes back and feels the kiss of mother once again, goes back and hears the sermon in the old church, goes back to the very day when the preacher talked about hell and the man believed it not; goes back to opportunity and sunshine and light again. Oh, memory, memory, memory! Oh, if a man could go to hell and leave his memory behind him it would not be hell. After all, hell is memory and memory is hell. Take the debauchee. How does he feel this morning? Ah, if he had no memory! But before he can get up and set his blood on fire again with the hellish liquor, he begins to think and think and think, to think of his little wife at home, his ragged children, and his wrecked manhood; think of the strewn pathway of his life, beset all the way with thorns and tossed about with tempests. Memory! Brother, hear me now. Draw a line fifty years from now and we will all be in heaven or in hell—everyone in this house, certainly every adult in this house; just fifty short years and there will come to the sinner in this house to-day the memory of that quiet summer Sunday, when the preacher in the best way he knew, talked about hell, and the man in hell, and he will say, "Oh, give me back the life of that Sunday," but it will be too late. Oh, may things terrestrial be made luminous with the light of eternity to-day, that men may see where they stand in the sight of Almighty God. May there come from the very throne of God a flash of supernal light, sped by his Spirit, that will seek the hearts of sinners in this house and cause them to fall down and say, "Oh, let me escape from the wrath to come!"

Out of the very fullness of my heart I plead with you to-day. Do not go with Dives into hell. Take your mother's hand, lean on the Saviour, and to-day plead for mercy from the throne of God; for there is mercy to-day, and there is love to-day, and there are blessing and salvation to-day. But in hell, no answer to the prayer. There is something sad, oh, awfully sad, when you think about what this rich man said to Abraham. He thought somewhat about himself and said, "I am in torment here and I wish you would just let Lazarus come and give me a little sympathy, for I am tormented in these flames." But he did not stop there. He said, "Oh, Abraham, Abraham, send Lazarus back to the world again. I have one, two, three, four, five brothers, and they are just as I was. They heard the gospel and slighted it just as I did. And I led them into a thousand wrongs. I said to them, There is no hereafter. I said to them, There is no eternity. And, O God, I am in hell, and they are still unrepentant. And though I know that I cannot escape it, oh, send Lazarus down there to preach to them." Oh, memory, memory, memory! Light it up with a flash of eternity. But the man became a missionary just a day too late. Just a day too late he thought about the awfulness of the fact that his five brethren were not saved. Solemnly, earnestly, prayerfully, I press this scene on your hearts this morning: A lost man. Time is over. Riches all gone. They are of no use now. Once he could have bought a whole county; he cannot buy a drop of water now. Once men followed him; now he is beset about with the evil men of all ages, and he wails out: "Here they are with me. Once I had opportunity. Once I had a mother's love. Once the Spirit of God came and moved my heart and said, 'After all, it is true. After all, you had better be a Christian. After all, you had better give your heart to God.' And I said, 'No, I will just close it up. I won't hear any of it.'" All the wealth of the Indies and the gold of Ophir could not buy for him a single mercy now, because the end has come.

And even poor Lazarus, oh, think about it! Lazarus was God's missionary to that man. Do you know what that poor fellow would have done if the rich man had just opened his gate that day and said: "Come in, poor fellow. You can have more than the crumbs. You can have a seat at the table. Just come in and we will help you. And now bring him something to eat." Do you know, if he had gone and lingered by his side and bound up his wounds, Lazarus would have told him about God, and Lazarus would have been there in that house a very electric current between that home and God, and the wires would have flashed with prayer and the rich man need never have been in hell at all. And he remembered that, and so he wanted the very beggar that he had cast off and scorned, to go back to his brethren and say to them, "Oh, don't you go where your brother has gone!" It seems to me that the saddest thing, when all the sum of our life shall have been cast up and the end shall have come—that the saddest thing of all will be the separation between loved ones. At the gate of death the unrepentant goes into hell to take up his abode with devils, and the penitent goes into the glory world to be with Jesus forever. There will be the separation of fathers and sons there. There will be the separation of wives and husbands. There will be families torn asunder. O God, may all in this house of every family be united in heaven. May every sinner in this house to-day flee from the wrath to come, for I tell you, dear friends, that it is true, every word of it is true, every word.

Now the last thought in this sermon. Why have I preached it? Why preach such a sermon? Why talk to men about a subject as harrowing as this? Why remove the veil and lift up the covering from the seething mouth of hell that we may gaze into it for a moment? I will tell you why. Why is it that when yellow fever comes it is flashed on the wires into a million homes in an hour? Why is it that when contagion makes its home among us that the news passes from lip to lip? It is done that we may escape it. Why is it that men warn each other against the blight and deadliness of temporal destruction? Why is it? It is to save them. And so I have come to-day to preach this sermon, because I know—and I realize it more and more as I grow older and come nearer to the end of my own life—I know that very soon the sums of your lives will have been made out forever and for eternity.

A word to the Christians just here. Why don't you talk more to sinners? Why don't you warn men? I tell you there is reality in it all; that there is a real, literal hell; and that the broad sweep of its eternity on the one hand is just as long as heaven on the other.

You say—and that is what this man thought—even in hell he thought that if somebody would just rise from the dead and go down there and tell those five brethren, they would all believe it. That is a great fallacy. Do you know that if a man were to die here in this house to-day, and stay dead a day, and after he had been dead a day should come back to life again and stand in this pulpit where I am standing, and talk to you and say: "I have been in heaven; I have seen Jesus; I have heard the angels sing; I have clasped hands with Abraham and Elijah and Moses, and men, it is all true; and I looked over that great gulf and I saw into hell, and lost men are there, and they are to-day raising their fruitless cries to heaven"; if he should come and stand here, you would say the man never was dead, and you would not believe him. You would say, "It is all a fraud, that fellow was never dead; he is lying." I tell you, brethren, if men hear not Moses and the prophets; if they hear not this book, these burning truths of the word of God, they would not hear if the whole graveyard should rise from the dead and come and proclaim the gospel with the cerements of the grave around them. If men cannot be convinced by the fact that Jesus Christ rose from the dead, by the militant tread of God's army for two thousand years, and by the testimony of a million men who, on the border line of death, have said, "I see heaven, and I hear the angels, and I know that heaven is real," nothing would convince them. I never shall forget how old Brother Watson died—a man whom some of you knew. When the last hour of his life came and he had no more sight in his eyes, except as he saw into eternity, he called his daughter to him and said, "I see Kitty." That was his wife who had gone to God. Was it a lie? Was it a lie that the old and venerable man of God told when the death-damp was on his brow? Oh, no! And I remember how M. V. Smith died, that consecrated man whom so many loved. In the very last moment almost of his kingly life, he said, "Safe in my Saviour's arms at last." Was it a lie? Blessed be God, it was true. There is salvation to-day and life eternal to-day, and there is hope to-day for every sinner.

One of the saddest things about hell is that there is no hope in hell. And men have committed suicide to get away from a hopeless world and gone straight to a hopeless hell. I point you to-day, dear sinner friend, to light and life and hope. I point you to Jesus Christ on the cross, the living Saviour. But for his mercy you would be in hell to-day. He has been very good to you. He has been very kind to you. He has given you health and prosperity and he has made you glad many a time because life has been so pleasant; and he gave you a Christian home and a Christian mother. Through his mercy you have heard the gospel many a time, and it is only through his mercy that we are here to-day. And in his name I plead with you to-day to come and forsake your sins; come and forsake your skepticism if you have it. Come and with humble spirit fall at the feet of Jesus and say, "O Jesus, here I am, an undone sinner with only a few years to live. Take me as I am and give me life eternal to-day." Is there one to-day in all this audience who wants to escape from the wrath to come? Faster than the breath of any cyclone, speedier than the flash of any lightning, deadlier than the embrace of any anaconda, is coming the last day, the last death, the unutterable and eternal death to sinful men. With all the power of my heart to-day, let me impress the transcendent truth of this text, "In hell he lifted up his eyes." And this gleam of hope: "God so loved the world that he gave his only begotten Son, that whosoever believeth on him should not perish, but have eternal life." Will you take him to-day? Take him as your Saviour. Take him for now, for to-morrow, and forever.

XXVI

GODHOOD IN CHRIST

BY J. J. TAYLOR, D. D.

"But the men marvelled, saying, What manner of man is this, that even the winds and the sea obey him!" Matt. 8 : 27.

THE miracle recorded in this connection is mentioned by three evangelists, whose accounts differ only in minor details. It was the crowning work of a busy day. Jesus had answered objectors, uttered and expounded parables, and declared the doctrines of his kingdom; and, as the evening shadows lengthened in the vales, he felt the need of retirement and repose, and gave orders to embark and pass over to the other side of the sea. On the way he retired to the hinder part of the ship, and

> As the vessel o'er the waters crept,
>   While the swelling sails they spread,
> The wearied Saviour gently slept,
>   With a pillow 'neath his head.
>
> But soon the lowering sky grew dark
>   On Bashan's rocky brow;
> The storm rushed down upon the bark,
>   The waves swept o'er her prow.

In **kind it** was a common occurrence. The intense heat generated in the basin about the lake rarified the atmosphere, and under favorable conditions according to natural law, the colder air from the surrounding mountains swept down the ravines with a violence that lashed the waters into fury, and some-

J. J. TAYLOR is of Welsh descent. His great-grandfather came to America about 1772, and settled in Henry County, Va. He is the son of Rev. D. G. Taylor, and brother of President S. F. Taylor, of Stephens College, Columbia, Mo., Rev. J. Lee Taylor, Spencer, Va., and the late R. R. Taylor. Was brought up on his father's farm in Henry County, Va., and prepared for college at the Jacksonville High School, Floyd C. H., and took the A. M. degree from Richmond College in 1880. He entered the Southern Baptist Theological Seminary, September, 1880; became pastor of the Upper Street Church, Lexington, Ky., in 1881, and remained until September, 1887, more than doubling the membership. He has been pastor of the St. Francis Street Church, Mobile, Ala., since October 1, 1887, during which time some five hundred members have been added and efficiency of the church greatly increased. He is the author of an "excellent" (Broadus) biography of his father, "Daniel G. Taylor, a Country Preacher," and several sermons in tract form.

times seemed to shake the solid land. In this case the tempest was strangely severe. The word used to designate it means an earthquake; as if the foundations of the sea were suddenly broken up, and its waters heaved aloft. The fishermen disciples, familiar with the freaks of the weather, and inured to the dangers of the deep, lost their fortitude and almost their faith. Alarmed and helpless amid the thickening peril they turned to Jesus, and awoke him, saying, Master, Master, we perish! Yielding to their entreaty he calmly arose, and in the language of personal appeal as if addressed to sentient beings, he spoke to the raging elements and ruled them with his word. The psalmist had said: "The Lord on high is mightier than the noise of many waters, yea than the mighty waves of the sea." "O Lord God of hosts, who is a strong Lord like unto thee? or to thy faithfulness round about thee? Thou rulest the raging of the sea; when the waves thereof arise, thou stillest them." In the light of these utterances the deed possessed a startling significance. It identified the man so lately asleep on a pillow as the mighty God extolled by the sacred bard. It forced upon the astonished spectators some weird conception of Godhood in Christ, and evoked the pertinent question, "What manner of man is this, that even the winds and sea obey him?"

As a disclosure of godhood this miracle is worthy of devout study. It is a parable crystallized in deed, and its teachings touch the heart of all religion. By nature men are worshipers, and by the same nature they desire to know the object of their devotions. In the earliest historic times Job cried, "Oh, that I knew where I might find him, that I might come even to his seat!" Philip prayed, "Lord, show us the Father, and it sufficeth us." The poet sings,

> Where shall I find him, oh, my soul,
> Who yet is everywhere.

Men have searched in the heights and in the depths, tracing every beam of light into the trackless void; and yet they have a common experience of vagueness in their conceptions of God. He seems like an evanescent glory, without form or center or local habitation. He is a vast and shadowy something, lying beyond the apprehension of the senses and eluding the shrewdest search; and he utters no voice and reveals no outlines of his person. The whole brotherhood of inspired writers agrees that God is not disclosed outwardly. He is a spirit, immortal, imponderable, immanent, and transcendent, whom no man hath seen or can see, and whom no earthly measurement can compass.

Some of the emptiest things in theological literature—and certainly that realm has its share of stupidity—are found in the documents which undertake to declare the divine essence, as for example, that Christ is "very God of very God, begotten not made." Such utterances display a genius for nonsense. It is difficult to form a conception of God, and impossible to fill out the lineaments of his being. Parts of his ways are shown in his works, but how little a portion is heard of him, and the thunder of his power who can understand? On this idea the commandment says, Thou shalt not make any graven image or likeness of anything in the heaven above or the earth beneath as an object of worship. Such objects, even when idealized and carried up to the highest perfection, fall short of the reality and belie the divine character. A block of wood or stone or metal bears no new relation to Jehovah, when it is graven by human device and carved into the form of men or monsters, crosses or crucifixes. It is simply a part of his creation, and it becomes a fetich in proportion as men become idolaters. In the realms of superstition a cat or a calf, a clam-shell or a cracker, may be an object of worship, but it cannot be an embodiment of him whom the heaven of heavens cannot contain.

In the absolute, God is forever the same without variableness or shadow of turning; he reveals himself without respect of persons, yet in some sense he is different to different men. The sunlight falls alike upon all objects; but it appears red or orange, yellow or green, according to the media through which it passes. In the same way the disclosures of God are interpreted according to the individual mind. One of the noblest announcements concerning the divine character is found in the book of Exodus. Moses stood trembling at the beginning of that work which gave his name to immortality. He desired such a view of Jehovah as would strengthen his heart for the allotted task. "And the Lord descended in the cloud and stood with him there . . .; and the Lord passed by before him and proclaimed, The Lord, the Lord God, merciful and gracious, long-suffering and abundant in goodness and truth, keeping mercy for thousands, forgiving iniquity and transgression and sin, and that will by no means clear the guilty; visiting the iniquity of the fathers upon the children and upon the children's children unto the third and to the fourth generation." Here certainly the milder aspects of the divine character predominate; yet they made but little impression on that coarse and callous age. In the Old Testament generally God is set forth as a mighty man and a man of war, whetting his sword, bending his bow and making ready his arrows. He is a God of armies, who flashes his fury in the lightnings and sounds his resentment in the thunder. He is a God of vengeance, whose anger burns into the lowest hell and consumes the foundations of the mountains, and whose hand is uplifted for the destruction of his enemies. In the ruder times, when men lived in Sodom and were degraded below the brutes which follow their natural instincts, when religion degenerated into legalized lust and violence succeeded law, when there was no established authority in society and every man did what was right in his own eyes, only the sterner phases of the divine character were competent to stay the course of wickedness and work reform in the ways of life. Stubborn iniquity was met with inflexible righteousness. God went forth in the greatness of his strength, red in his apparel as one that treadeth in the wine-press, uttering the doom of transgressors: "I will tread them in mine anger, and trample them in my fury; and their blood shall be sprinkled upon my garments, and I will stain all my raiment. For the day of vengeance is in mine heart, and the year of my redeemed is come."

In this miracle God is disclosed in power. The cleansing of the leper, the restoring of sight to the blind, the healing of the centurion's servant and of Peter's mother-in-law were amazing displays of power. Previously it was never so seen in Israel. But in these cases he had the co-operation of sentient beings. When he cast out unclean spirits or unstopped deaf ears, he had intelligence as an ally; even in raising the dead he hardly spanned a gulf so wide as that which separates between man and the forces of the physical world. We may not undertake to weigh his miracles and determine their relative merits; but I can conceive of no higher display of authority than this, that a word should control the winds and the sea. By observations extending through many years men have judged that certain adequate causes may be set in operation to regulate the clouds and claim to produce rain at will; they have learned also to pour oil on the troubled waters of the sea and abate the fury of the storm; but no daring inventor, no wizard of science, has found a way to bridle the forces that rule the winds. Yet a word from this man is mightier than the euroclydon. Spoken in perfect calmness, it brings a perfect calm.

Beyond the display of supreme power there is also a disclosure of beneficent wisdom and divine sympathy. The storm had power, ruthless power to break and terrify and destroy; power operating blindly, pitilessly, inexorably. In such a display the heathen saw only the great and awful God. They perceived his goings in the whirlwind, and heard his plaints in the plash of the waves; and they crawled in the dust before him, and suffered all manner of agony to appease his dreaded wrath. But there is power to rule the fiercest storm that ever swept the seas, or broke the rocks upon the shore. It lurks in no enormous engine, and operates through no mighty machine. It abides in a will, and is expressed in the voice of a man. It is subject to prayer; and it is exercised in compassion for weakness and needless alarm. God in Christ disclosed his sympathy as he puts forth his power to rescue imperiled men. He is a merciful Mediator, touched with a feeling of our infirmities, tempted in all points and tender with those who are tried.

> The pity of the Lord,
> To those that fear his name,
> Is such as tender parents feel;
> He knows our feeble frame.

And there is no man contending against the storms of life, and no man bowing his shoulders to the burdens of poverty or disease, and no man sweating blood in an agony of prayer for deliverance, that may not come, that may not have the assurance of divine sympathy in Jesus Christ.

The prophets of the Old Testament were chiefly reformers. They arose to rebuke corruption in government, hypocrisy in religion, and uncleanness in individual life. They uttered protest against the oppressions of power and the cruelties of man to man; and they came with a whip for the horse and a bridle for the ass and a rod for the fool. Nevertheless they came with a message of mercy and love and forgiveness for the penitent. It is not John, but David who says, " The mercy of the Lord is from everlasting to everlasting upon them that fear him, and his righteousness unto children's children, to such as keep his covenant and to those that remember his commandments to do them." It is not Matthew, but Isaiah who calls the wicked to forsake their ways and return unto the Lord, and assures them of mercy and pardon, abundant and free. It is not Paul, but Jeremiah who says, " Oh that my head were waters and mine eyes a fountain of tears, that I might weep day and night for the slain of the daughter of my people." The God who slew famous kings, Og, king of Bashan, and Sihon, king of the Amorites, is a God of compassion : for his mercy endureth forever. But the highest reach of might and of mercy is shown in Jesus Christ; and these qualities are blended in the miracle on the sea, as Jehovah wills and works according to the good pleasure of his will.

The disclosure of divine power and compassion in the plenitude of grace is not conditioned absolutely upon shipwreck or upon the hazard of the dearest things in life, but somehow it does depend upon conscious need. If from some steadfast cliff, beetling above the stroke of the fiercest wave, these men had watched the storm, what would they have cared whether it raged in fury or sank in repose ? But when they were adrift and helpless, spent and despairing, the Master's majestic words, " Peace, be still," and the ensuing calm, marked an epoch in their experience. In the man who stood before them as their teacher and familiar friend they saw not the full measure of divine character, but the outshining of a divinity which ruled the forces of nature with a word; and out of their disaster they came into a nobler conception of God in Christ.

They that are whole call not a physician; and they that are safe seek not a saviour. It is written: "I spake unto thee in thy prosperity, but thou saidst, I will not hear." If a man has ridden perpetually on the crest of the wave, and has never felt the shock of a storm; if he has never yielded to temptation and infirmity, and has never turned aside from the path of righteousness, what does he care for the friendship of One who rules the storm, and who, tempted in all possible points, is moved with a feeling of human infirmity, and brought into sympathy with the helpless and the wayward? But when

> He has been to the funeral of earthly hopes,
> And entombed them one by one;
> And then alone by the cold hearthstone
> Has wooed the midnight gloom;

when he has felt the burden of guilt, and the impossibility of mastering the forces that are bearing him down, no voice is so sweet as that which says, "Peace, be still."

Before such a disclosure men are swept with a sense of amazement and awe. Moses, the illustrious champion of righteousness, trembled before the burning bush, and durst not behold. Later, at Sinai, so terrible was the sight that he said, "I exceedingly fear and quake." Conscious of the divine presence at Bethel, Jacob exclaimed, "How dreadful is this place." Measuring himself by human standards, Job gloried in his own perfections, and challenged Jehovah to an argument, that the mysteries of providence in human suffering might be disclosed. But when in the end God appeared, Job was utterly abashed, and said, "I have heard of thee by the hearing of the ear, but now mine eye seeth thee; wherefore I abhor myself, and repent in dust and ashes." In his earlier life Peter was not noted for his humility. He rather boasted of his excellence as a disciple. But there on the lake shore, as Godhood flashed out in the miraculous draught of fishes, he fell down at Jesus' feet, saying, "Depart from me, for I am a sinful man, O Lord." And here before the outshining of divine power, the men marveled, "What manner of man is this?"

Many a soul, awakened to the importance of salvation, has been oppressed with a sense of unworthiness and has reflected, "What am I, that God should care for me? I am nothing, and worse than nothing before him. My sins have been many and grievous, and I have no claim upon his mercy." But what sort of a God is it who doles out mercy according to merit? Sometimes a weak and witless woman, whose husband has stumbled upon a little money and bought a house on a fashionable street, undertakes to put on airs, and she thinks she cannot afford to associate with her old friends in the humbler walks of life. Probably she cannot, for she is not secure in her new place; but the true aristocracy have no fear of losing caste. The God disclosed in Christ, whose soft voice outsounded the roar of the storm, can afford to help even me. He cares for sparrows, and not one of them falls to the ground unnoticed. "Fear ye not, therefore; ye are of more value than many sparrows." This he said to the multitude as well as to the disciples, and he demonstrated his care by his actions. He allowed publicans and sinners to draw near unto him, and when his conduct was questioned, he said he came not to call the righteous, but sinners to repentance. The stream of his compassion flowed toward the needy; and he folded back the veil and disclosed more joy in heaven over one sinner that repents, than over ninety and nine unsinning souls. He awoke from needed sleep at the cry of distress, and he exercised his power to dispel torturing fear. He showed himself always the helper of the helpless, merciful and gracious.

And after all, helpfulness is the supreme office of God in Christ; as it is written: "Himself took our infirmities, and bare our sicknesses." Viewed in their best estate, as the offspring of piety and health and culture, as moral and upright and saintly, men are weak and needy. They are disappointed, overthrown, broken upon the wheel, plunged into torments, baptized in blood; and gentle spirits on the rack of pain grow faint or fierce, and pray and curse by turns. Under the best conditions life is full of besetment and agony, and each heart has its own burden and its own bitterness. Lower down in the scale, where ignorance and squalor and sin prevail, the agony augments, and the victims of wretchedness struggle on in the failing fight, until at last with every aspiration crushed, and

> With not a trace upon the page,
> From desperate youth to loathsome age,
> But of sin and sorrow, wrong and chance,
> And the cruel blight of ignorance,

they drop down and pass out of sight. The march of mankind is undertoned with minor chords. Dumb tears enough have been shed to make an ocean. And in comparison with these things the fiercest storm that ever swept down from the heights of Hermon becomes feeble and insignificant. But to this host of helpless ones, drenched, drooping, and ready to despair, there is revealed a God of compassion, whose voice is omnipotent. He comes not in the bush that burns with fire and strikes terror to the stoutest heart, nor yet in the majesty which no man can see and live; he speaks not in the tones which once shook the earth and also the heavens, and echoed in the thunder of the skies. But he comes in Jesus Christ, who walks and talks with men, who sleeps on a pillow as a man, who awakes as a man, and with the voice of a man speaks as God the potent words which rule the storm. **The high hills are a refuge for the wild goats,** and the rocks for the conies.

> God is the refuge of his saints,
>   When storms of sharp distress invade;
> Ere we can offer our complaints,
>   Behold him present with his aid.

The divine administration on earth is based upon the ignorance, the helplessness, the guilt of men. They are the workmanship of divine hands, the objects of divine regard. Christ has been anointed of the Spirit to heal broken hearts, to bring deliverance to captives and recovering of sight to the blind, to set at liberty them that are bruised of the adversary, to proclaim the acceptable year of the Lord. The same yesterday, to-day, and forever, he still says, "Come unto me, all ye that labour and are heavy laden, and I will give you rest."

W. P. WALKER was born in Jackson County, Va., May 14, 1834. His father dying when he was eleven years old, he grew to manhood without an education. He was married to Miss Mary Jane McClung, March 9, 1855; was baptized by Rev. Allen Wood, pastor of the Mount Pleasant Church in Nicholas County, October 30, 1857; was licensed to preach March 13, 1858, and was ordained January 21, 1860. He was a student at Alleghany College in the session of 1859 and 1860, and of the following session till it was closed by the war. From 1862 to 1866, he preached in the counties of Nicholas, Fayette, and Greenbrier. In 1866 he took charge of the church at Williamstown, on the Ohio River. He spent the year 1876 as agent of Sheton College. In May, 1877, he took charge of mission work in Huntington, where he is still pastor of the church which grew out of his labors. The degree of D. D. was conferred upon him by the State University in 1889. He is highly esteemed and has been frequently honored by his brethren in West Virginia.

W. P. Walker, D. D.

XXVII

ABANDONED OF THE LORD

BY W. P. WALKER, D. D.

"Ephraim is joined to idols: let him alone." **Hosea 4 : 17.**

MAN is the crowning work of creation. He is the last and noblest work of God. He alone is endowed with intelligence. He can think, reason, and feel. God placed him in authority. He is to have dominion over the fish of the sea, and over the fowl of the air, and over the cattle, and over every living thing that creeps upon the earth. And just in proportion to his exalted position are his privileges and responsibilities. He is made the arbiter of his own destiny. Good and evil, life and death, are set before him, with the power of choice.

2. But he is not left to himself in this matter. His Maker wishes him well and follows him up with invitations and incentives to choose that which is good. He communicates with him, revealing his will and offering to him his blessing, guaranteeing support in time of need, and protection in time of danger. He even seeks his companionship. In the beginning God walked with man in the garden of Eden.

But all this may be lost. Man may resent the approaches of his Maker until he, offended, may turn away and leave him to himself. Ephraim was favored with every opportunity of blessing. He was set before his brother by the blessing of his grandfather, Jacob, and subsequently his tribe gained prominence in Israel by the favor of God. But after centuries of blessing and ages of opportunities, we hear his sad doom, in the words of the text, "Ephraim is joined to idols; let him alone." How sadly these words fall on our ears. May the Lord help us to learn profitable lessons from them. For this purpose they are written in the book of God.

I. GOD IS SEEKING MAN'S BEST INTERESTS.

Man has never been left wholly to himself. His Maker has followed him even into the depths of sin, commending his love toward him, that while he was yet a sinner Christ died for him. In every age of the world, in one way or another, he has kept open a way of communication with our race. Sometimes these communications were intermittent, but they did not wholly cease. To the glory of his name be it said, as the ages passed, they became more frequent and more distinct, until now we are blessed with the abiding revelation of the "glorious gospel of the blessed God." But what means all this? What good is intended to man?

1. *It is to save him.* The salvation of man was not an after-thought, but it was an after-act. God, foreseeing the entrance of sin into the world and the consequent fall of man, prepared beforehand the plan of salvation, and in the fullness of time all the details of that plan were wrought out. But this scheme of redemption must deal with men as individuals, and must be addressed to each one through the intellect and the affections, leaving the matter of choice with us. There is no coercion in matters of religion. God's revelation to man is sufficient to convince his judgment, conquer his will, and win his love. These obtained, his salvation is secured. This salvation implies the redemption of the whole man, body, soul, and spirit. It saves from sin, from the love of sin, from the stain of sin, from the consequences of sin, and from mortality. Moreover, it changes the indi-

vidual from an enemy to a friend, from an alien to a citizen, and to fellowship with God. God hath set apart him that is godly for himself. Blessed fellowship—blessed results of God's salvation.

2. *It is to make man better.* It is true that God is glorified in the salvation of men and for his name's sake, he saves them. But it is true also, that his love for man and desire for his welfare runs through the whole scheme of redemption. God so loved the world that he gave his Son to save it. The salvation of man necessarily involves the betterment of his condition. Man was made pure, in the likeness of his Maker. This likeness he lost by sin, and he became evil. Hence, salvation means an utter change in his mind and heart and life. For this purpose, God would put his law in his mind, his grace in his heart, and his spirit in his life. An opposer has sneeringly said: "The religion of the orthodox is absurd, in that it takes the miserable sinner from a life of vice and shame, and gives him an immediate pass to heaven." This is not a correct statement of the case. It is true that Christ came to save sinners, but he did not come to save them in their sins, but to save them from their sins. The sinner is invited to repentance and faith in the Lord Jesus, with the offer of regeneration and a new nature. Man must have this change of his nature before he can be saved; indeed this is his salvation. Thus, in the salvation of man, he is made better as well as happier.

3. *It is that he may do good to others.* God said to Abraham, I will bless thee, and thou shalt be a blessing. Paul said, the grace of God which was bestowed upon me was not in vain. The reason given is, that he labored abundantly. Just as soon as a man is brought over to the Lord's side, he is taken into partnership. "For we are laborers together with God." Converted men are made messengers of God,

with the word of life to their fellow-men. They are Christ's witness to the saving power of the gospel.

So it is, that God follows men up with his word, with his providence, with his Spirit, and with the persistent warnings and pleadings of his people, not willing that any should perish, but that all should come to repentance.

After all this, there are still those who, like Ephraim, not knowing that the goodness of God leads to repentance, by hardness and impenitence of heart, treasure up to themselves wrath against the day of wrath and revelation of the righteous judgment of God. Holy Spirit, forbid that any of us should do so! But if we would escape, we must cease our opposition and yield to God, lest he say, He is joined to his sins; let him alone. Grieve not the Holy Spirit of God, lest he leave you to your fate.

But we want to inquire further as to how God urges his claims upon men. What means does he use? Where and how is he speaking to us?

1. *In the Bible.* The Bible is God's plainest and fullest revelation to man. In it he reveals to us his will, our true condition, our destiny, and everything essential for improving our condition. From the beginning to the end it abounds in warning, in instruction, in invitations, and in promises. It is so plain that wayfaring men, though fools, need not err therein. It is wonderful how God has followed man with the Bible. It was given in olden time by holy men as they were moved by the Holy Spirit. And notwithstanding it has been hated and resisted in every age, and every device that wicked men and demons could invent has been used for its destruction, yet it is in the world, a standing protest against the sins of men and a perpetual offer of mercy and pardon to any who will accept it. In these later days it is being multiplied and cheapened until it can be had in any home where it is wanted. Through it

the world's Redeemer knocks at the door of every heart asking admittance. After the gift of his Son and the Holy Spirit, it is God's best gift to man. It perpetuates truth and light in the world. By the truth we may be made free, and by the light we may walk in the ways of God.

2. *But he speaks to men by his living ministry.* It has ever been so; the patriarchs were made ministers of God to their families. Thus a whole tribe was selected in Israel and made to minister in holy things. And still in this latest and best of the dispensations, God has selected whom he would then and there, and put them into this work. He put within them the power of an endless life, put in their hearts a warm love for truth and righteousness and an unconquerable zeal for the salvation of men, impelled by which they go everywhere preaching the word. Thus are these ceaseless agencies always urging men to be saved.

3. *God speaks to men in providence.* God made all things and he has not resigned his right to control them, but is ordering them in the interest of mankind, not to supply temporal wants only, but to win men's hearts and save their souls as well. In the effort to win the Jews, Jesus did not leave them with his word alone, but appealed also to his works. He had greater witness than that of John, even the works which he did. It was his works that left the Jews without excuse. Paul declared that God left us not without witness, in that he did good and gave us rain from heaven and fruitful seasons, filling our hearts with food and gladness. Every returning season, with its fruit and food supply, is God's testimony to his goodness to man and his invitation to submission and trust.

4. *By the Holy Spirit.* All of the agencies, powerful though they be, would not avail without the agency of the Holy Spirit. The Spirit has always

been interested in men. Patriarchs and prophets were subjects of his care and guidance. His restraining influence was felt by the wicked in the days of Noah, and his helpful presence was with the tribes of Israel until he was grieved away by their wickedness. But we live in the special dispensation of the Spirit. God, in speaking of the reign of Messiah by the prophet Ezekiel, says: "A new heart also will I give you, and a new spirit will I put within you, and I will take away the stony heart out of your flesh, and I will give you a heart of flesh." This is one of the "exceeding great and precious promises" by which we may be partakers of the divine nature. We are helpless in our fallen nature, and all of the means used to win us from sin will fail without the Spirit; but with his aid we can turn to God. This blessed Spirit is ever present to use the word of God, his providence, and his ministry, making them, each of them or all of them, his power unto salvation.

So then we are left without excuse. Every provision has been made. The plan of salvation is "finished," the way of life has been made plain, the dangers of sin have been pointed out, and the heart has been pressed by the claims of God's infinite love and the invitations of the Spirit. Who can, who will dare continue to resist all of these? God calls upon the heavens to witness man's irrational course. "Hear, O heavens, and give ear, O earth: I have nourished and brought up children, and they have rebelled against me. The ox knoweth his owner, and the ass his master's crib: but Israel doth not know, my people doth not consider. Ah, sinful nation, a people laden with iniquity, a seed of evildoers, children that are corrupters: they have forsaken the Lord, they have provoked the Holy One of Israel unto anger, they are gone away backward."

Such are the provoking circumstances under which divine love is forced to withdraw these saving influences and leave man to himself. Wretched condition, who can endure it? Who must endure it? "He that being often reproved hardeneth his neck, shall be destroyed, and that without remedy." Let Ephraim alone; he is joined to his idols.

III. *Let him alone—what does it mean?* The danger to us is, that we shall not fully understand this, nor appreciate what of it we may understand.

1. *Man left to himself.* He is left with the accumulated guilt of a lifetime of sin, helpless in his depraved nature, loving darkness rather than light, because his deeds are evil. Men may not realize this while in life and engaged in sin, but it is a reality, and the time will come when it will be felt. There is nothing more dreadful than for a man to be left to himself. He does not need to be punished. All the necessary conditions of penalty for his sins are in him. Whatsoever a man soweth that shall he also reap. The elements of destruction are in him. He that soweth to the flesh shall of the flesh reap corruption. Utterly helpless and hopeless he is.

2. *In the hands of Satan.* There is no middle ground. Every man is either in the hands of God or he is in the hands of Satan. The Jews claimed to be the seed of Abraham, but instead they were not doing the deeds of Abraham, but they had forsaken his teaching; and so they were of their father the devil, and the deeds of their father they would persist in doing.

In this slavery the mind is blinded, that truth cannot be seen. The affections are perverted that the truth is hated, and the will is paralyzed that it cannot be obeyed. The only relief is in God. "If the Son therefore shall make you free, ye shall be free indeed." But to be abandoned of the Lord is to remain the victim of Satan—led or driven to deeds of wickedness while in this world and to become the victim of fiendish hate in the world to come. This condition of things is not only taught in the Bible, but it is verified in the scenes of every-day life. Note the deeds of men and women as they occur day by day, and you will see signs of a spirit that is worse than human —it is devilish. It is unnatural, inhuman; and there is no accounting for it except upon the supposition that they are abandoned of the law and have become captives to Satan. Crimes are committed which promise no present or prospective good to the perpetrator; there is absolutely nothing to actuate but the love of sin. God forbid that any who hears this warning should persist in the downward way till too late.

1. *There is a sin unto death.* "If we sin willfully after that we have received a knowledge of the truth, there remaineth no more sacrifice for sin, but a certain fearful looking for of judgment and fiery indignation which shall devour the adversaries." Blasphemy against the Holy Spirit has no forgiveness neither in this world nor in the world to come. We may not be able to explain these statements to those who are disposed to quibble, but the facts remain. They stand out as signals of danger, and my business and yours is to heed them and avoid the wreck. They are not put in the Bible to amuse the curious, but they are there for the warning and safety of all who honestly seek for life and immortality.

2. *How may we know the approach of danger?* When the instructions, warnings, and invitations of God have come to us and have been unheeded, we may know that danger is nigh. Every opportunity given leaves one less to be improved. Therefore, we ought to give the more earnest heed to the things which we have heard, lest at any time we should let them slip. When all of the means appointed of God have been employed, the appeals of his messengers, the lessons of his providence, and the warnings of the Holy Spirit, when these have been multiplied and unheeded, know that the end is nigh.

3. *A word to all.* Unsaved friend, the door of mercy is still open, the invitations of grace are still extended. You may, perhaps, feel it in your heart. If so, yield, accept, and be saved. This may be the last opportunity. O Holy Spirit, restrain reluctant hearts.

Brethren and sisters, you know something of what you have escaped through grace, and of what you have obtained through Christ. Now you are the Lord's, and he will never forsake you. He will **never** say of you, "*Let him alone.*" But his infinite store of blessing and glory is open to you, and it shall not be shut at all, by day or by night, blessed be his holy name.

> And so, through all the coming days,
>   Thy love shall fail me never,
> And be the theme of all my praise
>   Within thy house forever.

XXVIII

THE SUBLIMITY OF THE LIFE OF FAITH

BY REV. DAVID M. RAMSEY

"For he endured, as seeing him who is invisible." Heb. 11 : 27.

THIS simple statement in the text is the key to a great career. It helps us to understand the life of a very unusual man. Taken all the way around, Moses has not a superior among the sons of men. Consider what he gave up and what he endured. He was truly an accomplished man. We read that he was versed in all the Egyptian learning. You may think that this statement means little, but upon reflection you will change your opinion. The discovery of the Rosetta stone, and the success of a great scholar in deciphering it, aided by the infinite patience of his co-laborers, enable us to know something definite of the superior civilization which belonged to this ancient land of the Nile in that far-off day when Moses lived.

Moses could write. I mean that he understood the art of penmanship. This was no mean accomplishment even for a great man in his day. Homer, the father of Greek literature, lived two hundred years perhaps after Moses, and yet he could not write his name. Not until three hundred years after the death of the blind bard of Greece were his poems reduced to writing, being preserved from oblivion by the traveling singers, an order corresponding to the Minnesingers of Europe, those nightingales of the Middle Ages, who went about singing of love, joy, and sorrow. The Egyptians were well versed also in

DAVID M. RAMSEY is a native of Greenville County, S. C., an alumnus of Richmond College, Richmond, Va., and a full graduate of the Southern Baptist Theological Seminary. During his last year at the seminary, and for a few months after finishing his course, he was the pastor of Glens Creek and Hillsboro churches in Woodford County, Kentucky. On February 9, 1888, Mr. Ramsey was married to Miss Mary R. Woodfolk, of Versailles, Ky. In May, of the same year, he became the pastor of the Tuscaloosa Baptist Church of Tuscaloosa, Ala., which he resigned in the summer of 1892 to accept a call to the Citadel Square Baptist Church of Charleston, S. C., entering upon his duties Oct. 1, 1892, where he still labors. Mr. Ramsey is a genial and cultured gentleman, an effective speaker, and a successful pastor.

THE SUBLIMITY OF THE LIFE OF FAITH 315

mathematics. The annual overflow of the Nile making it necessary to re-survey their lands frequently, occasioned practical use for this kind of knowledge. The pyramid of Cheops was a thousand years old in Moses' day and is still standing. Likewise the Egyptians were familiar with the science of medicine. If you have treated yourself to the reading of Mr. George Ebers' beautiful and instructive story, "Uarda," you have been impressed with the skill of their medical men. In this early day they had learned the practice of dentistry. Recently a tooth has been found in the mouth of a mummy that was well plugged and in a good state of preservation. Our boasted civilization is a stranger to their marvelous skill in the art of embalming the dead. They also knew something of chemistry and mineralogy for they worked their mines successfully. As for astronomy, our scholars are still quoting those of the Nile as authority.

Now, remember that a young man versed in this knowledge, and what is more, with a keen and refined taste to enjoy it all, with a fondness for such charmingly congenial society and with high social position, turned his back on all of it. He perhaps threw away a crown that he might be a blessing to his fellow-men and blood kindred who were suffering serfs in this proud land. Contrast, I pray you, the brilliance of that career which might have been, with the hardship which he actually endured, and you understand in some measure what the record means which says that he chose rather to suffer affliction with the people of God than to enjoy the pleasures of sin for a season.

With this splendid career of Moses before us I wish to discuss the life of faith and try to get you to see its sublimity.

I. Consider first the nature of the life of faith.

1. It is an unselfish life. Unless the forces are

strongly counteracted, the natural tendency is for us to become intensely selfish in this world. The struggle for existence, in this grinding life, where all business is conducted on the quite questionable principle of the semi-savage law of competition, has the effect of paralyzing our sympathy and stanching the flow of the milk of human kindness. If you do not look above and beyond your daily work you will surely and speedily become coldly selfish. The man who cares nothing for the eagle sailing in God's deep blue heavens but thinks only of the eagle on the dollar he is grasping, will have no high and holy impulses. The woman who sees only the diamond flashing which decorates the bosom of the devotee of fashion in the gay and festive hall, and is blind to the diamond tears sparkling in the eyes of hungry orphans, will soon and surely shut from her heart all love for God and all sympathy for her fellow-beings. There is nothing that weans our hearts away from sordid selfishness like the life of faith.

Faith made a man of Moses. When he was forty years old, having arrived at the years of manhood, he walked abroad in the land of Egypt. He heard the groans of his suffering brothers, while the taskmaster's whip was falling heavily on the backs of Abraham's children who were attempting the impossible task of making brick without straw. His blood tingled with the flush of righteous indignation. He arose to deliver the children of promise. But at present he is doomed to disappointment. Too impulsive by half he slays the offending Egyptian and tries to conceal the body in the sand. The next day he begins his work for his people again when two of his brethren are having a difficulty. He learns that they know his awful secret. He must fly for safety. What the slave knows to-day the taskmaster will know to-morrow, and the authorities the following day. The truth was the people were not ready to be delivered. They misunderstood Moses' good intentions. Stephen said in his speech that Moses supposed that they would have understood that God by his hand would deliver them. But it took forty years more to prepare the people, and that period of patient waiting in exile in the wilderness was not lost on Moses. You may remember Goethe's words: "Talent develops itself in solitude; character in the stream of life."

How will you explain such a life as that which Moses lived? It must be very puzzling to the men of the world. Is it fanaticism? Some have called Paul a fanatic, but I am not aware that any one has made this charge against conservative Moses. He is not a *crank*. A crank is one who does not regulate his acts by any well-defined principle, but is erratic and chaotic in his conduct. Men of the world, if you had seen Dr. Judson in Burma, toiling for weary years without converts, you might have thought him a fanatic. If you had seen him toiling on after he had laid Ann Hasseltine, the faithful wife, under the Hopia tree, near the murmuring sea; toiling on after Boardman had fallen; toiling on when the brethren in America had become despondent and were saying that there was no use trying any longer to save Burma, and had heard him say with Pauline faith: "Wait twenty years, brethren, and you shall hear from Burma again;" would you not have exclaimed, No fanatic this, no crank here, but a hero of faith in the Son of God?

Many years ago, now, there was born in that South Carolina city which bathes her feet in the sea, a young man of excellent and wealthy parentage. The young man could have been a princely merchant. Looking about him he saw a crying need, and said that if God spared his life he would give to a great denomination a seminary wherein to educate its sons for the ministry. To this end he toiled and prayed, but when his hopes and plans were about to ripen into blessed fruition the country was scourged and devastated. The smoke and dust of battle having cleared away, he took time only to wipe his eyes to look on the ruin that had been wrought, and went to work again. It is a story full of pathos and heroism, but never mind about the details. When that shattered man lay down to rest on the sunny slopes of France, no man said that his life had been a failure. The other day while riding on a street car in the city of Louisville, a stranger asked, "What buildings are these?" as he pointed to the proudest structures in that beautiful city on the Ohio. I hardly heard the answer. I was thinking of Jas. P. Boyce and his heroic struggles. It is fitting that in Louisville's city of the dead should stand to his memory a plain grannite shaft bearing this simple inscription: "In thee, O Lord, do I put my trust." Some such man as this was Moses. These three, Moses, Judson, Boyce, became synonyms of unselfishness by faith in God.

2. Again, the life of faith is unworldly. I am not now using the word unworldly in any technical or theological sense. It is used as an artist might use it. By unworldliness I mean freedom from entanglement with the visible world of sense.

How often have we felt some demand set up by the soul for freedom from the binding, galling world of contact! What freedom and joyous release of the soul have come to us sometimes when gazing out at the stars in boundless space! At such hours we have felt immortality surging in our breast. So we have felt while looking at the broad expanse of the sea.

Break, break, break,
On thy cold gray stones, O Sea!
And I would that my tongue could utter
The thoughts that arise in me.

Those who are gifted and well versed in higher mathematics, a science which contains truths independent of time and space, things which have no connection with weight and quality, contemplating eternal principles and laws, have become entranced with rapturous delight with the sense of relief from the bondage of this material world. This is what I call the rapture of unworldliness.

This is the great mission of music. A friend of mine who is a skilled performer on the violin and is blessed with an æsthetic soul, being approached by a young coxcomb and asked what he would charge to play for a "german," replied with calm indignation: "Sir, I have never yet allowed my music to be trampled under foot." Music, that seraphic mystery, was never designed to be an incentive to sensible men and women to make a whirligig of their bodies. Music was made for the soul. You remember that a great scientist said that he had no time to make money. That statement is almost incredible to this utilitarian age, but it is the truest unworldliness.

Brethren, have you observed the signs of the times? This is not a spiritual age in which we live. It is not an age of great poets. The work of the seer is below par. There is a widespread materialism abroad that is positively alarming. It threatens to turn Christian progress back toward paganism. There has been an effort to introduce into this country the barbarous Spanish bull fight. The greatest hero among us, it would seem, is a "slugger." The most popular form of philosophy is materialistic evolution. In some quarters there has been a great effort made to ignore the Christian Sunday. All this means something, and it is not wise to try to blink the fact. Men's morals are much in accord with their thinking. History shows that life follows doctrine as night tracks the day. This gross worldliness is liable to become destructive of morality. Seed sown in this generation will ripen in the next. The influence of Lucretius' philosophy in Rome on the morals of the people may be seen to-day in the frescoing on the walls of the exhumed buildings of Pompeii. France wrote over her cemetery gates, "Death is an eternal sleep!" and soon her streets were flowing with blood. The sovereign remedy for these evils of worldliness is the life of faith such as Christ offers.

II. Turn now to see the reasons for choosing the life of faith.

1. The principle of faith adds a new sense to the soul. It gives the power of seeing the unseen. It is plainly stated that the Christian walks by faith and not by sight. Faith is the substance of things hoped for, the evidence of things not seen. This seeing the invisible is a paradox; worse still, if there is nothing but this material world, the statement is sheer nonsense. Believing in the invisible may seem to be credulity, but it is good sense and sound reason. We believe in the existence of many things which we have not seen. The invention of the microscope has opened up a new world as large as that one Columbus discovered. We now talk of our neighbors' animalculæ and microbes with great familiarity, which reside in a thimbleful of ditch water; but did you ever see a microbe? You never will with your natural eye; still you believe that it exists. You act in accordance with this belief. Yet when asked to believe in the supernatural and spiritual world you reply that you are an agnostic, and that by the very laws of your mind you cannot believe in what cannot be demonstrated. You make yourself ridiculous, according to my thinking, when you laugh at the simple faith of my sister and then readily accept so much else that you do not know. "But," you reply, "scientific men who have fitted themselves for it have taken the appropriate instruments and have seen all these objects in this microscopic world." "Yes," I reply, "and spiritual men fitted for seeing have taken this instrument, the word of

God, and have looked straight through it into the spiritual world and seen such things as they have not the power to fully relate." Consciousness is as genuine and as reliable a source of information as sense-perception. I believe the philosophers have at last about agreed to that, and whether they have or not I know that it is so. What I have felt I know. When old Thomas Cranmer was being led to the stake, to die for his faith, some one asked him to repeat a passage of Scripture upon which he reposed his faith in Jesus Christ. The old man's memory proving treacherous at the moment he could not do so. "What," said the other, "dying for your religion, and still you cannot give me one passage which comforts you in such an hour!" "Yes," replied the martyr, "dying for it, but though my memory fails me, I know that Jesus Christ is the Son of God and the Saviour of my soul." "How do you know it?" he was asked. Tremblingly laying his hand on his breast he replied, "I feel it here, sir."

2. Again, the choosing of the life of faith is urged because it gives steadiness of nerve and confidence amid earth's hardships. Moses chose to suffer with the people of God, and we read that he endured. You know the rest. How well he endured is a matter of imperishable history. The cheerful fortitude of the Christian has ever been a source of surprise to the uninitiated. He stands serene in the wildest storm of trial. The moral sublimity of his conduct in adversity is not due to pagan stoicism but is normal, cheerful, and healthful. Poor and oppressed, he talks calmly of some unseen possession to which he will fall heir not many days hence, when his right to hold a wingless fortune shall be forevermore unquestioned. Homeless, he possesses a home in a city that hath foundations, whose builder and maker is God. Afflicted sorely, he exclaims: Though he slay me, yet will I trust him. Bereaved, he meekly says:

The Lord gave and the Lord hath taken away, blessed be the name of the Lord. Moses endured as seeing him who is invisible and thousands have done the same and others will until the ransomed of God shall be gathered to mansions in the skies.

Yes, brethren, we have a noble heritage in our Christian biographies. I am all admiration for the heroes of the Cross and I am persuaded that we do not make enough of these. We might learn a lesson from secular orators and writers, if we prefer to take them as examples rather than to imitate the author of the eleventh chapter of Hebrews. All the way along through our history we can find scores of whom the world was not worthy.

When Charles Cotesworth Pinckney said to Talleyrand at the Court of France, on refusing to promise money to settle a difficulty between this country and France: "War be it then! Millions for defense, sir, but not one cent for tribute," he made a noble speech for which he has been sufficiently praised; but a nobler one far was that made by a Baptist preacher who, having been imprisoned for preaching and being offered his freedom if he would promise to desist from preaching, exclaimed: "I will lie here in this dungeon till the moss grows over my eyes before I will make such a promise!"

3. And too, when the Christian comes to die it is in the fullness of the power of this sustaining faith. Paul's immortal words as he stood in the shadow of death, come to your mind. The hysterical fickleness of the dying sinner is not characteristic of the Christian. Ofttimes Christians have passed away with rapturous joy. Have you considered the departure of our brother Stephen? It was a thrilling scene. He saw the heavens opened and the Son of Man standing at the right hand of the Father. While praying for his enemies in almost the very words of his dying Lord, amid an avalanche of stones, he fell asleep.

Ah, brethren, I know that this invisible One is a reality in this present world and that he has a power that may be ours. The time is and will ever be when the support of this invisible arm is needed—in life, in death, at the bar of God. Oh, that the sons of men would call upon him while he is near and seek him while he may be found!

XXIX

THE FAITHFULNESS OF GOD[1]

BY J. P. GREENE, D. D., LL. D.

"God is faithful."   1 Cor. 1 : 9.

GOD is true. His word of promise is sure. In all his relations to his people he is faithful. No one ever trusted him in vain.

We find this doctrine everywhere in his word. He has revealed himself as a faithful God, because faithfulness is an essential part of his character, and his people must know that he is faithful in order that they may trust him. He is not like the gods of the heathen, capricious and untrustworthy, but is the same yesterday and to-day and forever. "It is impossible for God to lie."

While we accept this doctrine as most reasonable and true, we do not always realize that it is true for us. He is our God. We are depending on him for daily grace. He has made many exceeding great and precious promises to us. Will he do for us all that he has promised in his word? Can we, in our daily trials, lean with sweet assurance on his word and know that it is as firm as the everlasting hills? A theory is good, but practical knowledge is better.

It is not always easy to believe that God is faithful. Sometimes we are inclined to charge him with folly. Our faith is sorely tried; our eyes are bedimmed with tears, and we cannot see our Lord; our ears are dis-

---

[1] Preached in Washington, D. C., during the Jubilee Session of the Southern Baptist Convention.

JOHN PRIEST GREENE was born in Scotland County, Mo., in 1849. He was educated in private schools, Memphis (Mo.) Academy, La Grange College, Southern Baptist Theological Seminary, and Leipzig University, Germany. Was pastor of the East Baptist Church, Louisville, Ky., for four years, and of the Third Baptist Church, St. Louis, Mo., for ten years; became President of William Jewel College in June, 1892. In 1895 he received the degree of LL. D. from Wake Forest College, having already been honored with the doctorate in theology. He is a man of broad scholarship, and is held in high esteem by his brethren.

tracted with the noises of the world, and we cannot hear his word. He has **spoken to us.** He is not far from us. Yes, yes; but **we** are **confused**; we stagger; we fall. This is not what we expected. We are sorely disappointed. How can we harmonize this with the word of promise? Bitter disappointments for the time obscure the faithfulness of God.

But **we** must believe that he is true. Our very souls depend on his faithfulness. What shall we do if he fail us? To whom shall **we** go? In whom shall we trust? He has the words of eternal life. If he is unfaithful, then there is no **God.** He that comes to God must believe that he is, and that **he** is the rewarder of those that diligently seek **him.** We may not be able to reconcile our circumstances with his promises, but we cannot, on this account, believe that he is unfaithful. We will wait for more light. In his own good time he will show us that he has not deceived us nor forsaken us. He knows that our faith is based on his faithfulness, and he will not disappoint us. It may seem that he has forsaken us for a small moment, but he will soon gather us with everlasting mercies. Clouds obscure his face—vapors that his breath will drive away. But if mountains should rise between him and us, even these mighty barriers shall vanish before his almighty word. His people shall all know that he is a faithful God, keeping his word **unto a** thousand generations.

Let me point out to you several ways in which God has shown his faithfulness. It is necessary that you should know that "He is faithful that promised." He has given the world a record of his faithfulness.

The unwritten word of God, nature, is a sure testimony. "The heavens declare **the** glory of God"— and **also** declare his faithfulness. It is night now. **The sun** has **gone down, and** darkness **is** over the earth. **But the** morning **will** come and drive the darkness **away.** How sure is the rising of the sun?

You have already planned your work for **to-morrow.** You will lie down to-night in perfect confidence **of the** coming day. May not God forget to **send the** sun? You can trust him **for** the morrow, "O ye of little faith"! why can you not trust him for spiritual light? It is springtime now. Was **it** delayed a little? Were you afraid that winter would never loose his grasp on the earth? God did **not** forget to send **us** the seed-time. Men are now turning over the soil, **and** committing the seed to it in faith. They believe that nature will do her work, and confidently expect to reap a harvest. The seed will not fail, but the germ of life will spring up and grow and bear grain of its own kind. God giveth it a body even as it pleased him, and to each seed a body of its own. He has expressed his faithfulness in the laws of nature. **Men** sow their seed **in** faith **and** hope, and thus bear witness to his faithfulness. But shame on them! they do not look up to the faithful God that made these unerring laws of nature. Read his record aright, and **you** will not fail to see that he has given every creature good reason for trusting his word.

There is another record, the written word. The witness of nature is strong and convincing to those who will receive it. But wicked men have ever persisted in excluding God from his world. They will not read his unwritten and inarticulate word. So he added his spoken word, and then wrote it down, **that** all might be without excuse. Here it is, the word **of** the Lord which endures forever. He began thousands **of** years ago **to** make this record, and added **to** it **from** generation to generation. It **is a solemn** thing **to make** promises, especially **to those that will** and **must** depend **on** them. It is **more solemn** to make promises that **will go down** from generation to generation. But **how very** solemn to write down the promises in plain words. Men not only read them, but also look for their fulfillment. God promised this.

Has he done it? Has he kept his word? Times change. Customs change. Nations come and go. Many things that were written centuries ago are foolishness now. How many religions have come to naught! How many systems of philosophy have perished! How many strongholds of unbelief have been leveled by the hand of time!

But God was not afraid to write a book. He knew the end from the beginning. Here is his signature. Let his adversaries read it, and bring in their indictment. They are indeed even now—as for ages past—attacking the record. Destructive criticism is working hard to destroy the foundations of the Old Testament; fear not. The old Book is a record of God's faithfulness, and criticism will dash itself into a thousand fragments against the impregnable rock. Let men use pick and spade, and dig up the records of the past; let them bring to light the laws and customs and gods of the long-buried nations; let them trace the course of history and disclose the "environment" of the word in every age; the record will not suffer, but will shine the brighter, and we shall see more clearly than ever that "God is faithful." "All flesh is as grass, and all the glory thereof as the flower of grass. The grass withereth, and the flower falleth: but the word of the Lord abideth forever."

There is a peculiarity about the written record of God's faithfulness; The promise of a Redeemer. Sin entered this fair world, then sorrow came, and despair would have followed had not God in his mercy promised a deliverer. In the garden where man sinned, God gave him the promise of victory over the evil one. When the transgressor left that beautiful home and went out into the thorny world, he carried this sweet promise with him, the only consolation of the sinful race. As time went on the promise was renewed. The call of Abraham was a forward step, a pledge that God had not forgotten his word. "In thy seed shall all the nations of the earth be blessed." Moses was a nearer approach. God said, through Moses, "A prophet like unto me shall the Lord your God raise up unto you." In David the promise was repeated. And so on till the last prophet of the old dispensation spoke plainly of the coming of the Lord. In due time Jesus Christ came to save his people from their sins. He is the fulfillment of all of God's promises of deliverance. Some think that God is slack in his promises; but he is not; he is long-suffering, a faithful God, keeping his covenant with the children of men. Now that we have Christ, how can we ever doubt the word of our Heavenly Father?

Let me mention one more witness to his faithfulness. Every child of God "hath set his seal to this, that God is true." The record of the past is valuable. It is an indestructible monument of God's fidelity. But there is also an individual, experimental, and spiritual witness in the heart of every Christian. For many years you have had dealings with God. You have trusted him for his grace. When you believed in Jesus for the first time, you committed yourself to him, and since that time you have been following him. He promised to be with you, to make his grace sufficient for you. How long have you walked with him? Some of you are gray with age, and I know that you have been a long time in his service. Answer me! Has he ever failed you? Even when you feared and almost despaired, did he not verify his promise to you? Has he not been the kindest and truest of masters? Are you not more convinced than ever that he will do to trust? Experience is an excellent teacher. We know best what we have learned through experience. You have heard and seen enough; your soul is satisfied. Suppose all the servants of God could rise up now and

THE FAITHFULNESS OF GOD

bear witness to his faithfulness, what a cloud of witnesses would fill the horizon. There would be no room left for doubters and unbelievers and adversaries of the Lord.

We have a faithful God. We can and do trust him. All our hope is in him. "Some trust in chariots, and some in horses; but we will make mention of the Lord our God." All that is dear to us we have committed to him, and we have the assurance in our hearts that he will never fail us.

1. *We have committed our lives to him.* Once we thought that we could direct our own steps. But this self-trust brought us to confusion. It is not in man's power to direct his own steps. He is ignorant and weak and sinful. He does not know what is best for him, and he is not able to do all that he knows to be right. The sinful, unregenerate man is at sea without compass or chart, driven about by every wind, and is often finally dashed to pieces on the rocks of unbelief. As children need the guidance and protection of a father, so do the children of men need the guidance and protection of their Heavenly Father. Worldly wisdom and prudence cannot take the place of faith in God. The Lord must guide us with his eye, because our eyes cannot see the way of love.

When we come to Jesus we turned over all our interests to him, our business, our families, life itself. Now we try to manage all our affairs as he directs. The life that we now live we live by faith in the Son of God, for he alone can guide us unto success. This enterprise shall prosper, if he wills it. Our children shall come to usefulness and honor with his blessing. Once a dying man said to me, "I could die in peace if I did not have to leave my wife and these two little girls to the cruel fortunes of this wicked world." I said to him, "God reigns in this wicked world. He has promised to care for the widow and the orphan. Let us commit them to him." We prayed. Then, smiling through his tears, he said, "I can trust him. He will do what he has promised." His faith was not in vain. God cared for his wife and children better than he had ever cared for them. Will you not fully commit your whole life to him now? If your life has been a failure, you have not committed all your ways unto the Lord, but have leaned upon your own understanding. Entrust all to him and trust him for all.

2. *We have committed our souls to him.* If life, with all its important concerns cannot be intrusted to human wisdom, of course the immortal soul must find a higher and a safer guide. Failure in this life is bad enough—we must not fail in the life to come. Jesus is a faithful Saviour. He cleanses us from our sins, washes us in his own blood. Then he preserves us from the evil one during our earthly lives. Your soul is in his keeping. Paul said, "I know whom I have believed, and am persuaded that he is able to keep that which I have committed unto him against that day." The apostle did not keep himself,—he could not,—but committed himself to the faithful Saviour. And this is salvation. We are saved now through faith in the Son of God, and through faith in him we shall be saved in the world to come.

Where is that land of blessed immortality, the home of the soul? Jesus knows. He is leading us to that happy place. We can trust him as we follow. If any one asks, "How do you know that you are going to heaven?" we point to Jesus, "He is the way, the truth, and the life." So when death comes to the Christian he can only say, "Into thy hands I commit my spirit!" With perfect confidence he steps out of life into eternity. Surely at this time we need a faithful Saviour, for we are beyond human help. Jesus does not forsake his people in the last extremity. How many in the dying hour have borne witness to his faithfulness! How great and good and true he looks as he stands at the gate of death and causes his people to triumph over the last enemy!

God's faithfulness should inspire us to be faithful to him. He keeps every promise. But, alas, we have been untrue to him. Perhaps unfaithfulness is the most common fault of Christians. It has certainly injured the usefulness of many of us, and caused us much unhappiness. Let us try every day to be true to him. We know how our all depends on his faithfulness. So all his work in the world that he has committed to us depends on our faithfulness to him. Be faithful in every place, in your business, in your home, in your church, and God will love you and honor you. And on the last day he will say to you, "Well done, thou good and faithful servant: thou hast been faithful over a few things, I will make thee ruler over many things: enter thou into the joy of thy lord."

And now, my unsaved brother, let me remind you of God's word to you: "If we confess our sins, he is faithful and just to forgive us our sins and to cleanse us from all unrighteousness." Is this not a blessed promise? God is speaking to you. He knows that you are a sinner. He knows that you love sin and hate righteousness. Or perhaps you have become tired of sin. You have enjoyed "the pleasures of sin which are for a season," and wish that you were a Christian. But you do not see the way to Jesus. Many times your heart has cried, "What must I do to be saved?" Here is the way. Go to him and tell him that you have sinned against him. Confess your sins to him. This is all you can do. You cannot purify your heart. The leopard cannot change his spots, nor the Ethiopian his skin. Give up your hope in human help. Go directly to the Saviour. There is no other way. Why should there be another way? This is simple. You can do it, and you must do it, brother. The Lord has not required much of you, but you must do what he has required. "Tell him you are a wretch undone."

Do you not remember when you disobeyed your mother? How did you make your reconciliation with her? When you could bear the separation no longer, you ran to her, and buried your face in her lap, and sobbed out your confession of sin. Then she wiped away your tears and gave you the kiss of pardon. Go in this way to Jesus. Will he receive you? Hear his word again, "If we confess our sins, he is faithful and just to forgive us our sins, and to cleanse us from all unrighteousness." "Faithful is the saying, and worthy of all acceptation, that Christ Jesus came into the world to save sinners." How can you longer doubt? Try him. Since the fall of man penitent sinners have found him faithful to forgive sins. He will not fail to keep his promise to you.

R. R. ACREE was born in King and Queen County, Va., in 1852. When twelve years of age he was baptized by Rev. R. H. Bagby into the fellowship of the Bruington Baptist Church in 1865; licensed to preach in 1873, and ordained in 1876. He was educated at Aberdeen Academy, Richmond College, and the Southern Baptist Theological Seminary. His first ministerial work was done as State missionary in Loudon County. He has since served with much acceptableness and efficiency as pastor in Lynchburg, the First Baptist Church, Petersburg, in the Calvary Baptist Church, Roanoke, Va. In 1893 he entered his present inviting and important pastorate, Knoxville, Tenn. Dr. Acree is a genial gentleman, a consecrated Christian, a fine preacher, and enjoys a wide popularity. In Mrs. Acree he has a pastor's helper. She is a woman of unusual devotion to Christ and his church, and of skill in church work.

XXX

THE CLEANSING BLOOD

BY R. R. ACREE, D. D.

"And the blood of Jesus Christ his Son cleanseth us from all sin."
1 John 1 : 7.

THE Bible is the book of the blood. The one theme out of which all its other themes grow is the blood.

It is the scarlet thread that binds its parts together in unbroken unity. Take it out and the great book falls apart, a confused and dismembered mass without the power to bless or to save.

The blood of Christ gives to the Bible its highest value. It gives to its types and shadows the substance; to its symbols their sign; to its prophecies their promise; and to the gospel its good news. Take the blood out and the star of human hope, eclipsed by an impenetrable cloud of despair, drops into an eternal hell. Take it out, and God is a terror, and heaven a mockery of our misery. Without his blood we can do nothing but despair and die and be damned.

Yes, friends, the blood, the blood, the blood of Christ that makes atonement for the sins of the whole world, is the foundation of our faith, the inspiration of our hope, and the ground of our confidence. Not Christ, but Christ crucified is the power of God unto salvation to every one that believeth.

The blood of Jesus Christ his Son cleanseth us from all sin. If sin shuts us up to death and hell, his blood opens the gates to eternal life and heaven.

If sin has polluted and defiled us, his blood **can make us** white and clean. If sin has enslaved **us, it is his** blood that redeems us and makes us free. If sin condemns us under the law and alienates us from God, his blood justifies **us** before the law and reconciles us to God.

The Bible, **as** you so gladly remember, uses many illustrations **to** show how completely the blood of Christ delivers us from the power and penalty of sin; it gives life, justification, redemption, reconciliation, peace, pardon, purity, and sanctification. No one of these illustrations gives a complete idea of what Christ does for those who lovingly believe in him. Each **one** of them shows some phase **of** his work, and all of them emphasize the fact of complete salvation, of how entirely the blood of Christ removes every obstacle from between God and **our** possible salvation.

This text, regarding sin as guilt, as filthy defilement, and the relation of the blood of Christ to it, says: And the blood of Jesus Christ his Son cleanseth us from all sin.

The text teaches:

1. The defilement of sin.

Sin! What a word that is! What **a** history **it has!** In what anguish it has been written. Every letter **a** pang, every sentence a sob, every page wet with human tears and red with the blood of crushed and mangled hearts.

Who is the grim-visaged monster that lights **the** torch of war and bears it blazing over a trembling land? **Sin!** Who is the masked enemy lurking in the shadow of the night, sowing seeds of discord among friends and transforming faith and love into suspicion and hate? Sin!

Who is the painted temptress that steals virtue from the pure, the fair siren who, seated on the rock by **a** deadly pool, smiles to deceive, sings to lure, kisses to betray, and flings her arms around our neck to leap with us into perdition? Sin!

Who transforms homes into hell, fathers into fiends, mothers into monsters, brothers into brutes, and sisters into sirens, and then gathering them into its arms flings them weeping and wailing into perdition? Sin!

> Sin! What a monster she is!
> Her home is in the deep, damp dark, where
> Slimy things begot of hell rave and rot.
> Look, if you can, upon her foul progeny!

The leer of Lucifer is in their eyes and the slime of the pit befouls their garments. There they go, the liars, the slanderers, the thieves, the fornicators and adulterers, the murderers, the infidels, and blasphemers! Name me, if you can, a sorrow that sin has not caused, a defilement it has not made.

Every anguish that rends the brow, every pain that pierces the body, every shame that shadows life, every tear that scalds the cheek, every guilt that pollutes the soul; the maniac's chain, the felon's cell, the lazar house, the coffin, the hearse, the grave, hell itself, are the fruits of sin.

Nor is this all, nor is it the worst. The work begun here is consummated in eternity, when sin casts both soul and body into hell, "where the worm dieth not and the fire is not quenched."

Think on these things and tell me if sin is not guilt. Think on these things and tell me if we do not need to be washed from our sins and cleansed from our iniquities.

But some one says, I am not so guilty as that. The picture is overdrawn. Perhaps no individual is guilty of every sin, but all are guilty of some sin. There is none pure; no, not one. The seeds have been sown, what shall the harvest be? The wages of one sin is death. Some man put into his window as an advertisement some earthenware pigs, and wrote this sentence under them: "We are not hogs." Some other man passing by saw the sign and the sentence, and wrote under it: "No; but you will be if you live." The wages of sin is death. Look at that company of lepers, once so young, so beautiful, and so fair. As yet no sign of any malady appears. Wait and see. Look now. "The hair and eyebrows have fallen from a once beautiful countenance, the face once so fair is livid and bloated and covered with festering ulcers; the lips once firm and strong are gone, and the end is not far away." Sin is pollution. Sin is death.

The text teaches:

2. That the blood of Jesus Christ his Son cleanses us from the defilement of sin.

I see the light kindling in your eye, and I feel the joy and thankfulness that is rising in your hearts. I join with you in blessing the name of the Lord for this gospel. Listen, listen all ye who have seen your defilement and bowed your heads in shame and fear. Take courage and rejoice, for the blood of Jesus Christ his Son cleanseth us from all sin. Guilty, grimed, all unclean as we may be, his blood can make us clean and pure.

As Naaman, the leper, came up from the Jordan's waters with the pure flesh of a little child, so shall they who are washed in the blood of the Lamb be made every whit clean.

You have seen the men who work in the coal mines come home from their work. The grime and soot of the mine is upon them. Their faces and necks, arms and hands are grimy and black. So disfigured are they that one scarcely can recognize them. But when they stand beside the open fountain and wash and are clean, then the old smile comes back to the kindly face, and the same eye beams upon you, and the same honest hands grip your own.

> There is a fountain filled with blood
>   Drawn from Immanuel's veins;
> And sinners plunged beneath that flood,
>   Lose all their guilty stains.

Yes, yes; it is true; the prophets and apostles say it is true, the saints in all ages say it is true, the Lord God Almighty says it is true—the blood of Jesus Christ his Son cleanseth us from all sin.

During the late war a chaplain went among the soldiers in a hospital and preached unto them the way of Christ. He found one man whose eyes were closed and who was muttering something about—blood—blood—blood—and the chaplain thought he was thinking of the carnage of the battlefield, and going to him he tried to divert his mind; but the young man looked up and said: "Oh, doctor, it was not that that I was thinking of; I was thinking how precious the blood of Christ is to me now that I am dying. It covers all my sins."

The text teaches:

3. That the blood of Jesus Christ cleanseth us from all sin.

The cleansing is complete. The salvation is perfect. He saves "unto the uttermost all them that come unto God by him." Their robes are "washed and made white in the blood of the Lamb." One day Queen Victoria visited a paper mill, and when she saw the filthy rags, exclaimed, "How can those be made white?" "Ah, your majesty," was the reply: "I have a powerful chemical process by which I take the color even out of those red rags." Some days after, the Queen found on her writing-desk a lot of the most beautifully polished writing-paper she had ever seen; on each sheet were the letters of her own name and her likeness. There was also the accompanying note: "Will the Queen be pleased to accept a specimen of my paper with the assurance that every sheet was made from the dirty rags she saw on the back of the poor rag-picker. Will the Queen allow me to say I have had many a good sermon preached to me in my mill. I can understand how the Lord Jesus can take the poor heathen and the vilest of the vile and make them clean and white. And I can see how he can put his own name upon them; and just as these rags transformed may go into a royal palace and be admired, so poor sinners can be received into the palace of the Great King."

And his blood cleanses from all sin of every kind. He is not able to save from some sins and unable to save from other sins. His blood cleanses from all sin: from sins of omission and commission, sins of thought and of desire, sins of words and of deeds, sins of childhood and of youth, sins of manhood and of old age. His blood cleanses from all sin.

Finally, let us consider how the cleansing blood is applied.

And yet I need not tell you. You know. Familiar as your own name is that text which carries with it the power of God and the promise of eternal life.

"Believe"—ah, yes, that is it, "Believe on the Lord Jesus Christ and thou shalt be saved." An old herdsman, it is said, was taken to a London hospital to die. His granddaughter used to visit him there and read the Bible to him. One day she read the first chapter of first John and when she came to the seventh verse, the old man asked very earnestly: "Is that there?" "Yes, grandpa," was the reply. "Read it again," and she read: "And the blood of Jesus Christ his Son cleanseth us from all sin." "Are you sure that is there?" "Yes, quite sure." "Then take my hand and lay my finger on the words that I may feel them." And she took the bony finger of the blind old man and put it on the precious words. "You are sure they are there?" "Sure." "Read them again. If any one asks you how I died, tell them I died in the faith of these words: 'And the blood of Jesus Christ his Son cleanseth from all sin.'" Then the old man withdrew his hands, his gray head fell softly upon the pillow and he went out and went up to join those who have "washed their robes and made them white in the blood of the Lamb."

XXXI

THE MEAT AND MISSION OF THE MASTER

BY H. F. SPROLES, D. D.

"My meat is to do the will of him that sent me, and to finish his work." John 4 : 34.

THERE are three pictures in this chapter worthy of the painter's brush.

The disciples had gone into the city of Sychar, about two miles away, to buy food for the little company. It was about noon on the third day of the journey from Jerusalem to Galilee through Samaria. Jesus sat down on the low wall around Jacob's well, hungry and thirsty, with relaxed body, and with weary yet gentle face. That is an impressive picture. The mighty Son of God, tired and resting.

When the disciples returned they found him, with animated countenance, eagerly talking with a sinful woman, who came from the town for water. He came to seek the lost, and was always especially anxious to find those who had gone farthest away. With marvelous skill, he had quickened and satisfied the spiritual thirst of this soul, and was full of joy. In response to the disciples' entreaties to eat of the food which they had brought, he said: "My meat is to do the will of him that sent me." For this I hunger; this is my nourishment, my strength, my satisfaction. To carry on that work, step by step, according to the Father's will, and to have in prospect its completion on the cross, is my food; by this I have been nourished and quickened. That too is an attractive picture.

H. F. Shupard D. D.

H. F. SPROLES was born near Castilian Springs, Holmes County, Miss., January, 1844. Raised on a farm, accepted Jesus Christ as personal Saviour and Lord, and was baptized at the age of thirteen ; studied in neighborhood schools until seventeen years of age, when he expected to enter Mississippi College, but went into the Confederate army, and served to the close of the war, in which he was severely wounded. Studied four years in Southern Baptist Theological Seminary, then at Greenville, S. C., from which was graduated in full, May, 1870. Was ordained in August, 1867. During vacations of the seminary he remained in Greenville, S. C., and studied under Dr. William Williams, professor in the seminary, and Prof. D. T. Smith, of Furman University. Was pastor in Carrollton, Miss., nine years. Thence he went to Jackson, Miss., where he has since remained as pastor. Is now member of the Board of Trustees of Southern Baptist Theological Seminary, and also of Mississippi College, from which he received the honorary degree of D. D. in 1890, and is president of Convention Board of Mississippi Baptists. Was married to Miss R. A. Pickell, Williamston, S. C., in May, 1870.

THE MEAT AND MISSION OF THE MASTER

He was sent. "My meat is to do the will of him that sent me." His coming was not the caprice of an impulsive soul, nor the doubtful experiment of an ambitious seeker of fame: it was in fulfillment of a divine mission. "God sent not his Son into the world to condemn the world; but that the world through him might be saved." He said that he was sanctified, separated, and sent into the world by God the Father. He insisted that he came down from heaven to do the will of him that sent him. At the close of his earthly mission, he said with great satisfaction and joy, "I have finished the work which thou gavest me to do."

When it is said, however, that Christ was sent, it is not meant that he was compelled to come on an unpleasant mission, but merely that his work was in accordance with divine counsel. As Paul says, his mission was "according to the eternal purpose which God purposed in Christ Jesus our Lord." As Mediator in human redemption, he willingly and joyfully came to bring God's message to men, and to do his work among them, shouting: "I delight to do thy will, O my God." "My meat is to do the will of him that sent me."

To do the will of him who sent him, to deliver his message to men, to declare him, to open his heart unto men, to complete God's work among them, was the food of his soul, the supply of its truest needs, the satisfaction of the deepest desires of his nature. Meat nourishes, strengthens, refreshes, satisfies. The bodily hunger and thirst which our Lord had felt, when wearied with his journey he sat down on Jacob's well, was forgotten in carrying on the divine work in the soul of the woman of Samaria. His soul was full of other thought which drove away all sense of hunger. He had been eating that meat, he had been doing that will, when the disciples were away. So grateful had it been to him to be thus engaged;

so earnest and happy had he been in leading a solitary woman, and in sending her away in full belief of his Messiahship to go and bring others to him, that bodily appetite ceased to solicit, and the hunger of an hour ago was no longer felt. This was his meat—that he might be constantly doing God's will, and at last complete his work. We know with what joyous emotions he said at the close of his mission on earth, "I have glorified thee on earth: I have finished the work which thou gavest me to do."

The third picture is inspiring. A crowd of Samaritans set out with the woman for the prophet at the well. Jesus and his disciples looked at the people coming to him through the green fields. They saw only the crowd and the fields of springing corn, which in a few months would be ready for the harvest. He saw the wide fields of the world's nations already white unto the harvest. Raising his hand, he said with trembling emotion, "Say not ye, There are yet four months and then cometh harvest? behold, I say unto you, Lift up your eyes, and look on the fields; for they are white already to harvest." Lift up your eyes, that you may see far. Look, and you will become interested and prayerful. Becoming interested, you will wish to enter the fields crowded with ripe, golden, and perishing grain.

As was the Master, so are the disciples. He was sent; so are they. In his prayer for all those who should believe on him in every age and place, our Lord said: "As thou hast sent me into the world, even so have I also sent them into the world. And for their sakes I sanctify myself, that they also might be sanctified through the truth." It is his desire and prayer that every one of his disciples should enter upon the mission which he had fulfilled on his own behalf; and, in preparation for that work, that they might receive the same sanctification. It is the mission of every Christian to do God's will on earth.

Can there be anything more solemn, more thrilling, than the conviction that God has a purpose in one's life, and has given him a commission to fulfill that purpose? This purpose, this mission, from our exalted Lord is to carry his message to men, to convey his Spirit unto them, to reveal his great heart unto them, to do his will among them. A more important commission was never given to an angel.

The intense desire of the true Christian's soul, the satisfaction of the deepest yearnings of his nature, the meat which nourishes and refreshes, is to do God's will.

Three things are essential to obedience. (1) There must be an obedient spirit. Only such a soul can have insight into God's will. Jesus said, "If any man will"—is willing, anxious, determined to—"do his will, he shall know of the doctrine." Christ's will was always in harmony with God's will. The will of man is brought into harmony in his regeneration. He asks with the converted Saul, "Lord, what wilt thou have me to do?" God's will becomes the law of his spirit. He says, "I delight to do thy will, O my God: yea, thy law is within my heart." (2) The obedient spirit must have an expression of God's will. God's written law is the authoritative expression of his will, the transcription of his nature. (3) There must be honest effort to do God's will. An obedient spirit alone will not satisfy the disciple, nor will the performance of deeds which are required. The spirit without the doing would be only intention; doing without the spirit would be compulsion; but the spirit going out in the execution of God's will is obedience and satisfaction, the food of the soul. Be not satisfied with any feeling, with a mere movement of the soul toward God; aim at doing his will. Many persons seem to think that the great attainment is to be on the top wave of feeling. It is a greater privilege to be in the performance of duty. "To obey is better than sacrifice." Doing the will of God is more acceptable to him than any story one can tell about his enjoyment of religion. There is a morbid religious sentiment which will set aside the expressed and recognized will of God for its own gratification. Often the disobedient revel in emotion, and esteem themselves as Christians extraordinary because they are on a high wave of feeling. There is no nourishing, strengthening meat in this. To do God's will is food.

This food satisfies. But can we ever do the will of God perfectly and therefore eat of that meat which Christ ate? See what he did say. Not the accomplished mission, not the perfected work of God among men, but the end which he ever kept in view was the food of his soul. "My meat is that I may be doing the will of him that sent me, and that I may finish his work; that I may be constantly doing his will, and may at last complete his work." This food is accessible to the weakest and most imperfect among us. We may in everything seek to know and do God's will.

This purpose and effort give nourishment and refreshment. There can be no higher function of the human soul than to obey God. To recognize him, to believe in him, to love him, to commune with him, to come into harmony with him, is to live. Otherwise, man no more truly lives than the horse which he rides, the ox which draws his burdens, the dog which guards his house. The man who can say that "God's law, his expressed will, is not a terror, which makes me an outlaw, a fugitive; not an outward necessity, which makes me a slave; but an inward force, which makes me an obedient child"—that soul feeds. To him God's will is not an external necessity, but an inward power; not an unpleasant medicine to prevent death, but a pleasant food to nourish life. Such a man obeys God to appease the hunger of his soul. He feeds, grows, is joyous, and becomes strong.

Watkins, in Ellicott's Commentary, speaks of analogies in human experience. "The command of duty, the charming power of hope, the stimulus of success, are forces that supply to weak and weary nerves and muscles the vigor of a new life. Under these the soldier can forget his wounds, the martyr smile at the lion or the flame, the worn-out traveler still plod onward at the thought of home. We cannot analyze this power, but it exists. They have food to eat that those without know not of." We are not surprised when the Holy Spirit says through the Apostle John, that those who do God's will shall last. Other things will fail. "The world passeth away, and the lust thereof: but he that doeth the will of God abideth forever." He links himself with the divine order of things, and becomes as enduring as God himself.

XXXII

THE CRUCIFIED CHRIST [1]

BY C. A. STAKELY, D. D.

"The Jews require a sign, and the Greeks seek after wisdom; but we preach Christ crucified, unto the Jews a stumblingblock, and unto the Greeks foolishness; but unto them which are called, both Jews and Greeks, Christ the power of God, and the wisdom of God." 1 Cor. 1 : 22-24.

IT was not until the fullness of the time had come that God sent forth his Son. The wisdom of Heaven in having the Christ appear just when he did has doubtless occurred to us all. It was the right time. Not only was it the time specified in the prophets, and came after the chosen seed had been sufficiently long in the preparatory school, but it was after the world had had ample opportunity to test every human system of faith. Within the period from the creation of man to what is known as the Augustan age, in the closing days of which the Saviour appeared, the world had invented and tested every man-made religion now known to it. We have in this day no new religions. There may be new forms, but no **new** principles of religion. The religions which **now** exist in the world are only developments or modifications of principles long ago recognized and practised. None of the man-made religions ever relieved human misery, none ever brought spiritual peace to human hearts, none ever worked permanent reform in human lives. It was

---

[1] Preached before the English Baptist gathering at Manchester, in June, 1898, when the author was one of the fraternal delegates from the Southern Baptist Convention.

CHARLES AVERETTE STAKELY, **pastor of the First Baptist** Church of Washington, D. C., is among the younger ministers of the Southern Baptist Convention. He was born **at** Madisonville, Monroe County, Tenn., **on** the third day **of** March, 1859, but was **reared in** Alabama and Georgia. At about thirteen years of age he was baptized into the fellowship **of** the First Baptist Church of Montgomery, Ala., by Dr D. W. Gwin. Soon afterward, his father dying, the family moved **to** La Grange, Ga., where young Stakely entered upon high school studies, and where, after having studied law under Hon. A. H. Cox, he entered the bar, being scarcely nineteen years of age. He practised in La Grange until he was nearly twenty-two years of age; in the meantime, at the age of twenty, he was made county solicitor, which office he resigned to enter the ministry. His first charge **was at** Elberton, Ga., the church at this place calling him to ordination. During his pastorate in Elberton, in 1882, he was married to Miss Jessie Davis, daughter of Rev. William H. Davis, of Richmond County, Ga. From Elberton he went to Augusta, where his labors were brief, and from Augusta to Charleston, S. C., where he was **pastor** of the Citadel Square Church for about four years.

Dr. Stakely lent well-known and valuable aid to **the** Baptist churches of Charleston in their recovery from the earthquake of 1886. In 1888 he was called to the pastorate of the First Baptist Church of Washington, D. C., where he still remains. Dr. Stakely received his degree of A. M. from Mercer University, Georgia, in 1884, and his degree of D. D. **from** Richmond College, in 1889. The magnificent building **of** the First Baptist Church of Washington, D. C., in which the Convention held its Fiftieth Anniversary, was erected during Dr. Stakely's pastorate, and is largely the result of his own enterprise and zeal.

when every plan of men had signally failed, when human ingenuity had made the final draft upon its resources, and the last hope of the world for spiritual recovery through its own wisdom and power had gone, that an all-gracious God introduced, upon the foundation of an older true but undeveloped faith, that amazing salvation which has for its center a crucified Christ. The Cross has been on trial these nineteen centuries; its influence is known; many of its accomplishments have passed into history; its fruits are abroad in the earth. That it has been an unspeakable blessing its candid enemies can scarcely deny.

The passage of Scripture which has been chosen for a text invites us to consider the crucified Christ, whom it presents in three aspects; first, as the burden of the ministry, "We preach Christ crucified"; second, as the contempt of the world, "unto the Jews a stumblingblock and unto the Greeks foolishness"; and third, as the admiration of the elect, "but unto them which are called, both Jews and Greeks, Christ the power of God, and the wisdom of God."

I. *The burden of the ministry.* Jesus Christ and him crucified was the distinctive burden of apostolic preaching. In the text the crucifixion of the Saviour is put, by a common rule of rhetoric, as a part for the whole. The sublime transaction of the cross is employed as the designation of the gospel in its entirety. The cross is the center of the Scriptures and around it all the doctrines and duties cluster as kindred and dependent principles. The blessed lines of both Testaments meet in it. Hence to preach the crucified Christ fully and faithfully is to proclaim every inspired doctrine and to urge every scriptural duty. But why is the death of Christ singled out and made the distinguishing mark of the gospel? Evidently on account of its moral significance. The mere execution of a reputed malefactor could amount to nothing.

We should have no sympathy with the idea that the Saviour went to the cross as Socrates did to the hemlock, merely as a proof of his sincerity and firmness. The death of Christ cannot be accounted for on the ground of martyrdom. As a matter of fact, the Saviour was not a good specimen of a martyr. "Father, if it be possible, let this cup pass from me" was his thrice-offered prayer in the garden of Gethsemane. Surely this cannot be regarded as the utterance of a martyr. Nor would a martyr have cried out as the Saviour did upon the cross, "My God, my God, why hast thou forsaken me?" thus confessing failure in the supreme moment, when all the angels of God should have come to his support and the flush of victory should have been the glory of his countenance. The death of Socrates was an accident, but that of Jesus Christ was a great divine purpose. Speaking of his own life, Jesus said: "No man taketh it from me, but I lay it down of myself. I have power to lay it down and I have power to take it again." Neither should we sympathize with the position, so popular in some quarters, that the death of the Saviour, in all the awful circumstances of the same, was only a demonstration of divine love. Demonstrations of love, however impressive they may be in themselves, cannot be an adequate provision for redemption from sin. It is consoling to know that the love of God for the children of men was expressed in the crucifixion of his Son. But there was something more in the crucifixion than the love of God. Indeed this was in it only because something more was in it. The death of Jesus Christ struck deeper than a display of heroism or a demonstration of love. Isaiah expressed it when he said: "He was wounded for our transgressions, he was bruised for our iniquities: the chastisement of our peace was upon him, and with his stripes we are healed. All we like sheep have gone astray; we have turned everyone to his own way: and the Lord **hath laid on** him the iniquity **of** us all." The Saviour of sinners **was** the lamb of God not only for innocence, but for sacrifice. He was slain from the foundation of the world. His death **was vicarious**. He took our place in the day of execution. He carried upon his soul the accumulated guilt of the world. His sacrifice was an atoning **sacrifice**. The purpose of his manifestation in the flesh was, primarily, that he might die, and dying, to expiate the guilt of the world. It is **not** wonderful then that the apostle should say, "We preach Christ *crucified*."

II. *The contempt of the world.* Naturally enough such a gospel as this would provoke opposition, and opposition of the most radical and persistent kind. Beyond all things else it was the object of Hebrew prejudice and pagan hate. To the Jew, who required "a sign," it became the occasion of stumbling, while the Greek, who sought after "wisdom," viewed it with feelings of utter disdain. The Jew and the Greek in their forms of opposition to the cross of Christ, were representative characters. They have a numerous progeny in the world to-day. In these two characters some of the most popular forms of opposition to the cross of Christ find illustration.

In the Jew we may behold the power of human prejudice. Had it not been for this, he would probably have embraced the truth. "Can there any good thing come out of Nazareth?" was the voice of the Jewish heart. It was enough that **the** so-called Christ was of humble parentage, born **in** a stable, and crucified as an offender. This ascertained, the argument was closed and the issue settled. The claims and doctrines of the Saviour, however well founded, could only provoke additional contempt. Prejudice had shut out the disposition to investigate with honesty and fullness. In the Jew, again, we may behold one blinded by traditional teaching. His own inspired

Scriptures, had they been consulted, would have led him to the Christ; but these he left for the uninspired and, in most cases untruthful, traditions of the elders. For this God-dishonoring custom the Saviour often reproved and threatened the Pharisees, who made void the law of God by their traditions, substituting the commandments of men for the commandments of God, and the institutions of men for the institutions of God. These human amendments led them away from the true character of the Christ and gave them unworthy ideas of his kingdom. Furthermore, the Jew was an advocate of self-righteousness as a means of salvation. In his own estimation he needed a temporal saviour, but the idea of a spiritual saviour was far from it. He did good works; he kept the law; he said prayers; he paid tithes. The unclean Gentile may have needed a more perfect righteousness, but not he. From this entrenchment of prejudice, blindness, and self-righteousness he could not be dislodged without a sign from heaven; but his demand for a sign was all a subterfuge. Miracles had been worked in his presence by Jesus and the apostles. Oh, the thousands to-day who are demanding additional evidence of Christianity; who are saying that if an angel from heaven should descend and whisper "the gospel is true," or God were to write in letters of light across the sky, or in some other supernatural way bear witness to it, they would accept it! Clearly they are mistaken. "I pray thee, therefore, father (Abraham), that thou wouldest send him to my father's house, for I have five brethren, that he may testify unto them, lest they also come into this place of torment." "They have Moses and the prophets, let them hear them." "Nay, father Abraham, but if one went unto them from the dead, they will repent." "If they hear not Moses and the prophets, neither will they repent though one rose from the dead." If one receives not gospel on the evidences which are already presented, he will not receive it at all. Christianity does not profess to convince the perverse and headstrong, but only to offer such evidences as will satisfy the plain, the teachable, the humble in mind. The existing evidences of Christianity are all that can be reasonably demanded.

But what of the Greek? The Greek represents in general the conceit of human wisdom. He is set forth as an admirer of philosophy. He was a rationalist, so to speak. He worshiped reason, or rather what he called reason. The reason which he worshiped was, of course, his own, for he recognized no other standard. The reason of a Roman or Egyptian or Jew was unreasonable to him unless it accorded with his own. The Greek is represented as delighting in that which has the ring of science about it and is capable of demonstration. He would have things reduced to the level of man's comprehension and would reject what he could not understand. The fact is, the Greek has already ordained in his own mind who and what God ought to be, how he ought to work and act, and what and how he ought to teach. He prescribes for God and rejects any and everything concerning God which does not accord with his prescriptions.

But it may be noticed that the Greek, though paying his devotion to reason, is one of the most unreasonable of men. He practically repudiates probability and faith, without which the operations and enterprises of the human world must cease. If absolute and infallible proofs were required in all cases, we could scarcely recognize anything on earth as truth. Few indeed are the truths which rest upon mathematical certainty. In our temples of justice, when a human life is at stake, the highest certainty which the law requires is probability. A man is blind indeed not to see that outside of religion, faith is a commoner thing than reason, and probability is relied upon a thousand times to positive demonstration's one. Furthermore, the Greek is not happy, nor does he make anybody else happy. His principle would blight all hope and freeze out all love in the hearts and lives of others.

And still further, he is an example of glaring inconsistency. Religion is the only thing in the broad universe which he rejects because he does not understand it. Here is light, a subtle influence pervading all space. The Greek does not understand it, yet he is not disposed to reject it. Yonder is electricity, now illuminating the heavens with sublime splendor, now splitting the giant pine of the forest into fragments. The Greek does not understand it, neither does he reject it. Life is a mysterious principle which no man can put under the glass of analysis; it is beyond human comprehension, yet under no circumstances can any one doubt its existence or its power. The Greek should abandon his rule or be more consistent in its application.

3. *The admiration of the elect.* "But unto them which are called," continues the apostle, "both Jews and Greeks, Christ the power of God, and the wisdom of God." Through the effectual calling of the Holy Spirit both Jews and Greeks are brought to embrace the gospel. God in his own mysterious way is able to remove prejudice and break down pride. By the clause, "them which are called," the apostle evidently means such persons as under the operation of grace have been brought to know Christ and to love him. The effectual call is that internal persuasion of the Spirit which is answered with repentance toward God and faith toward our Lord Jesus Christ. Just where the divine element in conversion leaves off and the human begins, no one is able to determine. It is not wise to say that a person is altogether passive or altogether active in the great change. The spirit of God effects regeneration, but at the same time the blessings of

the gospel are ours through the exercise of faith. It is enough to know that every regenerate person is a believer and every believer is a regenerate person. While it is true that we are "born, not of blood nor of the will of the flesh, nor of the **will** of man, but of God," it is also true that "Christ is the end of the law for righteousness to every one that believeth."

The prejudice of the Jew being now removed and the pride of the Greek overcome, they discern with an appreciative mind, they cherish with a delighted heart, they confess and advocate with an enthusiastic soul. Now that they who were "sometime darkness" become "light in the Lord," the gospel is possessed of admirable features. They now behold in the cross, once contemptible, the fullness of power and the perfection of wisdom. They now realize that "the foolishness of God is wiser than men and the weakness of God is stronger than men." In that which to them was once the symbol of weakness they now discern the power of God; once the perfection of folly, now the wisdom of God. The Jew freely confesses he knew not what power was until he saw it on the cross, and that the most marvelous of all signs is the cross itself. The Greek now proudly acknowledges that the wisdom which he knew was utter foolishness and that the **true** wisdom is the philosophy of the cross. What mighty and marvelous changes divine grace can work in the thoughts and feelings of each!

The crucified Christ is represented **as** the power of God and the wisdom **of** God. The cross is power indeed. Behold its accomplishments on the day of Pentecost and in every conversion since. Every new birth **is a** miracle. Every saved soul **is a** monument to the power of the cross. Things physical may have strength, which **is** the ability to resist pressure. Power, on the **other** hand, **is** the ability to produce motion, and in **the** nature **of** things, is spiritual.

The highest display of power is beheld when the Lord God Almighty reaches down to this world of darkness and with the long arm of his grace rescues a soul from sin. "The cross of Christ is to them that perish foolishness, but unto us which are saved it is the power of God." And even to the end of the world it is going to please God by "the foolishness of preaching to save them that believe." It is the despised gospel whose distinguishing mark is the crucified Christ, that shall demolish the strongholds of sin, achieve the victory over death and the devil, and finally restore the world to God. "And I, if I be lifted up from the earth, will draw all men unto me." Jesus was beautiful in his character, in his life, in his moral teachings, and through these he must of course exert a corresponding influence and charm; but the power which shall overwhelm and subdue is Jesus hanging upon the cross, bleeding, dying, dead, and in his passion making atonement for the guilt of the world.

The wisdom of God in the crucified Christ is seen in the perfect adaptedness of the cross to the necessities of the case. The effects of the cross, both manward and Godward, are all that could be desired. It secures all the blessings of mercy and at the same time answers every demand of justice. It is only upon such a basis that God can be just and yet justify sinners. The cross presents terms of reconciliation to which both God and man can subscribe,—man to the complete salvation of his soul, and God without violating his rights, or compromising his character. The wisdom is seen again in the ability of the cross so to save a man as to give him all of his time for self-improvement and the performance of good works. He is not required to spend one moment in doing penance, in making atonement for his sins. The anger of God has already been appeased by the death of Christ. Once for all time, for all men, Christ hath put away sin by the sacrifice of himself. In our Christian life we are entirely relieved of the burden of atoning for sin, and all the golden opportunities of life can be used in developing ourselves in grace and promoting the kingdom of truth.

Still further, as a mark of divine wisdom, the cross so saves us as to give the credit of saving to God. Every human consideration is removed as a ground of boasting, so that no flesh should glory in his presence. In the pulpit and in the books we sometimes talk works, but never at the throne of grace. When we are on the knees in prayer before God, we cry grace, not works; we say, "O Lord, thou hast done it, take thou the glory." In the long eternity of heaven there will not come up from the bosom of any redeemed soul the suggestion of personal merit, but the beautiful and endless life will be spent in magnifying the Lord for his amazing grace.

> Grace first contrived the way
>   To save rebellious man,
> And all the steps that grace display
>   Which drew the wondrous plan.
>
> Grace led my roving feet
>   To tread the heavenly road,
> And new supplies each hour I meet,
>   While pressing on to God.
>
> Grace all the work shall crown
>   Through everlasting days,
> It lays in heaven the topmost stone,
>   And well deserves the praise.

XXXIII

CONSECRATION AND ENTHUSIASM [1]

BY H. M. WHARTON, D. D.

"God forbid that I should glory, save in the cross of our Lord Jesus Christ, by whom the world is crucified unto me, and I unto the world." Gal. 6 : 14.

IT falls to my lot to-night, dear friends, to give to you a message from God which you will carry to your homes and which I trust may be a blessing to you in the ensuing year. I pray that God may lay it upon your hearts, and that this service may honor his name and bless you and me.

You will find the message in the letter to the Galatians, the sixth chapter, fourteenth verse : "God forbid that I should glory, save in the cross of our Lord Jesus Christ, by whom the world is crucified unto me, and I unto the world." A consecration that grows out of crucifixion, and a glorious enthusiasm crowning all! He dead to the world, the world dead to him! He consecrated to Christ and glorying in his Christ! It is a wonderful thing; that which was the very synonym of sin and shame eighteen hundred years ago and more has now become the pride and glory of many millions on earth.

I was walking once through the Corcoran Art Gallery, in Washington, and I saw a calm, pale face pressed against the grated window of a jail. It was the face of Charlotte Corday. A letter appended to the picture, written to her father, said : "Dear father,

---

[1] Preached at the Convention of Christian Endeavor held at Boston, July, 1895.

H. M. Wharton, D. D.

Henry Marvin Wharton, pastor, evangelist, lecturer, editor, and college president, is one of the best-known men in the Southern Baptist pulpit. He is a native of Virginia and is now in the prime of life. Among the various instances of signal success which have marked his eventful career one scarcely knows which to select as the most notable. His achievement in building up a magnificent church of nine hundred members, in the heart of Baltimore, out of a beginning of but thirty, and of so wisely planning and faithfully laboring that they to-day worship in a superb temple valued at seventy thousand dollars, is almost unprecedented. His orphanage enterprise does credit to his tender Christliness, and the products of his authorship glow with strength and beauty. But H. M. Wharton is most widely known as the matchless Baptist evangelist. The elements which go to make up his wonderful success in this regard are partly manifest and partly hidden. A superb personality, a simple, pathetic, and often humorous style, an intense earnestness ever under dignified restraint, and a voice musical as a lute, are things seen and appreciated; but united to these is that subtile factor we call magnetism, and the sanctifying, crowning power of the Holy Spirit.

do not be distressed about me. It is the crime and not the scaffold that brings disgrace. I have committed no crime; I shall suffer no disgrace." In a higher and more glorious sense it may be said of Jesus that, instead of himself being disgraced by the cross, he lifted it into glory and glorified it, making it ever the conquering sign of all his followers.

Paul was wonderfully enthusiastic; and, my friends, I believe in enthusiasm—an enthusiasm that has a backbone to it, an enthusiasm that has life in it, an enthusiasm that has weight and power in it, an enthusiasm that has usefulness in it. Paul was wonderfully enthusiastic, but his enthusiasm was simply the atmosphere in which the wonderful man lived. A physician cannot be very successful unless he is enthusiastic about his profession. A lawyer will never accomplish much unless he has some enthusiasm about his profession; and I tell you a Christian will never amount to much unless there is enthusiasm in his Christianity. It is just as true of you who sit in the pew as of the preacher who stands in the pulpit. I love to hear a man's heart beat in his sermons when I hear him preach, and I love to see Christians whose hearts are in their religion when they go forth to work for God.

"God forbid that I should glory, save in the cross of our Lord Jesus Christ." Why, the fact of the matter is, there is nothing else in which we can glory. Look around you, if you will, in the world, and where will you find anything else in which you can glory?

Will you young people glory in your health? You are here now, in the very morning of your life, many of you; your faces are toward the rising sun; your hands are stretched forth toward the opening day, and there are many days and years of usefulness for you, let us hope; and yet, ere the morrow's sun may rise, some of the strongest, some of the best, some of the most useful, may have been called to the other world. We cannot glory in our health; we cannot glory in our strength, in our young manhood, in our young womanhood.

Can we glory in pleasure? It is said in these days pleasure is fairly running away with most of our young people; and I will tell you that most of us who have tried it have come to the conclusion that Burns was right when he wrote:

> But pleasures are like poppies spread;
> You seize the flower, its bloom is shed;
> Or like the snow-fall in the river,
> A moment white, then melts forever.

We cannot glory in the pleasures of this world.

Can you glory in fame? Why, let those who have accomplished something of fame in the walks of this world answer. Go to the very heights of fame and what will you find? The man who, to-day, leads in all the affairs of the nation is forgotten to-morrow. Why, it has not been long since a great president in this country, who was no longer a president, was so far forgotten that when he attended the funeral of one of our dead presidents he was only spoken to by one man in the whole crowd, and that was by a policeman, who requested him to get off the grass.

But perhaps another says, "How about wealth?" The whole world is running mad after wealth; but shall we glory in wealth? It was only a short time ago that the great leaders of wealth in this country were called upon by one of our most prominent daily papers to answer whether wealth brought happiness; and every man answered that wealth simply brings care and responsibility, but it does not bring happiness. Well did Mr. Astor say to a man who suggested to him that he must be a very happy man, "Would you attend to my business for your board and your clothes?" "Why," said he, "no, sir."

"Well, that is all I get." How much more can any man receive than what he can eat and what he can drink and what he can put on?

We cannot glory in wealth; but perhaps some one may say, "How about the home?" Already your heart is longing for the home and the dear ones, and happiness perhaps is there; but can we glory in it? Shall it endure? I can well remember in my old country home down in Virginia, sitting before the great log fire, father over in that corner, mother over in this, eight children sitting around the fire down to the youngest—and I was the youngest, in my little chair at mother's side. They talked of heaven, and mother, placing her hand upon my head and bending my head back until my face was turned toward hers, said, "Mother wants her boy to be a good boy, serve Jesus, and then go home to heaven." I utterly astonished her by saying, "Mother, I don't want to go to heaven." "What do you mean, my child?" "You are here, father is here, brothers are here, sisters are here; I don't want to go to heaven." It was heaven to my child-heart to have them with me. But where are they now? Mother has crossed over the river, and father and part of the sisters and brothers have passed to the other side; and if my home had been my heaven, my heaven is broken up.

Why, my friends, we cannot glory in the things of this world. I might mention them one after another, and you might write on every one of them, "This will perish with the using." The German poet, Schiller, said, as he stood one morning in the door of his father's home and looked far away to the mountain summit that touched the very sky as it seemed to him—he said in his heart, "Some day, when I get to be a big, strong boy, I will go up to the top of yonder mountain, and then I shall be in heaven;" and so one day he started from his home, across the fields, and up the mountain's side, over ditches and rocks, and through the brush. By-and-by he reached the mountain's top, and when he did, he said heaven was as far away as before. You may climb any height on earth, and you will find, when you have reached its summit, that heaven is as far away as ever. Therefore, Paul might say, as he took a view of the things in this world, "God forbid that I should glory, save in the cross of our Lord Jesus Christ."

And while it is true that there is nothing on this earth in which we can glory, it is just as true that there is every reason why we can glory in the cross. You are enthusiastic, wonderfully so. You have a right to be enthusiastic. But, my friends, this enthusiasm is intelligent, and the more we know of the rightfulness of it, the stronger will we be in the glorying of the blessed cross.

We should glory in the cross because of its doctrines. What are its doctrines? The blessed old doctrine of sacrifice. There can be no happiness in this world, in its highest sense, unless we sacrifice on our part for somebody else. Sacrifice! Down South a gentleman told me that in Nashville, Tenn., he attended the decoration of the soldiers' graves. I am proud to tell you, as a Southern man, that now, when Decoration Day comes in the South, and our beautiful young women go forth to scatter their roses upon the soldiers' graves, they do not stop to ask whether the man wore the blue or the gray, but on every grave they scatter the flowers, because the men were brave and true, and died for their country's sake, as they honestly believed.

A gentleman said to me that he was standing in the cemetery at Nashville. He saw a cart come through the gate with a marble slab in it. He followed the cart. By-and-by it came to a grave. A man was standing there, having a place prepared to put this slab. He said he walked up to the man, and said, "Your son, I presume?" "No." "Some near relative?" "No." Well, he did not like to be inquisitive, and did not further insist. The gentleman turned to him and said, " No. I was a member of a company during the war. When the time came for us to go my wife was ill, my children were young. All night long I spent at her bedside, knowing that in the early morning I must leave her. Just as the day was breaking I heard a knock at my door. I walked to the door, and there stood one of my young neighbors, a young boy of sixteen, knapsack upon his back, his haversack filled with provisions; and as he stood there in the early dawn of that morning, the ruddy glow upon his manly cheek, the fire of enthusiasm blazing in his eyes, he said to me, ' I have come to take your place. I am going and will answer to your name.' 'Why,' said I, 'my friend, I will give you my farm, I will give you my money, I will give you all I have. It is just what I have desired, that some one might be found to take my place.' 'Oh,' he said, ' I couldn't think of taking anything for it. Then I would not be going for you and your wife and children. No, sir; not a cent, not a cent.'" The young man was killed at the battle of Missionary Ridge, near Chattanooga, Tenn., and on that tombstone the gentleman had placed the young man's name, the date of his birth, the date of his death, and under all, " He died for me." And I tell you, every one of us here may place his hand upon his heart and say of Jesus Christ, " He died for me ; " and this blessed doctrine of sacrifice should pass into every act of our every life.

And then the blessed doctrine of substitution! Jesus Christ taking your place, you taking his place! He made sin for us that we might be made the righteousness of God in him.

And then the blessed doctrine of the atonement! That at the cross of Christ the poor sinner finds peace and pardon through reconciliation of the blood of Jesus Christ! Well might Paul say, who once was a blasphemer, who once, like you and me, was a poor sinner, without God and without hope—well might he say, since Jesus Christ had sacrificed himself and had taken Paul's place, had atoned for his sins—well might he say, "God forbid that I should glory, save in the cross of our Lord Jesus Christ."

And then another thing: this old cross has the power to attract. Jesus said, "I, if I be lifted up, . . . will draw all men unto me;" and isn't it a fact? I say it deliberately, I say it calmly: I do not believe that there is any other power on earth or under the heavens that would have drawn together fifty-six thousand four hundred and twenty-five souls in this July of 1895, save and except the Lord Jesus Christ. It is the drawing power, my friends, and it is this that attracts the human heart.

I read some time ago of a mother who went to the police officers in New York City and laid all her money at their feet. She said, "My daughter is gone. She has been betrayed, and now, with a broken heart and crushed spirit, she has left me." She sought for her child in every direction. She could not find her, and by-and-by, after the years had passed away, one said to her one day, "Perhaps your daughter may frequent some one of the dance halls and other places of that description in this city. Go there and seek her;" and one day there appeared in one of these halls this mother. She went up to the superintendent, the man who had charge of the affair, and said to him, "Will you do a poor, broken-hearted mother a favor?" "Why," said he, "what can I do for you?" She said, "My child; my child is lost to me. I have spent every cent; I have done everything; I have tried everywhere to get my poor child back. There is one more hope; perhaps she may come to this place." "Well," he said, "suppose she does; how could I find her?" She drew from under her shawl a picture, and said, "Will you let that hang on your wall? She might see it, and if she does, perhaps she might come back to me." "Why," he said, "that is not your picture!" "No," she said, "but it was my picture. She would hardly know me now, but that is as she did know me." Said he, "Yes, the picture may hang there." A few nights afterward, after one of the dances was over and the great crowd were promenading around, suddenly he noticed a commotion over in that part of the hall. He walked over there, and he said, "What does this mean here?" "Why," some one said, "a girl has fainted here just now. She stood looking at that picture there." He turned and said, "Bring me a carriage to the door there at once;" and they ordered a carriage. In a few minutes he was in the carriage with her. She came to, and said, "Where are you taking me?" He said, "I am taking you to your mother. She brought that picture and hung it there, and she said that perhaps it might bring her wayward child to her;" and in a few moments she fell into the arms of her loving, devoted, and forgiving mother.

I tell you, brethren, when Jesus Christ died on the cross God hung up a picture in this world which draws the poor, wayward, wandering ones from earth's remotest bounds up to the cross, and to the Father's forgiving and loving arms. God forbid that we should glory, save in the cross that does draw men from every nation and every clime. Moreover, it has the power to convict. If I wanted to persuade a man here to-day that he is a sinner, I wouldn't sit down and reason with him about it. I wouldn't have a long argument about his sinfulness, his depravity. I'll tell you what I'd do: I'd take him to Calvary; I would lead him up on the hill; I would let him see the dying Son of God; I'd ask him to look at those pierced hands, those feet that wandered homeless through this world, now crushed and bleeding and at rest forever; I would ask him to look at that pierced side and thorned brow; I'd ask him to listen to the groan of that dying One; and, as he looked upon that picture, I would say, "Your sin did that." Oh, I'd want no better argument.

Another thing about this glorious cross, dear friends: it makes us want to give up the world for Christ, "by whom the world is crucified to me, and I to the world." That is the idea which makes us give up everything for God, if truly we are consecrated to his service, and then, oh what a comforting power there is in the cross! You know what I am talking about; I can't tell you. It is in your heart, but there never was language that could explain it.

Young people, I sympathize with you. The world offers many allurements and inducements, but we are dead to the world. Let us not enter into any of its sinful ways. The cards should be utterly repudiated by you. The wine should be forever ostracized. The dance should be in no way indulged in. The theatre should be put back behind you; and these things forever given up. I trust that through your effort a new lesson may be taught to our churches, and that people when they give up card-playing, and drinking, and theatre-going, and dancing, out in the world, will not come to our churches to find that our church-members are doing the very things they have been called upon to give up. Leave these things, leave them behind. It is the cross of Jesus Christ that crucifies the world to us, and us to the world. That may be Puritan doctrine, but I stand on Puritan ground, and the blessed old Bible is a Puritan book. Let us give up the world to be consecrated to Christ.

Another word: Search the Scriptures; turn your enthusiasm to the Bible; study.

Another word: Be ready everywhere to go to work for the Lord Jesus Christ.

If you and I are going to do great work for God, let us do personal work, and let us see to it that every Endeavorer wins a soul for Christ.

And now good-bye until we meet again. Among all the sermons that I have ever heard in all my life, that which made its deepest impression upon me was preached by my precious mother. I remember one night being led, while yet a child, up to her bedside, and they said to me, "Kiss mother and tell her good-bye." I said, "Where's mother going?" They said, "She is going away." I never dreamed that mother could leave me. They said, "Mother, here's your baby boy come to say good-bye"; and, as I bent over her, I kissed her. It has been nearly forty years since then, and yet it seems to me this evening I can still feel the sweet, soft pressure of those dear lips on mine. They said, "Listen, she is saying something to you," and I put my ear close down to her mouth, and she said, "Meet me in heaven"; and they closed her eyes and laid her hands across her quiet breast.

www.ingramcontent.com/pod-product-compliance
Lightning Source LLC
Chambersburg PA
CBHW051740300426
44115CB00007B/641